IN THE
LAND OF ISRAEL
My Family 1809-1949

Nitza, age 9, portrait by Colm-Bialla, 1943

In the Land of Israel
My Family 1809-1949

NITZA ROSOVSKY

TidePool Press
Cambridge, Massachusetts

Copyright © 2012 by Nitza Rosovsky

Published in the United States in 2012 by TidePool Press

All rights reserved.

No part of this book may be reproduced in any manner whatsoever without written permission.

TidePool Press

6 Maple Avenue, Cambridge, Massachusetts 02139

www.tidepoolpress.com

For information, address:

TidePool Press

7 Front Street, Maynard, Massachusetts 01754

Printed in the United States

Library of Congress Cataloging-in-Publication Data

Nitza, Rosovsky, 1934-

    In the Land of Israel: My Family 1809-1949

    p.cm.

    ISBN 0-9755557-9-8/978-0-9755557-9-8

    1. Rosovsky, Nitza 2. Israel—History

    3. Memoir 4. Politics 5. Family Business I. Title.

2012941217

*For Leah, Judy, Michael, Rachel,
Benjamin, Sarah, Abigail, and Ella*

Israel, 1949 Armistice Lines

Contents

Introduction — IX

Part I: Tiberias

In Search of Family History — 3
Going Up to the Holy Land — 15
Weaving the Threads — 21
The World of Menahem Mendel Epstein — 29
The Family Ashkenazi — 39
From Beirut to Jerusalem — 47

Part II: Jerusalem

The Berman Family's Beginnings — 57
The Business and the Family — 69
The Great War — 91
In the Aftermath of the War — 102
The Early Thirties — 133

Part III: Within Memory

Home and Hearth — 157
Weekdays and Holidays — 177
The Early Years — 217
World War II — 235
Family Affairs — 259
The Road to Independence — 270
Jerusalem Besieged — 279
The End of a Chapter — 303

Epilogue — 318

Acknowledgments — 323

Endnotes — 325

NITZA'S FAMILY TREE

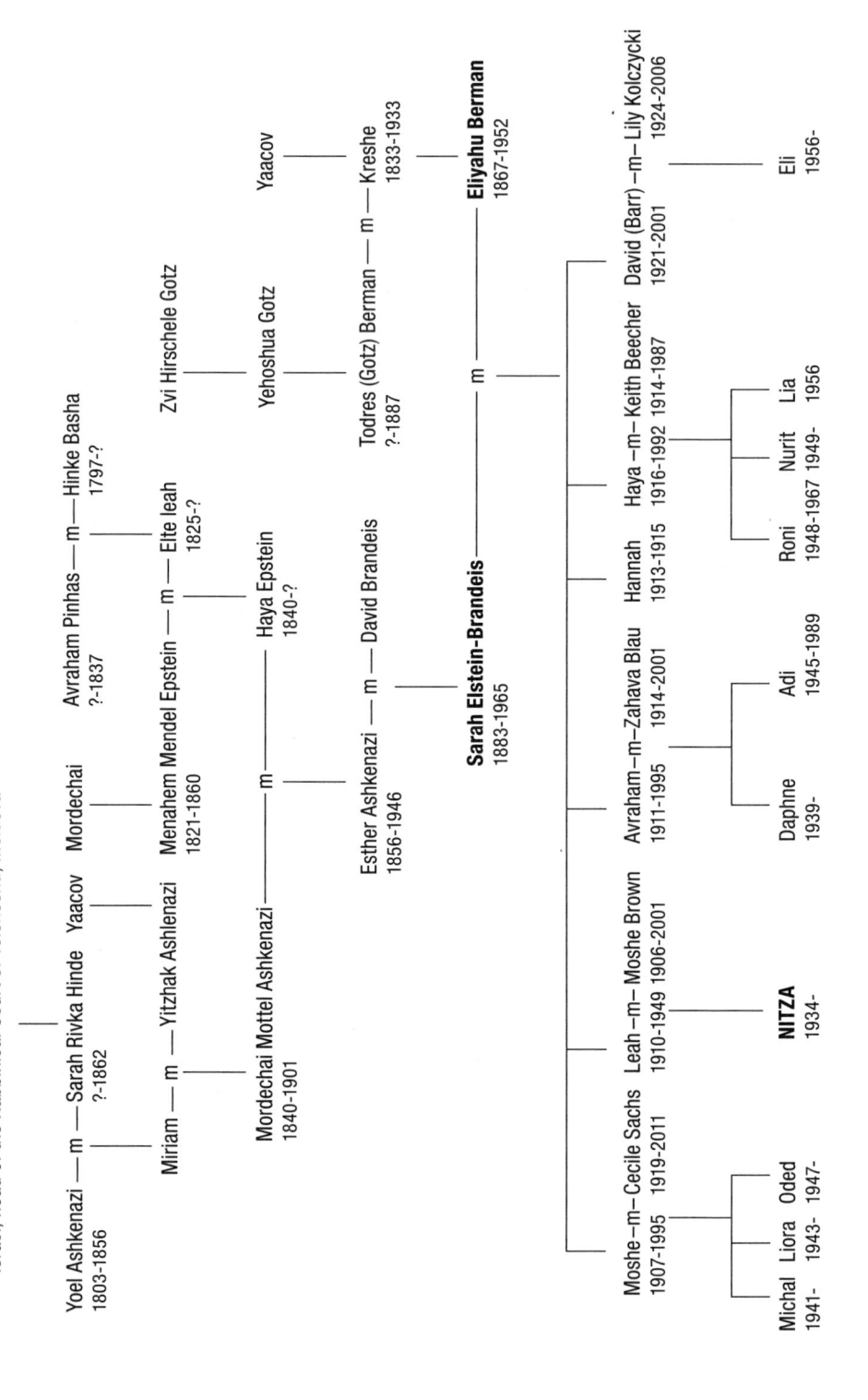

Israel, head of the Rabbinical Court of Teleneshti, Moldova

Yoel Ashkenazi — m — Sarah Rivka Hinde   Yaacov   Mordechai
1803-1856   ?-1862

Miriam — m — Yitzhak Ashlenazi

Avraham Pinhas — m — Hinke Basha
?-1837   1797-?

Menahem Mendel Epstein — m — Elte leah
1821-1860   1825-?

Zvi Hirschele Gotz

Haya Epstein
1840-?

Yehoshua Gotz

Yaacov

Mordechai Mottel Ashkenazi — m —
1840-1901

Esther Ashkenazi — m — David Brandeis
1856-1946

Todres (Gotz) Berman — m — Kreshe
?-1887   1833-1933

Eliyahu Berman
1867-1952

Sarah Elstein-Brandeis — m —
1883-1965

Avraham — m — Zahava Blau   Hannah   Haya — m — Keith Beecher   David (Barr) — m — Lily Kolczycki
1911-1995   1914-2001   1913-1915   1916-1992   1914-1987   1921-2001   1924-2006

Moshe — m — Cecile Sachs   Leah — m — Moshe Brown   NITZA   Daphne   Adi
1907-1995   1919-2011   1910-1949   1906-2001   1934-   1939-   1945-1989

Roni   Nurit   Lia
1948-1967   1949-   1956

Eli
1956-

Michal   Liora   Oded
1941-   1943-   1947-

Introduction

SOMEWHERE UP IN HEAVEN my great-grandmother, Esther Ashkenazi Brandeis, must be chuckling. During my childhood, whenever Jerusalem was in winter's icy grip, I used to crawl under her quilt at night and beg for a story. Baba Esther knew many tales, tales set against the mountains of Safed and the Sea of Galilee where she grew up, enchanting tales about shepherds and fishermen, shoemakers and washerwomen. But whenever she strayed into reality and reminisced about her own life, my attention wandered. Facts, after all, were so boring. Half a century later, as I was interviewing one relative after another, rushing from archive to library to cemetery in an effort to piece together my family's history, I could almost hear Esther saying: "Ah, Nitzaleh, if you had only listened!"

When I began my search for roots I also realized how little I knew about Jews in Europe, where my ancestors came from, even though I was a graduate of the Hebrew Gymnasium in Jerusalem, a well-known secular high school, where my classmates and I spent many hours a week studying the annals of the Jewish people. But it was almost as if history stopped in AD 70 when the Romans destroyed Jerusalem, bringing Jewish sovereignty to an end, and resumed in 1881, when the first Zionists left Eastern Europe for Eretz Israel, the Land of Israel. Eighteen centuries of Jewish life in the Diaspora hardly seemed to matter.

Another chapter of history that was neglected for a long time by the country's schools was Jewish life in Palestine before Zionism. Rarely mentioned were the Orthodox men and women who emigrated to the Holy Land over the centuries in the belief that by living there they would hasten the arrival of the Messiah or who just wanted to be buried in hallowed ground. The young Zionists who came to Palestine in the 1880s to till the ancient land looked upon the members of the old Yishuv, the local Jewish community, as idlers who lived off money from abroad, who spent their days praying in the synagogue or studying at the yeshiva, neither gainfully employed nor visibly productive. Even today, in the continuous battle between the ultra-Orthodox and the secular Israelis, neither side seems willing to recognize the achievements or even the aspirations of the other.

Although I was always proud to be a seventh-generation *sabra*, I was not at all curious about my family's history because whatever happened before the ascent of Zionism did not seem important. In addition, just dealing with my family's present was overwhelming. I grew up in my maternal grandparents' house that stood next door to the family's business, the Berman Bakery. Dozens of relatives streamed through the house: uncles and cousins were constantly dropping in for coffee, a cold drink, or just to find a quiet corner where a small cabal from the bakery could get together and conspire—alliances within the family were constantly shifting. In addition to the many Bermans, members of my grandmother Sarah's family sometimes showed up in need of help. "You have to be extra nice to those who are less fortunate than we are," Grandmother—who had married well—never failed to remind us. Even cousins twice removed were considered immediate family. Awed by their sheer numbers, I often tried to avoid kith and kin, with limited success.

My lack of interest in family affairs changed completely in the late 1970s, when I began to write *Jerusalemwalks*, a guidebook to some of the older parts of the city. I became fascinated by life in Palestine in the nineteenth century. I wanted to understand what made Jews come to live

Introduction

in that backward corner of the Ottoman Empire and to learn more about their struggles, their conflicts, and their dreams. I contemplated writing a book about that relatively less known period in Jewish history, a period overshadowed by the advance of Zionism in the latter part of the century. While searching through books, biographies, and newspaper accounts from those days, I occasionally came upon the names of relatives, minor characters in the unfolding drama. Then one day I read a contemporary account of the great earthquake of 1837 and I was really shaken—if you'll pardon the pun. I recalled stories Baba Esther had told me, stories she had heard from her own parents and grandparents, about *der groisser roysh*, "the big noise," as the disaster was known in Yiddish. One boy was pushed out of a window by his mother: "*Nemt meyn Motteleh*," the woman cried. "Take my little Mottel." The child was caught by some neighbors and survived. (For years I thought that this Mottel was Esther's father, but that proved to be wrong.) An uncle crawled under the kitchen table as the house around him collapsed and he survived for a whole week sniffing an onion—a tale I found very amusing when I was young. As I continued to read about the destruction of Safed and Tiberias I thought about Baba Esther's relatives whose stories she had passed on to me and felt that I was literally touching a moment in history. I then decided to see if I could find enough material about my ancestors so that I could use their narrative as a leitmotif, a thread in a vast tapestry of Jewish history in Palestine. But my journey of discovery became so personal that I soon found myself writing about what was happening in the country merely as background for the story of my family, rather than the other way around. Matters got even more complicated in the second part of the book, where I was writing about events I remembered. I have heard novelists claim that sometimes their characters take over the plot. When I began this book, it was not my intention to write an autobiography but somehow the story took over.

This book begins in 1809, in Tiberias, with the arrival of one of my great-great-great-great-grandmothers, Hinke Basha. It depicts the daily life of the Jewish community in the city in the nineteenth century; eventually it moves to Jerusalem and the arrival there, in 1876, of my great-grandmother Kreshe who established the Berman Bakery, the first commercial bakery in the country, which is still thriving. The story continues through World War I, the end of Turkish rule, the British Mandate and World War II, and it ends in 1949, shortly after Israel's War of Independence. I hope it will give the reader a sense of what it was like to live in Palestine—at least for one family—during the hundred and forty years before the birth of Israel.

Reader beware: the beginning of the book—the first fifty pages where I trace the family's sojourn in Tiberias—is complicated and dense. But I believe it is the most important part of the book since it is covers a period in Israel's history that is not well known, especially abroad. I became fascinated by the daily life of a small community of Jews in the city: where did they come from, how did they make a living, what did they eat, what was their communal life like? I hope that you, the reader, will find it interesting as well. And bear with me and continue reading since the plot thickens and the narrative picks up speed when it gets to Jerusalem.

In the Land of Israel
My Family 1809-1949

View of Tiberias, 1898-1914
Courtesy of the Matson Collection, Library of Congress

part one

Tiberias

ASHKENAZI FAMILY MEMBERS INTERVIEWED

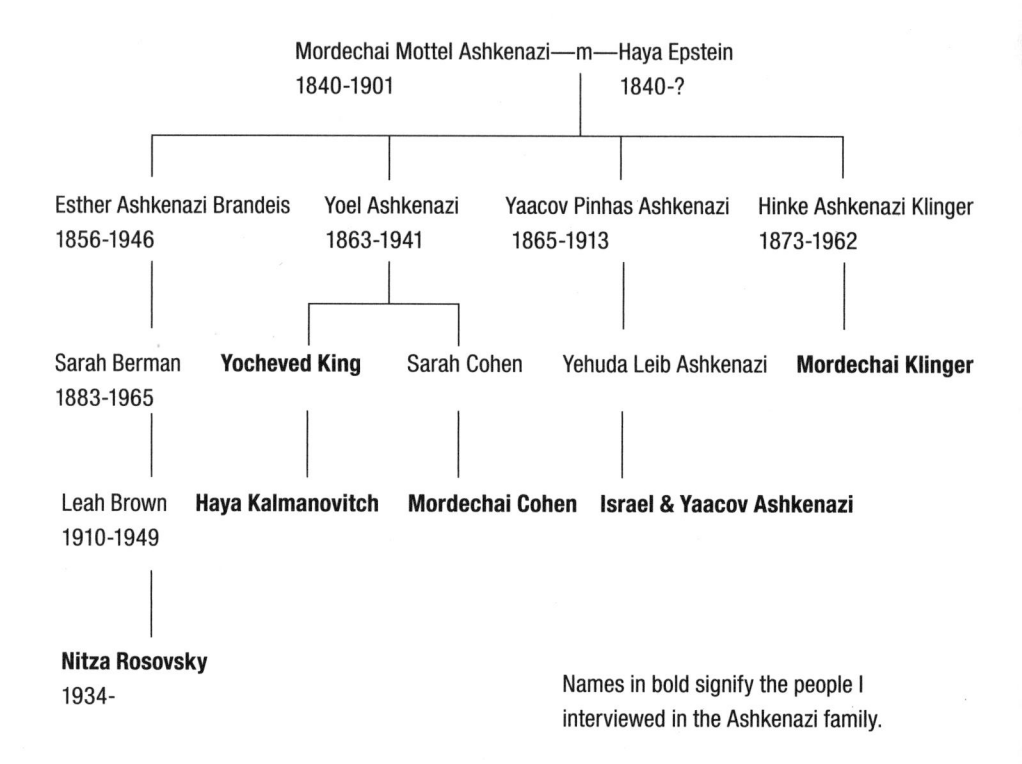

Mordechai Mottel Ashkenazi—m—Haya Epstein
1840-1901 | 1840-?

- Esther Ashkenazi Brandeis
1856-1946
- Yoel Ashkenazi
1863-1941
- Yaacov Pinhas Ashkenazi
1865-1913
- Hinke Ashkenazi Klinger
1873-1962

Sarah Berman
1883-1965

Yocheved King   Sarah Cohen   Yehuda Leib Ashkenazi   **Mordechai Klinger**

Leah Brown   **Haya Kalmanovitch**   **Mordechai Cohen**   **Israel & Yaacov Ashkenazi**
1910-1949

Nitza Rosovsky
1934-

Names in bold signify the people I interviewed in the Ashkenazi family.

In Search of Family History

Finding the beginning of the thread was not easy. As is often the case, my search began much too late, long after my grandparents and their generation were gone. By then I was living in the United States, busy with family, work, and other commitments. But starting in 1978, various projects brought me back to Israel several times a year, and each time I was there I interviewed some relatives. First I questioned my mother's siblings and a number of her Berman cousins. My mother Leah's oldest brother, Moshe Berman, confessed that he once owned a copy of our family tree that went back many generations, to the family's origins in Europe. In his twenties at the time, Moshe was not interested in family history and he lost the tree. He told me that he thought that the first person in our family settled in Palestine in 1777, but he was not sure.

It was my great-grandmother Esther Ashkenazi's side that intrigued me the most since they had lived in the country for seven generations. As a child I often went with my mother to visit Esther's surviving siblings—her brother Yoel in Tiberias and her sister Hinke in Safed—and I remembered their children's and most of their grandchildren's names, a great asset in the search for roots. On the opposite page is a "guide for the perplexed" with the names of the Ashkenazi descendants whom I eventually interviewed printed in bold, as is my name at the bottom.

Interviews

I will only mention a couple of the interviews. A key one was in 1983, with my mother's second cousin Haya Kalmanovitch, who possessed a trove of anecdotes about family members in Safed and Tiberias. She spoke of Esther's parents—and my great-great-grandparents—Mordechai Mottel Ashkenazi and his wife Haya, née Epstein, after whom she and several other women in the family were named. The Ashkenazis, she said, were Hasidim who came from Bessarabia, part of Moldova, and were descendants of the famous and influential rabbi, Hacham Zvi Ashkenazi. Haya then suggested that I visit her mother, Yocheved Ashkenazi King, who, to my surprise, was still alive.

It was only in January of 1985 that I got to see Yocheved. The nursing home where she was spending her last days was located in Petach Tikva, the first modern agricultural colony in Eretz Israel, founded in 1878 by members of the old Yishuv, the Jews who lived in Palestine before Zionism. Yocheved, then in her nineties, was delighted to have a visitor and knew who I was as soon as I said my name: *"Ah, Leah's tokhter,"* she said as she began to cry, "Leah's daughter." We spoke in Yiddish while we sat in the shade of an old eucalyptus tree, away from prying ears. Yocheved's voice was so soft that at times I was not sure that I was hearing her correctly, yet her memory seemed sharp and she mentioned a few names unfamiliar to me and clarified various relationships. She recalled her grandfather Mordechai Mottel, tall and handsome with a long beard. His wife Haya always kept sweets for her grandchildren in the pocket of her starched white apron. As I left I kissed Yocheved's wrinkled cheeks, the very cheeks touched by the lips of my great-great-grandparents.

Yocheved died in 1989. I did not see her again.

In the same year, after a long search I found Mordechai Cohen of Tiberias, nephew of Yocheved and great-grandson of Mordechai Mottel. The last time I had seen him was half a century earlier when I spent many happy hours playing with his three sons who were about my age. He showed me a *mahzor* from 1816, a prayer book for the High Holidays, which belonged to his great-grandfather and bore a trilingual stamp in Hebrew, Arabic, and Latin scripts: "Rabbiner M. M. Aschkenasi, Tiberias." He too mentioned the seventeenth-century rabbi, Hacham Zvi Ashkenazi: "We are all descended from him, you know. And Rabbi Kook himself once told me that if one of Hacham Zvi's heirs, even unto the tenth generation, would make a wish at his graveside, that wish will be granted." A wise man and revered scholar, Avraham Hacohen Kook was the first Ashkenazi chief rabbi in the country; he died in 1935. Mordechai did not know the location of Hacham Zvi's tomb and it was too late to ask Rabbi Kook.

Among the relatives whose names I remembered were the children of Yehuda Ashkenazi who was my grandmother Sarah's beloved cousin and confidant and a frequent visitor to our house in Jerusalem. I recalled that one of his sons was named Hillel and that he used to practice law in Jerusalem. When I opened the telephone book, I found two lawyers by that name, one married to a Claudette, the other to a Ruth. I gambled on Ruth and dialed the number. A woman answered. "May I please speak to Hillel Ashkenazi?" I asked.

"Who's calling?"

"My name is Nitza Rosovsky and I am Sarah Berman's granddaughter. I am collecting material about the Ashkenazi family, and I wonder if Hillel could help me." An awkward silence greeted this lengthy opening statement, and it gave me time to think of the numerous calls of this kind that I had received over the years from various people who claimed a Rosovsky ancestor and wanted to find out whether they were related to my husband. Since I had been blessed by an abundance of my own relatives, the prospect of discovering additional ones was not necessarily a priority, so I usually suggested that the potential kin call my brother-in-law Alex, explaining—truthfully—that he was the expert on

Rosovsky history. The prolonged silence ended when Ruth said: "Hillel doesn't know much about the family. Why don't you call my brother-in-law Israel? He is the one interested in family history." When I stopped chortling, I made the call.

Perhaps I should explain why in Israel I still identify myself as Sarah Berman's granddaughter. In her time, Sarah was a Jerusalem landmark who spent her days dealing with beggars who came to the house, with representatives of various charitable organizations, with genteel if poor relatives—the list goes on. In 1965, ten years after I had left Jerusalem, my husband and I were spending a sabbatical there. We lived in a small apartment where the nameplate on the door simply said "Rosovsky." One day the bell rang and a handsome gentleman, in a black coat and hat and with moderately long ear locks and beard, entered. He was collecting money for a religious girls' orphanage. I handed him a few dollars, a respectable sum, I thought, for a door-to-door solicitor. He took a long look at me, apparently recognized me, and announced that it was not fitting, *es past nisht*, for the granddaughter of Sarah Berman to give only a few dollars.

I did not need to recite my credentials to Israel Ashkenazi who remembered me as a small girl and greeted me like a long-lost relative—which I was. He and his wife Malka immediately invited me to their house and there we sat—over the mandatory tea and cake without which a visit in Israel is not a visit—and tried to catch up with all that had happened to the many descendants of Mordechai Mottel Ashkenazi. When I mentioned Hacham Zvi, Israel was astonished that I did not know more about him and suggested that I begin by looking him up in the *Encyclopaedia Judaica*.

When I asked about Ashkenazis who lived in the country during the nineteenth century, Israel recalled the Humashim, the first five books of the Bible—the Torah or Pentateuch—which belonged to his late father and where various names were recorded. A frantic search through well-stocked bookshelves eventually produced the Humashim that, ultimately, provided the key to the family's beginnings in Eretz Israel.

The "Family Bible"

The Humashim originally belonged to Mordechai Mottel Ashkenazi of Tiberias—Mordechai from now on with some exceptions—as was noted on the frontispieces of several of the volumes. They were inherited in turn by his son Yaacov, then by his grandson Yehuda, and finally by Israel. Listed on several pages, in three different handwritings, were many *yortzeiten*, the dates on which various family members had died. I recognized most of the names and all of the burial places: Tiberias, Safed, Jerusalem, Beirut. I copied a lot of the information and, once back in the United States, unsuccessfully tried to fit the puzzle pieces together. It took an additional trip to Israel before I began to understand the data.

The volumes were stamped with three different seals: The first was "Rabbiner M. M. Aschkenasi, Tiberias," the same trilingual seal that was in the prayer book Mordechai Cohen had shown me. Next came "Jacob. P. Aschkenasi, Tiberias," in English and Hebrew, and finally several different versions of Yehuda's seal with "Ashkenazi" appearing both in Hebrew and in the more contemporary English transliteration. In the Hebrew version Yehuda added: "Grandchild [descendant] of the Gaon, the Sage, Hacham Zvi." Eventually I was able to assign the three distinct Hebrew handwritings to the different seal owners. Mordechai's was an elegant square hand, as formal as that used by scribes to copy the holy words of the Torah; his son Yaacov wrote in small, even letters, in straight lines; Yehuda had a freer hand—the letters were larger and the lines sloped downward from right to left. Noted were the dates on which several of their grandparents, parents, or in-laws had died. Yehuda included the *yortzeiten* of a number of aunts and uncles, and in a shaky hand noted the passing of an infant son who had succumbed to pneumonia. Jews traditionally registered dates of birth and death in the *pinkasim*, the ledgers of their communities. But it is important for family members in later generations to know the exact day and month when someone died since, in addition to the Kaddish and other prayers said on the *yortzeit*, special liturgical passages appropriate to that very date are also recited. The year is not relevant and thus was not always noted in the Humashim, and neither were dates of birth.

Mordechai recoreded the *yortzeiten* in several Humashim: "The anniversary of my grandfather, the pious *rav* [an honorific title, not necessarily a rabbi], the renowned son of saints in the chain of distinguished lineage, Rav Yoel Ashkenazi of blessed memory, died 16 Tevet, Tarta"z [December 24, 1855], in the Holy City of Safed, may she be rebuilt soon, in our days, Amen." Next was "the anniversary of my modest and pious grandmother, the descendant of saints, Mrs. Sarah Rivka Hinde of blessed memory, daughter of the righteous Rabbi Israel, of blessed pious memory, the head of the rabbinical court in Teleneshti, died 10 Heshvan, Tarka"v [October 10, 1861]." (Teleneshti, I later found out, is a small town in Moldova, in the former USSR.) This was followed by the *yortzeiten* of Mordechai's in-laws: Menahem Mendel, the son of another Mordechai and his wife Elte Leah, daughter of Avraham Pinhas. Both Yaacov and Yehuda continued to record *yortzeiten* but the practice died with them.

Yoel Ashkenazi "the Elder" was the only person described as the "son of saints in the chain of distinguished lineage." Was it in order to remind everyone that the family descended from Zvi Ashkenazi? For a long time I researched the life of Hacham Zvi, hoping, in vain, that through him and his many descendants I could find out when my family arrived in Eretz Israel.

Zvi's was an amazing life. He was born in 1660 in a small town in Moravia where his family found refuge after the Cossacks' attack on Vilna five years earlier. When his maternal grandfather, Ephraim Hacohen, was appointed rabbi in Budapest, the rest of the family moved there and young Zvi was sent to a Sephardi yeshiva in Salonika where he acquired the title *hacham*, the equivalent of rabbi, by which he was known

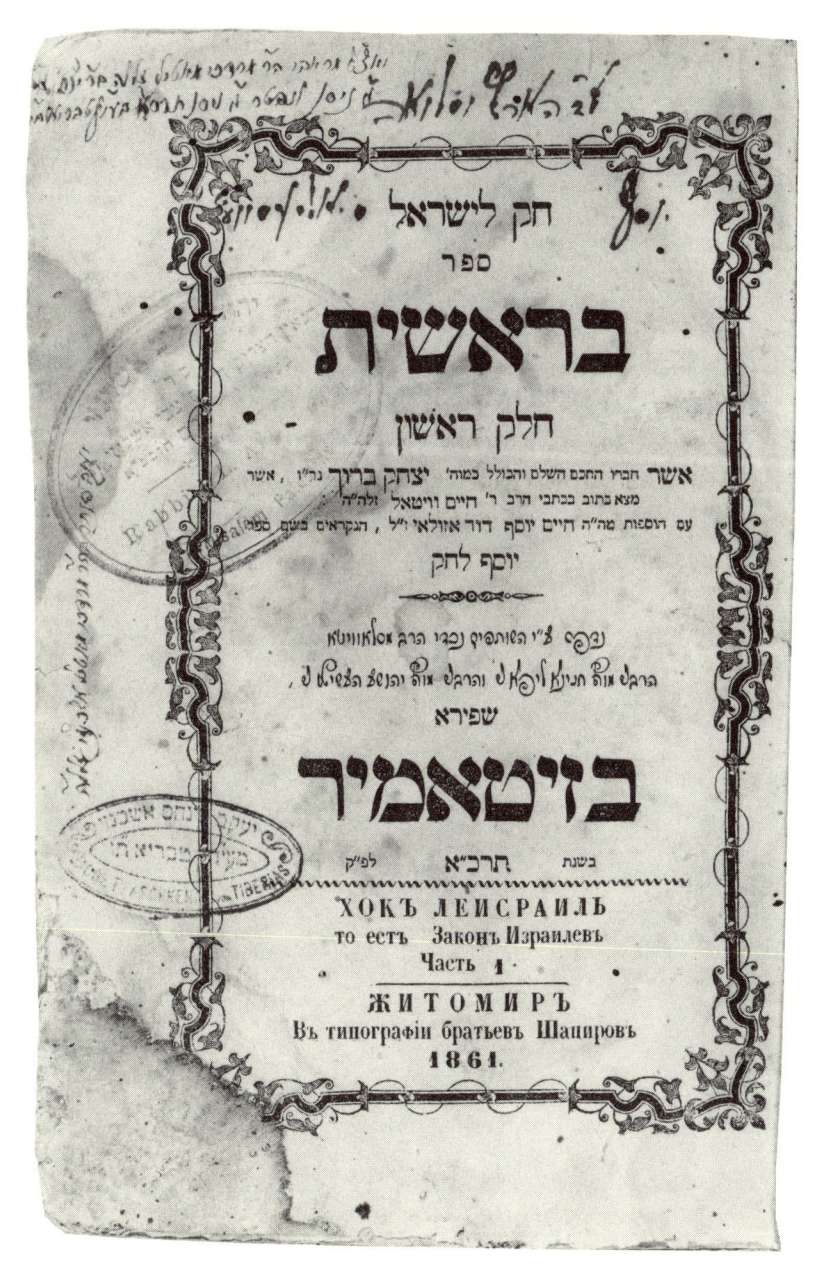

The book of Genesis which belonged to my great-great-grandfather, Mordechai Mottel Ashkenazi. Printed in Zhitamir, Ukraine, in 1861
Courtesy of Israel Ashkenazi, Jerusalem

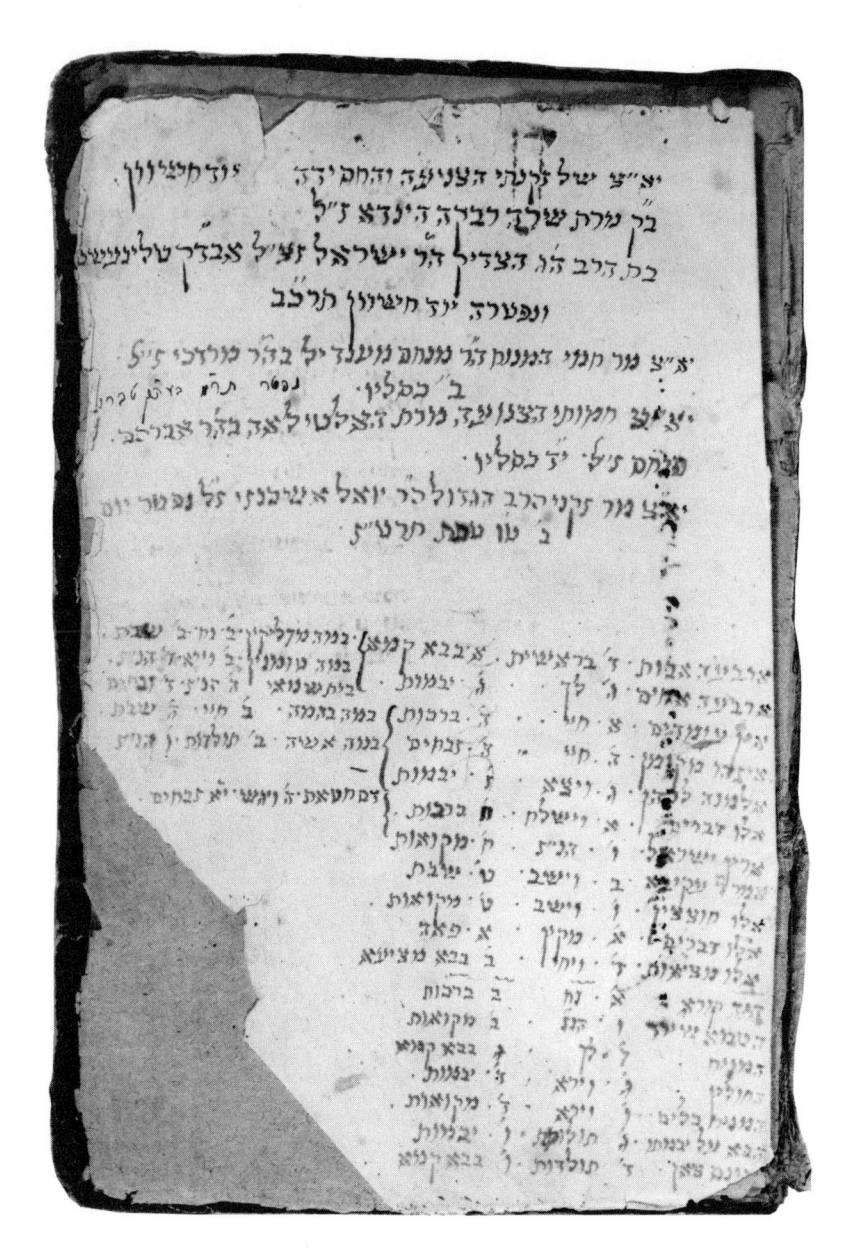

The dates on which several family members died, recorded by Mordechai Mottel Ashkenazi: his grandmother, his in-laws, and his grandfather
Courtesy of Israel Ashkenazi, Jerusalem

for the rest of his life. He eventually held the position of rabbi in Altona and Hamburg, then in Amsterdam, and finally in Lvov (also known as Lemberg, and now Lviv), under Poland at the time. He died in 1718; his wife Sarah Rivka, only thirty-nine years old, died a year later. They left behind ten children.

Zvi is best known for his collection of responsa, answers to Jewish legal questions, addressed to him from all over the world. *Megilat Sefer*, an autobiography written by his son, Jacob Emden—a brilliant if controversial figure—is the main source of information about Zvi's life. I followed as best I could the histories of Zvi's ten children and their descendants who lived in many different countries. Family stories, tombstone inscriptions, and individual seals all suggest a connection to Hacham Zvi, but I could not prove it. In the end it did not really matter because I eventually found out where different family members of the Ashkenazi and Epstein families came from and when they arrived in Eretz Israel.

Tiberias Cemetery

In the early 1980s, I twice went to visit the cemetery in Tiberias where I searched unsuccessfully for Mordechai Mottel Ashkenazi's tomb. I tried again in 1989 after I learned the exact date of his death from the *yortzeiten* list.

Tiberias is situated on the western shore of the Kinneret, the Sea of Galilee. The cemetery lies between the lake on the east and a rocky basalt mountain range on the west. Lakeside frontage is at a premium and modern apartment buildings and hotels are rapidly encroaching upon the ancient burial grounds. The modern part of the cemetery is filled with elaborately carved headstones featuring doves and other creatures that presumably watch over the dead. (This is a Sephardi, rather than Ashkenazi, custom.) In the older part of the necropolis, simple stone slabs mark the graves. Many headstones were washed away during a flood in 1934, as were many of the city's buildings and the archives of the Jewish community. A few years later, the Burial Society, *Hevra Kadisha*, whose written records vanished in the flood, numbered the remaining tombs and copied into new ledgers those inscriptions that were still legible. The deceased were listed alphabetically, mostly by first name and patronymic. Engraving last names on tombstones is a fairly recent custom.

At the small office of the Burial Society, located on the premises, I was courteously received once again by the elderly keeper; perhaps it is a relief to deal with the relatives of those who died long ago. I was asked, just as on my previous visits, if the family was of Sephardi or Ashkenazi origin, and the appropriate volume was produced. I did not find Mordechai Mottel. I found another Mordechai and another Yoel, both descendants of Hacham Zvi, but their dates did not fit. That reminded me that Mordechai Mottel's son Yoel, my great-grandmother's brother who used to feed me candy half a century earlier, was buried in Tiberias. The gentleman from the Burial Society pointed me in the right direction, and there was Yoel's headstone, surrounded by tombs of other relatives. The inscription said: "Here is buried the wise *rav* of the stock [*migeza*] of Hacham Zvi, may his righteous memory be blessed. Our teacher Rav Yoel son of Rav Mordechai Ashkenazi of blessed memory, died on 23 Heshvan, Tasha"v [November 13, 1941]. May his soul be preserved among the living." Having spent a lot of time trying to establish a link with Hacham Zvi, I was pleased to see the inscription on Yoel's tomb, stating that he was a descendant of the Hacham.

As I stood there, on a clear November morning, I was swept by recollections of earlier times in the city. It is another crisp winter day in Tiberias, near the end of World War II. And there is my mother, in her early thirties, elegant, vivacious. We are sitting at the Lido Café, by the lake. An old family friend takes us in a private motorboat—a great luxury in those days—across the lake to his man-made fishponds, a new experiment. We continue from Tabkhah to Kfar Nahum, or Capernaum, where fallen pillars and capitals lie strewn by the water's edge. Later that day I explore caves in the mountains with three of my distant cousins, the

Gravestone of Yoel, son of Mordechai Mottel Ashkenazi, 1941

Gravestone of my great-great-great grandfather, Menahem Mendel, 1879

sons of Mordechai Cohen, great-grandsons of the Yoel Ashkenazi whose tomb I had just seen. On that day long ago we picked wild anemones and cyclamens, before it was politically incorrect, until we saw a jackal in the woods and ran back home. My mother pinned a few of the wild flowers to her lapel.

I laid a small stone on Yoel's tomb in remembrance, as is the custom, and put to rest the shadows of the past. As I cast a final glance in the direction of the sparkling lake, over the older part of the cemetery which I had already explored, an inscription caught my attention, carved onto a tombstone which was slightly better preserved than the ones around it. On its side I could see the number assigned to it by the Burial Society, 1501. When I got closer I could actually read the inscription: "Menahem Mendel son of Mordechai, died on *rosh hodesh* Kislev, Taram. May his soul be preserved among the living." *Rosh hodesh* means the beginning— the first two days—of the month. I was almost afraid to check the photocopied pages of the Humashim that I was carrying with me. But there it was, in Mordechai Mottel's own handwriting: "The anniversary of my late father-in-law, Rav Menahem Mendel, son of Rav Mordechai of blessed memory, 2 Kislev, Taram [November 17, 1879], Tiberias." So while I did not find Mordechai Mottel, I did come upon the grave of his father-in-law, my great-great-great-grandfather. Was it a mere accident? Even though Professor Israel Bartal of the Hebrew University, who is an expert on the history of the Jews of Palestine, told me that many Hasidim claimed a relationship to Hacham Zvi whether true or not— I must confess that finding Menahem Mendel's final resting place and Hacham Zvi's name on Yoel's tomb seemed like an omen, a signal that I should persevere.

Going Up to the Holy Land

By 1989 I had spent a lot of time in archives in both Safed and Tiberias but found little useful material since natural and man-made disasters had caused much distraction in those towns: the great earthquake in 1837, the cloudburst and flood in Tiberias in 1934, wars and changes of regimes—between 1918 and 1948 the country had gone from Ottoman to British to Israeli or Jordanian rule. Still, by then I had learned that the Ashkenazis were Hasidim and that at some point they left Bessarabia to come to Palestine, so I tried to better understand the relationship between Hasidut—the religious movement which emerged in Eastern Europe around the middle of the eighteenth century—and *aliya*—"going up" to settle in Eretz Israel.

This chapter is not directly related to my family but it provides background information about the early years of the Hasidim in Safed and Tiberias.

Hasidut and Aliya

Since the sixteenth century, Safed, the city where my great-great-great-great-grandfather Yoel Ashkenazi died in 1856, had served as a magnet for Kabbalists, for Jewish mysticists. Among those who settled there, none was more influential than Rabbi Yitzhak Luria Ashkenazi—not a relative—who moved to Safed around 1570. Facts and fable mingle when the story of Luria's life is told: how he understood the talk of birds and animals, how he identified the burial places of many sages as he walked around Safed with his disciples. After he died his own tomb became a place of pilgrimage. His doctrine, known as Lurianic Kabbala, had great appeal for the masses because it made ordinary people feel that through *tikkun*, "restoration," they could influence cosmic events. *Tikkun* is a complex process consisting of spiritual actions among which are prayer and the observance of the *mitzvot*, of God's commandments. Since certain *mitzvot* can only be fulfilled in Eretz Israel, some Hasidim believed that they could affect events by settling there and, through *tikkun*, cause an awakening from "down below" and bring Redemption closer.

Hasidut has been called "the daughter of Kabbala" because, like the older movement, it differs from traditional Jewish rationalism. Founded in the middle of the eighteenth century by Rabbi Israel Baal Shem Tov, "Master of the Divine Name," it was an anti-establishment movement, a reaction against the physically dreary and spiritually arid life of Jews at that time, and it provided the common people with a sense of joy in worship. The popularity of the movement must be seen against the background of the desolate sixteenth and seventeenth centuries, beginning with the Expulsion from Spain in 1492 and culminating in the Chmielnicki massacres (1648-1658) when Cossacks from the Ukraine slaughtered tens of thousands of Jews in three hundred communities. The political situation of the Jews was dismal as well. Most were denied a dignified occupation; riots and blood libels—when Jews were accused of killing Christians to use their blood for ritual purposes—were common and the law offered little protection. Not allowed to own land and limited by law to a few occupations such as lending money and selling alcohol, the Jews were hated by the peasants who were in their debt and vilified by the church as Christ-killers. Their own religious leaders did not bring them much comfort, particularly in Poland where the rabbis were constantly engaged in the reinterpretation of the Law. The ordinary man in the street—and especially the one living in a remote and isolated village—could neither understand nor follow the rabbis' talmudic disquisitions. Instead, superstition triumphed, learning declined, and a wide chasm appeared between the scholars who dwelt in the city and the uneducated—if pious—masses in the countryside. All those conditions help explain the rapid spread of Hasidut.

The Baal Shem himself set out to go to Eretz Israel but for reasons unknown turned back. While he did not complete the journey, his brother-in-law, Avraham Gershon of Kutow did, and he settled with his family in Hebron in 1747. For centuries living conditions in Palestine were so difficult that it was mainly old men and women who went there, wishing to be buried in its consecrated ground. But this began to change, even before Avraham Gershon came, with the arrival of several notable groups such as the one led by Rabbi Yehuda Hasid of Poland—*hasid* here means "pious," not a follower of Hasidut which began half a century later—who arrived in Jerusalem in 1700 with perhaps several hundred followers, or that of Rabbi Haim Attar of Morocco—who came to the city with his two wives and his disciples—and established a yeshiva there in 1741. Avraham Gershon's *aliya* created a bridge between the ancient land and Hasidut, the new spiritual movement. Others followed him to the Holy Land and they too brought along their families. About thirty Hasidim left for Tiberias in 1764, then another group of three hundred Hasidim, led by Menahem Mendel of Vitebsk, arrived in Safed in 1777. I do not know whether one of my ancestors came with the latter group but sixty years later, yet another Menahem Mendel, my great-great-great-grandfather whose tomb I had located in Tiberias, became one of the leaders of the remnants of the 1777 *aliya*.

The 1777 Aliya

I have no family records from the eighteenth century, but I can still hear Baba Esther's voice: "They came in little boats across the Black Sea." Even if my ancestors arrived in the country later, their voyages and experiences would have been similar to those who came there with Menahem Mendel of Vitebsk.

In 1777, when the total Jewish population in Palestine numbered three thousand, the arrival of three hundred Hasidim was an important event. Led by Menahem Mendel along with Avraham of Kalisk and Israel of Polotsk, the Hasidim came from Belarus and Volhyn—a province once in Poland and now in northwest Ukraine. They began their difficult journey by land then crossed the Dniester, the river that marked the border of the Ottoman Empire. They continued to Galati where they boarded small boats and crossed over the marshy Danube delta and the Black Sea to Constantinople, the capital of the Ottoman Empire, now Istanbul. There they lingered until they could join some local Sephardi Jews who were going on pilgrimage to the Holy Places in Eretz Israel and together they sailed down the eastern shore of the Mediterranean.

A month before Rosh Hashana the Hasidim disembarked at Acre and, by donkey, crossed the Galilee to Safed. Their journey had lasted over five months. (The term "Ashkenazim" means Jews from Germany—*Ashkenaz* in Hebrew—and includes Jews from central and Eastern Europe. "Sephardim" means Jews from Spain—*Sepharad*—but it often refers to North African and Middle Eastern Jews as well. In Israel the term "Mizrahiym"—Easterners—is now applied to Jews from Egypt, Iraq, Syria, Turkey, Iran, and other Middle Eastern countries.)

Rabbi Israel described their state of mind upon reaching *Eretz Hakodesh*, the Holy Land: "This is the day we have yearned for, to rejoice and be happy in our land, the object of our delight, the desire of our hearts and joy of our pursuits, the holiest of holy, a land filled with a variety of fruits and other pleasures, and all of the commandments which one can fulfill only here."[1]

But reality stood in sharp contrast to the Hasidim's joy. Two earthquakes had wrecked Safed seventeen years before their arrival and even undamaged houses stood empty because their inhabitants had fled. Still, wrote Israel, it was a city where "one could earn a living if she [Safed] were settled, but we do not know the language nor the local customs." He was echoing the words of Rabbi Moshe Basola who was there in the 1520s: "Whoever does not have capital for commerce should have a profession—weaver, silversmith, tanner, shoemaker, or builder. Strong men can hire themselves out as day laborers and they will be well paid. Even a tailor can make a living. But he who cannot be a teacher or a servant in a shop or a home, should not come here ... and become a burden to the community."[2] The Hasidim soon ran out of money and Rabbi Israel was writing to Vitebsk for help, reminding his co-religionists that Jews everywhere should support their brethren who were risking their lives to redeem the Holy Land—a recurring theme in Jewish history, reiterated in every community, in every generation:

> Thus, our brothers, the Children of Israel, who are merciful and are the children of generous people, it is upon you and upon us to rebuild the House of the Lord, and for all of Israel to become stronger by settling the Holy Land. Cherish [those] ... who risked death and abandoned themselves [to danger] ... Feed them and dress them, so that they can stay in the Holy Land and beg for mercy from above, and pray for the whole community of Israel. After all, you have a major share in the welfare of this land ...
>
> And whoever was touched in his heart by the fear of God, should take pity of those remnants that stay and redeem the soil, who pray for peace over our land and over all of Israel, so that the entire nation will soon swell and come together in the light of Zion, in the House of the God of Jacob. And the virtues of those holy ones in the land will protect all those who make vows and donations ... And I pray for your peace from the Master of Peace. So say I, Israel, son of Peretz, my teacher and rabbi, may he be blessedly remembered in the next world.[3]

On top of their poverty, the Hasidim had other problems. Their Mitnagdim opponents in Lithuania had sent defamatory letters about them to the small Ashkenazi community in Safed. Then, the Sephardim in the city became suspicious of the Hasidim because of their nontraditional rituals, such as shaking their bodies and raising their voices during prayer. The Hasidim apparently received little help from the city's Sephardim and the *pakid*, the official representative of the Jewish community to the Ottoman authorities, discriminated against them. In 1781, along with many of his Hasidim, Menahem Mendel accepted the invitation from the Jews of Tiberias to move there. (On the whole, the Hasidim got along well with the Sephardi majority in the country and it is often noted that Menahem Mendel's son Moshe married the daughter of a learned and wealthy Sephardi from Jerusalem.) Five years later, Avraham of Kalisk moved to Tiberias where he was greatly admired and it was said that even the Sephardim came to hear him pray. Menahem Mendel died in 1788 and was mourned by Ashkenazim and Sephardim alike. Avraham became the leader of the local Hasidim. By then many of the original 1777 group had died.

In a book filled with descriptions of life in Tiberias during the eighteenth and nineteenth centuries, titled *Sefer Teveria*,[4] I came across one of Menahem Mendel of Vitebsk's favorite Yiddish songs, a song full of longing which my great-grandmother Baba Esther used to sing to us. (The verse reproduced here is not the one quoted in the book.)

Vot ikh gehat a shifale	If I had a little boat
Vot ikh tsu dir gekumen.	I would have come to you.
Voste gizeyn meyn fabitterte hartz	Then you would see my embittered heart
Und meyne farveynte oygn.	And my tear-filled eyes.

WEAVING THE THREADS

THE MONTEFIORE CENSUSES

Armed with the names of relatives and information from the *yortzeiten* recorded in the Humashim, I turned to the Montefiore Censuses to learn more about the Jews living in Palestine in the nineteenth century. The five censuses, or *mifkadim*, taken between 1839 and 1876, were commissioned by Sir Moses Montefiore and his wife, Lady Judith. The son of a successful Sephardi merchant, Montefiore grew up in England where he became well known for his contributions to civic causes and was knighted by Queen Victoria. He remained a committed Jew who tried to help his people, especially the ones in Eretz Israel who were living in poverty, spending their days in prayer and study.

Jewish immigration to Palestine had increased during the first part of the nineteenth century, but few newcomers could earn a living largely because of the poor economic conditions in the country. Most Ashkenazi Jews existed on welfare, on *haluka*, which further discouraged them from seeking work. Montefiore tried to motivate them to get jobs, to engage in farming and manufacturing. He and his wife visited the country in 1839, two years after the earthquake that had flattened Safed and Tiberias and killed thousands of people, the majority of whom were Jews. Montefiore

In the Land of Israel

ASHKENAZI - EPSTEIN FAMILY TREE

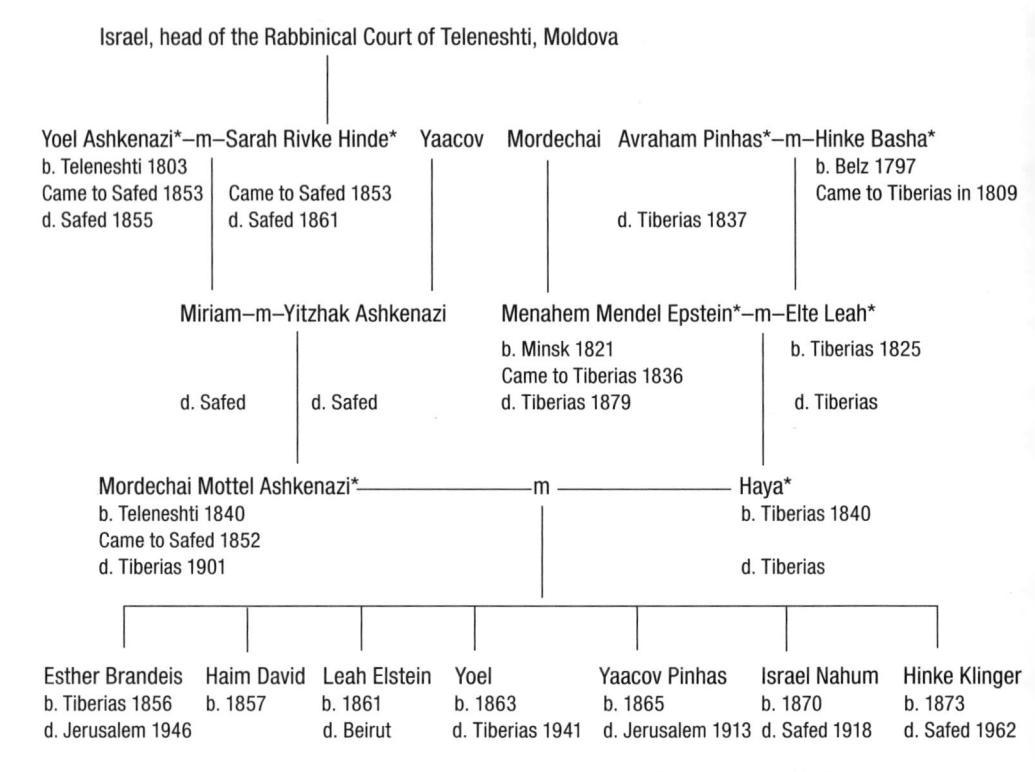

Israel, head of the Rabbinical Court of Teleneshti, Moldova

Yoel Ashkenazi*–m–Sarah Rivke Hinde*   Yaacov   Mordechai   Avraham Pinhas*–m–Hinke Basha*
b. Teleneshti 1803   b. Belz 1797
Came to Safed 1853 | Came to Safed 1853   Came to Tiberias in 1809
d. Safed 1855 | d. Safed 1861   d. Tiberias 1837

Miriam–m–Yitzhak Ashkenazi   Menahem Mendel Epstein*–m–Elte Leah*
                                    b. Minsk 1821   b. Tiberias 1825
                                    Came to Tiberias 1836
d. Safed | d. Safed   d. Tiberias 1879   d. Tiberias

Mordechai Mottel Ashkenazi*————————m————————Haya*
b. Teleneshti 1840   b. Tiberias 1840
Came to Safed 1852
d. Tiberias 1901   d. Tiberias

Esther Brandeis	Haim David	Leah Elstein	Yoel	Yaacov Pinhas	Israel Nahum	Hinke Klinger
b. Tiberias 1856	b. 1857	b. 1861	b. 1863	b. 1865	b. 1870	b. 1873
d. Jerusalem 1946		d. Beirut	d. Tiberias 1941	d. Jerusalem 1913	d. Safed 1918	d. Safed 1962

* name appeared in the censuses

wished to assess the damage caused by the disaster and provide aid to the victims. He might have also wanted to assure the fair allocation of funds. The first census was taken during that visit, recording the names of 6,048 Jews.

Community representatives in every town and village set out to list the first name and age of each Jewish male, the date and place of his birth and, if he was born abroad, the year of his arrival in the country. The man's occupation, marital status, and the number of children under thirteen living in his household were noted. Most of the later censuses included the names of wives and children as well. The inhabitants were divided into Sephardim and Ashkenazim. The latter were further divided into Hasidim and Perushim (also known as Mitnagdim), and into *kolelim*, groups organized by place of origin. The censuses were not perfect yet they provide priceless information.[5]

Combining the data I had from interviews and the Humashim with what I found in the censuses, I was able to construct a family tree (on opposite page). The names that appeared in the censuses are marked by an asterisk. And a reminder to help the reader: Esther Ashkenazi Brandeis, listed last in the segment on the left, was my great-grandmother.

Every researcher, detective, or crossword puzzle addict knows the sense of exhilaration when a bit of information falls into place and a picture begins to emerge. I was thrilled when I found my ancestors' names in the censuses. Not that I ever doubted the accuracy of the Humashim but they only contained evidence of death. When the same names appeared in the censuses it made their bearers' lives so very real: I found out when and where they were born, when they came to the Land of Israel, and where and how they lived.

Hinke Basha and Avraham Pinhas

Ironically, I almost missed the name of the first person in my family who came to Palestine (at least according to the information I have to date). In the 1839 census she was listed simply as "the widow of Avraham Pinhas," who was killed by the 1837 earthquake. How symbolic, I thought, of the lack of attention paid to women's role in history. According to that census, the widow was born in 1797 in Belz—a small town now in Ukraine, formerly in Poland, and the Austro-Hungarian Empire—and came to Palestine in 1809. Then I found her again, in the 1855 census, "the widow of Avraham Pinhas the Cohen," but this time her first name was given: Hinke Basha. (According to that census, she was born in 1795 and came to Palestine in 1805. Dates sometimes vary slightly in the different censuses. I use the dates from the first census, from 1839.) I do not know where her husband was born, only that he belonged to the Russian *kolel*, to the followers of Menahem Mendel of Vitebsk, leader of the 1777 *aliya*. (The term *kolel*, which means "community," had been used since the late 1700s to identify a group of people who originated from the same place in the Diaspora and who remained together as an organized group in Eretz Israel, largely for the allocation of funds: Jews abroad were more generous when the money they gave went to support people who came from their home town.)

My great-great-great-great-grandmother Hinke Basha—Hinke from now on—arrived in the country at a time of great uncertainty. At the dawn of the nineteenth century, Palestine was but a neglected corner of the Ottoman Empire. Corruption was rampant, reaching down from Constantinople to the outer edges of the sultan's realm. Local pashas imposed ever-higher taxes, the countryside was depleted, commerce was at a standstill, and poverty reigned. Epidemics periodically spread through the population and only three hundred thousand people lived there at the turn of the century: The vast majority were Muslims, about ten percent were Christians, and the Jews numbered three thousand.

In Tiberias Hinke would have lived in the Jewish Quarter, located at the edge of the Sea of Galilee, surrounded by a wall within the rebuilt Crusader wall. Tiberias is one of Judaism's Four Holy Cities, along with Jerusalem, Safed, and Hebron. It was founded around AD 18 and named in honor of the Roman emperor Tiberius. After the Romans destroyed Jerusalem in AD 70, many Jews sought refuge in the Galilee and Tiberias became their spiritual capital. The Sanhedrin, the Supreme Council, settled there in the third century and much of the compilation of the Mishna and the final editing of the Jerusalem (or Palestinian) Talmud took place there. Several sages are buried in Tiberias, and throughout the ages Jews came on pilgrimage to pray at their tombs. Saladin demolished the city in 1187, on his way to the nearby Horns of Hattin—a volcanic hill with two peaks—where his victory sealed the fate of the Latin Kingdom of Jerusalem.

Weaving the Threads

Several attempts had been made to rebuild Tiberias and by the time Hinke arrived, about fifteen hundred people were residing there: half were Muslims, the other half Jews, including Sephardim and more recent Ashkenazi immigrants, mostly Hasidim from Russia, Lithuania, and Poland. A number of Christian families lived there as well, and the city encompassed a Catholic church, two mosques, and several synagogues. Most houses were built of basalt blocks, hewn from the nearby volcanic hills, and the rough black masonry, held together by thick gray mortar, lent Tiberias a distinct air. The Sea of Galilee supplied the residents with fresh fish and, in the market, locally grown fruit and vegetables were available, as were oil, wheat, and cotton produced in the vicinity. But daily life was not easy, especially for the Hasidim: Few of them were gainfully employed and, in addition, they had accumulated large debts over the years, a situation aggravated by arbitrary taxes and fines imposed by the authorities.

Hinke and Avraham lived through several epidemics that plagued Tiberias in the second decade of the nineteenth century. Then, in 1826, a year after the birth of their daughter Elte Leah, a locust infestation devastated the crops in the Jordan Valley and hunger spread across the land. In 1831 a severe drought resulted in another famine. Kolel Reisin, the Russian community to which Avraham belonged, was among the poorest in the city and the family must have had a difficult time. Also in 1831 the Egyptian ruler Mohammad Ali rose against the Turks, and his armies, led by his son Ibrahim Pasha, conquered Palestine and Syria. Ibrahim introduced many reforms and brought a measure of stability to the land, but he also instituted compulsory military service for Muslims and levied certain taxes on them, previously paid by Jews and Christians alone. Those new laws caused growing unrest among the Muslims, resulting in a peasant uprising in 1834. When it reached the Galilee, Arab villagers, *falaheen*, attacked the Jews in Safed. Homes were looted, Torah scrolls destroyed, women raped, dozens of men killed and hundreds more wounded. The Jews in Tiberias escaped the riots by paying a large bribe to the rebels. After thirty-three days the forces of Ibrahim Pasha finally prevailed and thirteen rebels, including the ruler of Safed, were executed; the Pasha ordered that the Jews in Tiberias be given back their money.

According to the 1839 census, the earthquake that had killed Avraham also caused ten thousand piasters worth of damage to his property in Tiberias—now his widow's. (From 1825 to 1884, one hundred piasters equaled one Egyptian pound, which in turn was worth about $7; from 1885 to 1939, a pound was worth $5. For current value, see Samuel H. Williamson, "Seven Ways to Compute the Value of a U.S. Dollar Amount—1774 to the Present Time.")[6]

The two cities in the Galilee where the Hasidim—including my family—had settled were intimately related. Only twenty-two miles apart, their climates are very different since Tiberias is located some 680 feet below sea level, while Safed is at 2,650 feet above. Although it took six hours to climb up to Safed by mule or donkey, and three to come back down, people from Safed used to go to Tiberias to take advantage of its mild winters, while the citizens of Tiberias sought relief from hot and humid summers in Safed. There were many marriages between Jewish families in the two cities and events in one place affected lives in the other.

The Earthquake

It was the stories my great-grandmother Esther told me about the 1837 earthquake that got me interested in family history many years after she died. I had always assumed that the little Mottel who was thrown out of the window by his mother was Esther's father, which—as mentioned before—my later research found to be incorrect. But there were plenty of other Mottels in the family and the story must relate to one of them.

The earthquake, in which about one third of the country's Jews perished, was one of the greatest natural disasters ever to hit the area. Tremors were felt from Damascus to Hebron, but the most devastating effects were in Safed. The Jewish community there was the hardest hit because the neighborhood where most of the Sephardim and many of the Hasidim lived consisted of two-story stone houses that clung to the side of a mountain. When the quake came the buildings tumbled down to the valley, one on top of the other, trapping their inhabitants in layer upon layer of debris. The Perushim (or Mitnagdim), most of the Muslims, and Safed's small Christian community lived in other parts of the city which were also leveled but where fewer people lost their lives.

Haraash Hagadol, the Great Earthquake, occurred on Sunday, January 1, 1837, at five in the evening, just as darkness enveloped the land. In Safed, as elsewhere, most adult Jewish males were gathered in their synagogues for the evening prayers and few escaped. In addition to those who were killed instantly, others were caught under the rubble and could not be rescued. The women, children, and the aged who survived could do little to help, lacking manpower and equipment. The screams of the dying were heard for days yet no one could save them, not even their family members who were listening to their cries. There were no doctors, medicine, or food for the injured above ground, nor clothing to protect them from the icy January nights and many who could have been saved perished. Even some of those who escaped unscathed died of hunger or cold and, it was said, of sorrow.

For over two weeks the survivors were on their own. Under the primitive conditions in the country, news of the magnitude of the disaster took a week to reach Beirut and ten days to get to Jerusalem. Rescue teams were organized in both places. Two missionaries, William M. Thomson—who later wrote the bestseller *The Land and the Book*—and E. Scott Calman—a Lithuanian Jew who had converted to Christianity—led a small group from Beirut that arrived in Safed with some medical supplies on January 17. And Rabbi Israel of Shklov, the head of the Perushim in Safed who happened to be in Jerusalem when the quake struck, hurried back bringing with him twelve thousand piasters (about $840), which he borrowed from the Sephardim in Jerusalem to help feed and clothe the survivors. His group arrived in the ruined city on January 22, three weeks after the quake.

There are no exact numbers but it was estimated that between fifteen hundred and eighteen hundred out of Safed's thirty-five hundred Jews were killed. The majority were Sephardim, plus about five hundred Hasidim and fifty Perushim. Hundreds of Muslims in the city died as well, perhaps close to a thousand, and some twenty-five Christians. (According to the 1839 Montefiore census, 711 Sephardim and 571 Ashkenazim were living in Safed two years after the earthquake.)

The damage to buildings in Tiberias was almost as severe as in Safed. The earthquake destroyed all the synagogues and rendered streets and markets unrecognizable. Rabbi Israel of Shklov wrote that "the wall around Tiberias fell and a fire rose from the Kinneret and the sea flooded the city ... This one was left without a wife, this one without a husband, this one without sons, and sons without fathers."[7] Nearly a third of the city's total population of twenty-five hundred died. In Tiberias, too, the Jewish Quarter was hardest hit, and of about eight hundred victims, five hundred were Jews. Among them was Avraham Pinhas, my great-great-great-great-grandfather.

The World of Menahem Mendel Epstein

ELTE LEAH—or LEAH—the daughter of Avraham and Hinke, was already married in 1839 when the first census was taken. Her husband was Menahem Mendel Epstein who was born in Minsk, Belarus, in 1821 and arrived in Palestine in 1836. Jews had lived in Minsk since the sixteenth century and the city's Polish rulers granted them the right to own land and to engage in crafts and commerce. Even after 1793, when the city came under Russian rule, Jews continued to do well there, both materially and spiritually. When Menahem left, the Jewish community numbered about twelve thousand, one of the largest in Russia.

In Tiberias, Menahem joined the Russian *kolel*. By then, Hasidut itself had changed since splits began to occur among the Baal Shem's followers in Europe after his death in 1760. At first the leadership passed on to his disciple, Dov Baer, the Maggid of Mezhirech, but by the third generation, as the movement continued to spread, individual *zadikim*, the leaders of the Hasidim, set up their own courts where each interpreted the Baal Shem's teachings in his own way. Decentralization thus resulted in bitter disputes among various sects and, for both ideological and practical reasons, what happened in Europe affected the Hasidim in Eretz Israel. Near the end of the eighteenth century a major quarrel broke out in the country among the Hasidim over the division of funds collected in Belarus and Volhyn, and the Russian Hasidim broke away and established their own *kolel*, Kolel Reisin. Avraham of Kalisk, one of the leaders of the 1777 *aliya*, led the *kolel* until his death in 1810.

The Jewish Community of Tiberias

Bits and pieces of information form a mosaic that depicts life in Tiberias around the middle of the nineteenth century; there I could trace the annals of Kolel Reisin and Menahem's role within it. Most of the material about the *kolel* comes from a book by Aharon Surasky—*Yesud Ha'ma'alah: Divrei Hayamim Leyishuv Haharidim Be'eretz Israel* about the history of the Hasidim in the country.[8] Other data come from Montefiore's censuses and records of his journeys, reports by other travelers, residents' memoirs, family stories, and *Sefer Teveria*, already mentioned.

I knew Tiberias well as a child and I tried to picture my relatives living there a century earlier. How did they adjust to the city's notoriously muggy, hot summers, having come from northern climes? How did they deal with their Arab neighbors or with Turkish officials without a language in common? I have no precise answers, only general information about daily life in Tiberias.

The 1839 Montefiore census recorded 695 Jews in Tiberias: 316 were Sephardim, the rest were Ashkenazim divided between Kolel Volhyn with 310 people, and Kolel Reisin with sixty nine. When asked by the census takers to describe their financial situation, some Jews said "average," a few noted that they were "well-to-do," and one Sephardi rabbi stated that he "used to be rich" before the earthquake. But most—perhaps because they were hoping for a contribution from Montefiore—declared themselves to be destitute, needy, barely eking out a living, subsisting on charity. Menahem, married but still childless, gave his family's fiscal position as average, *beinoni*; his occupation was "studying the Torah." Kolel Reisin was the only subgroup in the country whose exact monetary

Census of Kolel Reisin in Tiberias, 1855. Menahem Mendel's name is third down on the right; Elte Leah is third down on the left.
Courtesy of the Montefiore Endowment, London

losses from the earthquake were noted, from five hundred to thirty thousand piasters per household or about $35 to $2,100. The damage suffered by Menahem was assessed at five thousand piasters. (The salary of the United States president in 1839 was $25,000, while the average price of a loaf of bread was under ten cents.)

The census noted the individual occupation of most males. In Tiberias, among the Sephardim, were a baker, grocer, tinsmith, goldsmith, builder, painter, tailor, miller, donkey driver, a man "going around villages"—probably a peddler—and a number of religious scholars and synagogue officials. There was also a *batlan*, which literally means "idler," but here it refers to someone living on alms whose duty it was to show up at the synagogue at prayer time in case he was needed to complete a *minyan*, the quorum of ten Jewish males. Among the city's Ashkenazim, many in Kolel Volhyn did not seem to have a profession and presumably survived on the *haluka*—the welfare-like system that distributed money collected from Jews abroad. But some did work: wine merchants, carpenters, tailors, a tinsmith, and a translator were among the 106 adult males recorded, including scholars and rabbis. But in Kolel Reisin, the Russian *kolel*, each of the twenty-four adult males was either studying the Torah or teaching it. This was not because it was difficult to find work. Rather, it was a matter of ideology that differentiated that *kolel* from most other Jewish groups in the country. Its leaders in Russia expected the Hasidim in Eretz Israel to devote their lives to worshiping the Lord—to pray, study, and fulfill the *mitzvot*—and not to engage in worldly matters such as earning a living. Support was to come from their brethren abroad. Those European leaders even discouraged other Hasidim from immigrating to the Holy Land unless their purpose was study and worship.

As noted, Sir Moses Montefiore held the opposite view. Lady Judith wrote in her diary that "... the general opinion of those who know the Holy Land is that agriculture, when properly attended to, can be considered the best means of securing a useful and comfortable life to the poor who for religious motives may prefer that country to any other." During their 1839 tour, on their way from Safed to Jerusalem, the couple stopped in Tiberias from May 27 to June 2. Their reputation preceded them and they were greeted like royalty; the Jewish community met them with song and dance, fifes and drums, and the city's Turkish governor, "well mounted and armed," joined the celebrants with his soldiers who skirmished up and down the sides of a mountain for the party's amusement. The couple stayed at the house of the Sephardi rabbi, Haim Nissan Abulafia, a roomy and clean place "furnished in the Turkish style," and there they met with representatives of the Jewish community and discussed Sir Moses's ideas about land cultivation. The Montefiores worshiped at the Portuguese [Sephardi] Synagogue on Friday afternoon and "attended divine service in the German [Ashkenazi] Synagogue" on Saturday morning. That afternoon, "having attended service in the Russian [Kolel Reisin] place of worship, they visited the heads of the congregation." Among them, I assume, was Menahem Mendel Epstein.[9]

At his request, Sir Moses was given a list of the Jews living in Tiberias, part of what was to become the first Montefiore census. He and his wife then spent one whole day—till ten at night—distributing money into "the hands of every man, woman, and child of the Hebrew, as well as of the Mussulman [Muslim] and Christian congregations." On their way to and from Tiberias they had passed by olive and mulberry trees, "apparently many centuries old," as well as almond and fig trees, prickly pears, and pomegranate bushes. In one place where the scenery was especially pleasing, Sir Moses observed, "... it might well have been termed, 'a garden of Eden,' a very Paradise."[10]

"Squalor and Poverty"

"Paradise" is not a word found in other travelers' descriptions. By mid-century, when the Grand Tour became fashionable, a growing number of "pilgrims and sinners"—to borrow a phrase from Mark Twain—arrived in the Holy Land, both the pious and the curious: missionaries and clergymen, writers and scientific investigators, painters and photographers, famous personalities as well as ordinary sightseers.

Twain, who descended upon Tiberias in 1867, recorded his scathing observations in *The Innocents Abroad*, published two years after his visit. There he described "the stupid village of Tiberias slumbering under its six funereal plumes of palms," its people "vermin-tortured vagabonds," who were best examined at a distance: "They are particularly uncomely Jews, Arabs, and Negroes. Squalor and poverty are the pride of Tiberias." Upon leaving he wrote in his notebook: "I have only one pleasant reminiscence of this Palestine excursion—time I had the cholera in Damascus." It turns out that Twain, under contract to a newspaper in California that had financed his trip, discovered on his way back home that several letters he had mailed to the paper from Italy were lost. To fulfill his word quota, he inflated his Holy Land notes by plagiarizing a little, and exaggerating his unfavorable impressions. As he makes clear in *The Innocents Abroad*, the land was so different from what he learned in Sunday school.

Many travelers—tormented by flies, mosquitoes, and bed bugs—quoted the tenth-century Arab geographer al-Muqadasi: "The King of the Fleas holds his court in Tiberias," where the citizens "danced in their beds" which they shared with legions of bugs. Some lucky visitors stayed at Dr. Haim Weissmann's small hotel that was clean, if simply furnished, where they consumed chicken, eggplant, tasty fish from the Sea of Galilee, and wine from Safed. The antiquarian Félicien de Saulcy slept at that hotel in 1850 and was bitten by fleas. The photographer Maxime Du Camp and his travel companion Gustave Flaubert stayed there as well.

Travelers noted the widespread poverty, mentioned the damage caused by the 1837 earthquake, and applauded the hot springs—famous since Roman times—with their elegant bathhouse, rebuilt by Ibrahim Pasha. Christian pilgrims praised the natural beauty of the lake and the mountains, scenery they assumed had changed little since the time of Jesus. The missionary William Thomson, author of *The Land and the Book*, described the Sea of Galilee and its environs: "To me, Gennesaret and its surroundings are ever fair" because there "our blessed Lord dwelt with men and taught the way of life." One midnight, when the thermometer stood at 100° Fahrenheit, Thomson wondered why so many people lived in Tiberias, then reflected: "They are chiefly Jews, attracted hither either to cleanse their leprous bodies in her baths, or to purify their unclean spirits by contact with her traditionary and ceremonial holiness."[11]

Some travelers commented on the strange dress of Ashkenazi men: either long black coats, striped silk ones, or Indian cotton coats tied with a sash, and hats, either wide-brimmed or trimmed with fur. (I read somewhere that the fur hats were called *gatos muertos* by the Sephardim—that is "dead cats"—for the way they looked and, perhaps, smelled in the hot summers.) Travelers observed that some Jews were fair-skinned, but many visitors preferred the darker ones—the Sephardim—who had better manners than the Ashkenazim. Most women wore long-sleeved dresses, with bright flowers on a white background, and shawls over their shoulders, though some wore European clothes. A few travelers found the women charming.

Jews revered Tiberias both for its spiritual role after the fall of Jerusalem and for the sages and martyrs who were buried there, and they came on pilgrimage to pray at the numerous tombs. One famous sage said to be buried in Tiberias is Rabbi Yohanan ben Zakkai who had himself smuggled out of Jerusalem in a coffin during the Roman siege, foreseeing the destruction of the Temple and fearing the disappearance of Judaism. He soon founded academies where his people were taught how to practice their religion without the central authority of Jerusalem and the Temple. One tradition, questioned by some, has it that the body of Maimonides—the famous philosopher and codifier of Jewish law who was a physician in Saladin's court in Egypt and died there in 1204—was brought to Tiberias and re-interred there.

Menahem Mendel and Kolel Reisin

By late 1839, my ancestor Menahem was one of the three officials, *memunim*, who led Kolel Reisin. The poverty-stricken *kolel* was then at one of its lowest points because the earthquake killed many of its members and only twenty-four adult males survived. Some Hasidim began to think that the whole idea of settling in Eretz Israel to try and hasten Redemption was a mistake and that the earthquake, which killed so many of them, was God's punishment.

In the 1855 Montefiore census, the names of Menahem and Leah's seven children were given, starting with Haya, aged sixteen. The census taker noted that Menahem "serves the needs of the community faithfully"—*osek betzorchei tzibur be'emuna*—and that "he needs [help] with the marriage of his daughter," *hu tzarich lenesuei bito*. Did he require financial aid for Haya's dowry and wedding, or did he worry that she was becoming an old maid? In either case, his wish was soon granted as Haya married Mordechai Mottel Ashkenazi. Esther, their first child and my great-grandmother, was born within a year.

The three officials mentioned above signed Kolel Reisin's 1855 census sheets to testify to the accuracy of the data. The *kolel* comprised of ninety-two people, including two orphans and six widows. It had four societies, manned by volunteers: *Hevra Kdosha*, the Burial Society; *Bikkur Holim*, Visiting the Sick; *Malbish Arumim*, Clothing the Naked; and *Olei Regalim*, a society which assisted people going on pilgrimage to Jerusalem during the festivals of Succot, Passover, and Shavuot, a tradition that goes back to biblical times. The more affluent Kolel Volhyn sponsored additional good causes, such as providing for poor brides and supporting needy Torah students. Both *kolelim* had small study houses or rooms where tutors instructed four to six students each, and were paid a pittance, between sixty and a hundred piasters a month, depending on whether they taught youngsters "from Alef-Bet to Torah," or guided older students through the intricacies of the Mishna and Talmud.

In 1862 Menahem's name appeared on a letter sent jointly by the Sephardi and Ashkenazi communities in Tiberias to the officials of Kupat Eretz Israel—the Fund for the Land of Israel—based in Trieste. The letter, another appeal for help, described events during the preceding year when a cholera epidemic had broken out in the city and the Jewish community had to borrow thirty thousand piasters in order to send its members to the mountains of Safed to escape the outbreak. The letter is preserved in Jerusalem, at The Central Archives for the History of the Jewish People, under "Trieste: Poveri di Terra Santa." (File IT/Ts

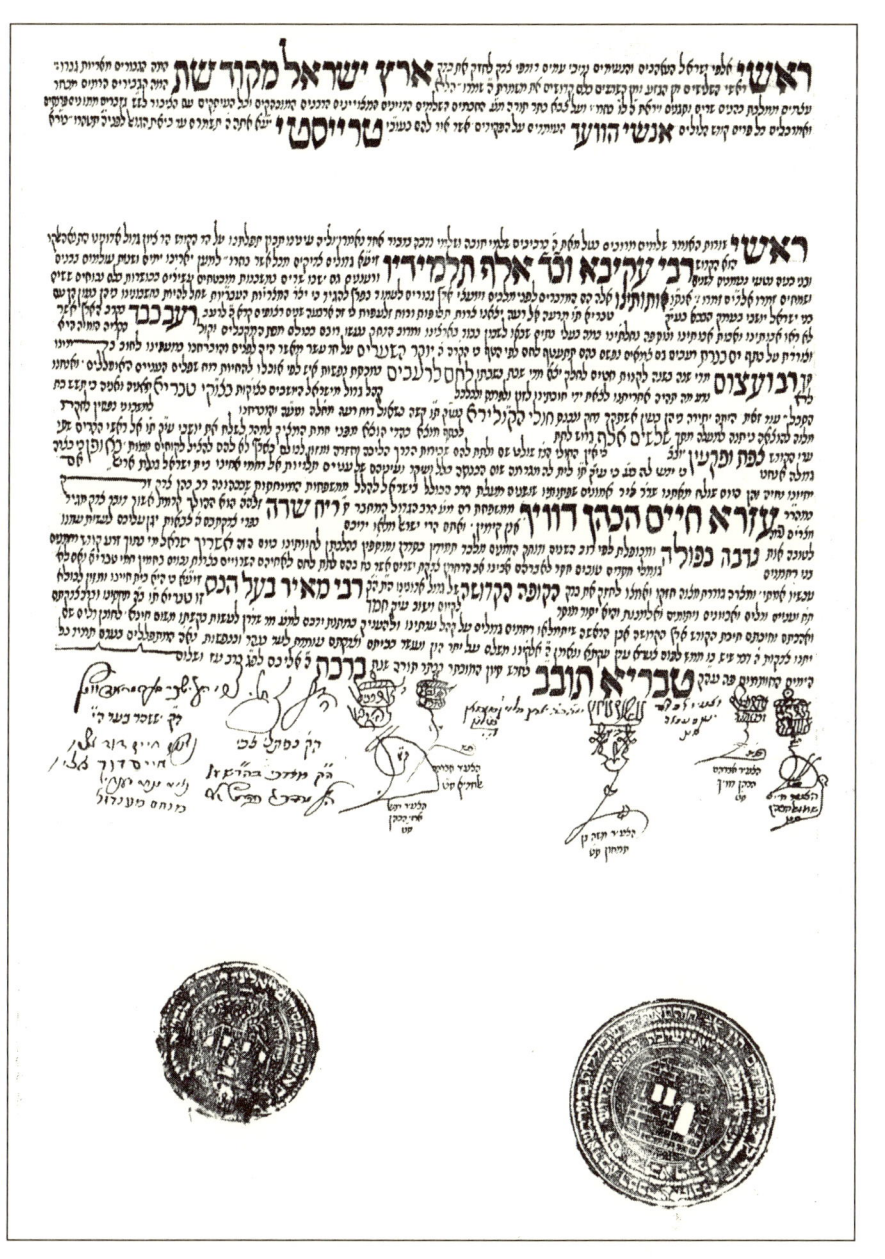

Letter from the Jewish community in Tiberias, 1862. Menahem Mendel's signature and name are the last two on the left.
Courtesy of the Central Archives for the History of the Jewish People, Jerusalem

161.) The last signature and name affixed to it is "Menahem Mendel." I saw the original letter at the Archives where I gingerly touched his pen strokes. When the 1866 census was taken, Menahem was still an official of the *kolel*, but Leah was dead by then. In 1861 her daughter Haya had a child whom she named Leah, after her mother.

I try to imagine Menahem, with a long beard and ear locks, wearing an ankle-length coat and perhaps a *shtreimel*, a fur hat, even during the oppressively hot summers. Menahem Mendel's word was said to be law and he was not only honored and respected by all the Jews in Tiberias, but even the Arabs admired him. Yet within the family, he was reputed to have been "a difficult person."

As one of the leaders of a tiny *kolel* completely dependent on charity from abroad, he surely worried about the welfare of his small community and his large family. Yet there must have been some bright spots in his life. From its very beginning Hasidut was a joyous movement whose followers worshipped God in ecstasy. They had communal meals and drank wine together, and they sang and danced. Rabbi Israel wrote in 1777 that the Hasidim were happy to be "in our land, the object of our delight, the desire of our hearts and joy of our pursuits ..."[12] In 1789 another Hasid described praying at the tombs of the sages in Safed: it was "like milk and fatness [overabundance]. And now my lips are full of joy and praise from what I tasted and my eyes are brighter [see the light better] than in all the days when I lived abroad."[13]

Menahem Mendel died on November 17, 1879, and was buried in Tiberias.

The Family Ashkenazi

Arrival from Teleneshti

According to the 1855 Montefiore Census, my great-great-great-great-grandparents, Yoel and Sarah Rivke Hinde Ashkenazi, came to Safed from Teleneshti in 1853. Their grandson, Mordechai Mottel, would later marry Haya, daughter of Menachem and Leah Epstein. Yoel was a learned man, a *ben Torah*, and an official of Kolel Volhyn, which included some Hasidim from Bessarabia. I do not know what Yoel's occupation was in Teleneshti, only that his father-in-law served as the head of the rabbinical court there (see Ashkenazi-Epstein family tree, p. 22).

Teleneshti is a small town in Moldova, located in a region once known as Bessarabia. The country itself lies between the Dniester and Prut rivers, bordered by Ukraine and Romania. Documents from the early seventeenth century show that the Ottoman authorities, which ruled part of the country before 1812, invited Jewish and Armenian merchants from Poland, especially from the area of Lviv—where Hacham Zvi died—to come and resettle the countryside, which for centuries had been depleted by attacks from neighboring countries. A 1794 *pinkas*, or register, of the Jewish burial society in Teleneshti attested to the existence of an established community.[14]

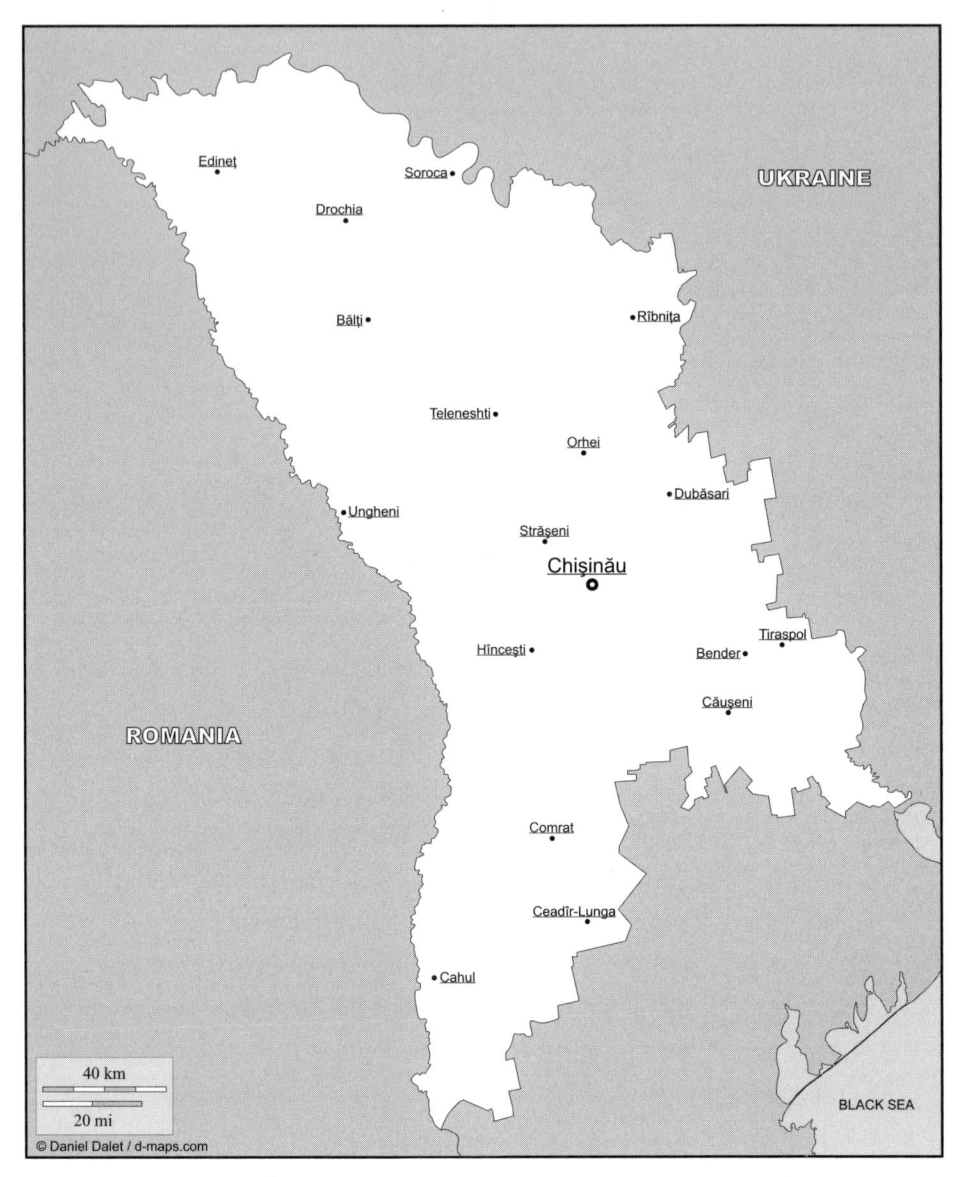

IN THE LAND OF ISRAEL

Map of Moldova, c. 2007
Courtesy of d-maps.com
(http://d-maps.com/carte.php?lib=moldova_map&num_car=27000&lang=en)

Anti-Semitism was prevalent all over Europe, and Bessarabia, under the powerful influence of the Orthodox Church, was no exception. Throughout Eastern Europe Jews often found themselves in the position of middlemen, dealing with aristocratic landowners on one side, and serfs, peasants, and merchants on the other. While the local peasant could see "God's will" in the feudal system that required him to work for the aristocracy and give up most of his crops, he looked upon the Jew as a "leech"—a moneylender, a tavern owner. Venomous sermons on Sundays reinforced the peasant's hatred and made the Jew a convenient scapegoat. Yet there were no state-sponsored pogroms in Moldava during the eighteenth century, and edicts show that the civic authorities warned against persecuting the Jews who were helping develop the countryside. The landowners were interested in the skills the Jews brought with them and granted them land for building synagogues, houses of study, ritual baths, and cemeteries. Jews engaged in agriculture, raised cattle, grew fish in ponds, and distilled and sold alcohol. Some were artisans, wagoners, and innkeepers.

Teleneshti was situated in a heavily wooded area with oaks, birches, orchards, and vineyards. Every year merchants from surrounding countries descended upon the town to buy the produce of the fertile black earth—wheat, maize, barley, flax, tobacco, fruit, wine—so the citizens were aware of events in the outside world. Life was relatively secure for Jews in the countryside. Even after Bessarabia was annexed by Russia in 1812, it managed to maintain an autonomous status and was not affected by the tsar's anti-Jewish legislation. But this began to change and by 1852 compulsory military service was imposed on Bessarabian Jews. This may have expedited the departure of the Ashkenazi family for the Holy Land. Six or seven other families from Teleneshti had settled in Safed in 1852 and 1853, according to the censuses.

Yoel died in 1855, followed by Sarah six years later. Their daughter Miriam had married Yitzhak whose last name was also Ashkenazi. According to the Humashim, they were buried in Safed but I am not sure about the sequence of events since I found their son, Mordechai Mottel, listed in the 1855 census under "Ashkenazi Orphans" in Safed. He was born in Teleneshti in 1840, arrived in Eretz Israel in 1852 and was the grandson of Yoel of Teleneshti.

Mordechai Mottel Ashkenazi

Baba Esther often talked about her father Mordechai Mottel who, after marrying Haya Epstein moved to Tiberias, where he joined the Russian *kolel* to which his father-in-law belonged. Years later he applied for British protection, a move made possible by the Capitulations which placed non-Ottoman citizens—as well as people under the shield of a foreign power—within the legal safeguards of their own consular representatives. Great Britain in particular became a patron of the Jews in Palestine and came to their aid on numerous occasions. Being under British protection had many advantages, which explains Mordechai's application addressed to the British consul in Haifa and dated April 1, 1872. I do not know whether British protection was granted to the family.

In 1865, many people died in Tiberias during a cholera epidemic. The city had no real medical facilities and the need for a hospital was acute.[15] In 1872, three *kolelim*, Volhyn, Karlin, and the Russian *kolel*—the latter represented by Mordechai—joined together in what was known as Hevrat Bikkur Holim, "Society for Visiting the Sick." A courtyard and four houses which belonged to the *kolelim* were made available to the society and soon some sort of a hospital was set up there with a doctor who appeared at irregular intervals. But the city's hot climate and poor sanitary conditions brought on many diseases which the small facility could not handle. So in 1883, several rabbis and officials from Jerusalem, Safed, Tiberias, and Hebron came out in favor of building a proper hospital in Tiberias since the city's therapeutic hot springs attracted a large number of sick people. Two years later, in the spring of 1885, Israel Dov

The Family Ashkenazi

Frumkin, the editor of *Habazeleth*, visited the city and wrote at great length about the need for a hospital. (His paper, an organ of the Hasidim, was one of the earliest Hebrew newspapers in the country, first published in 1863.) That summer a group of seven people wrote to Frumkin, hoping he would publish their letter in *Habazeleth* and get others to support building a hospital. In Tiberias, they noted, even those who came to the hot springs had no one who could tell them how long they should stay in the water, and since "there is no doctor, there are no drugs ... [and] people die before their time." Mordechai Mottel Ashkenazi was the first person to sign the letter. I came upon it unexpectedly, in 1989, while searching through the Zionist Archives in Jerusalem (File: Tiberias, A199 #59). I had just returned from Tiberias, after one of my futile searches for Mordechai's tomb, so finding a letter with his name on it was simply overwhelming.

The need to set up a Jewish hospital became even more urgent when a Scottish missionary group—the Committee for the Conversion of the Jews—decided to establish the Sea of Galilee Medical Mission in Tiberias. It opened a clinic there in 1885, headed by Dr. David Watt Torrance, and inaugurated the Scottish Hospital ten years later. Providing health care was a tactic often used by missionaries in the Holy Land. While most Jews shunned efforts to convert them, many were tempted to consult a doctor—even an evangelizer—if the life of a child was in danger and no Jewish doctor was available. Once a Christian health facility opened, the Jewish community galvanized to offer similar care, and so a Jewish hospital was finally built in Tiberias in 1896. Dr. Torrance, it turned out, spent little time on saving souls and devoted the next forty years of his life caring for the sick in Tiberias. He had a huge following among Jews and Muslims alike and was mourned by all when he died in 1923.[16]

I found Mordechai's footprints in another episode. In 1891, before the Jewish hospital opened, a Dr. Hillel Yaffe was invited to Tiberias to see if he might be interested in serving there. In his memoirs Yaffe described his first meeting with some forty men, all Orthodox, dressed in white

Little Jewish Boy in the Scots Mission Hospital, 1934-1939
Courtesy of the Library of Congress

trousers and cotton or silk coats, with long beards and ear locks. A secular Jew, the doctor hastened to assure the gathering that he would not break any religious laws in his clinic nor would he force any patient to do so unless illness dictated it. One of the more important people in the group, wrote Yaffe, a man called Mottel Ashkenazi, stood up and said: "Sir, we already have a wise and God-fearing rabbi in Tiberias. What we need now is a medical specialist." Pleased by this attitude, Yaffe accepted the position. Later, no one asked why he did not attend synagogue services: "They never worried about the relationship between God and me," wrote the doctor in his memoirs. Eventually, a deep affection developed between the physician and the community.[17] Dr Yaffe later became famous for his efforts to establish health services throughout the country.

The Family Ashkenazi

I do not know much about Haya, Mordechai's wife. Esther, her daughter—and my great-grandmother—claimed she spoiled her children and later her many grandchildren. She was an excellent housekeeper and learned how to cook local dishes from her Sephardi and Arab neighbors. (Esther was always quoting proverbs in Arabic that her mother had taught her. Concerned with good manners, she often repeated: *Duq al-bab qabil ma tudkel.* "Knock on the door before entering.") Many of Haya's female descendants were named after her, including my mother's beloved sister.

Mordechai was quite liberal when it came to the education of Esther, the oldest child in his family that eventually consisted of four sons and three daughters. While most boys began to study in *heder*—a religious elementary school—at age five, girls were taught at home, if at all. (According to one tradition, Jewish girls learned enough Hebrew to be able to follow the prayer book, and enough of the local vernacular to be able to address an envelope.) Esther had an inquisitive mind and fortunately, she told me, her father was sympathetic. Either because of the bad reputation of the local *heders* or, as I like to think, for Esther's benefit, he hired a tutor, a *melamed*, to come and teach his sons at home. Esther was allowed to sit in the same room and listen, so, indirectly she studied the Bible, Mishna, and Talmud. Due perhaps to poverty, the state of learning in the Jewish community in Tiberias was grim, especially among the Hasidim. Dr. Ludwig August Frankl, secretary of the Jewish community in Vienna who set up the Laeml School for Girls in Jerusalem, wrote after he visited Tiberias in 1856: "The city where the Sanhedrin, the Supreme Council, met and the great sages lived and taught, is now the seat of ignorance."[18]

Esther did not shave her hair when she got married, as was the custom among Orthodox families and I give her father some credit for that. But against the practical, progressive image of Mordechai stand the instructions he left his sons, written on the back pages of one of the Humashim: "My dear sons, be careful not to bathe in the sea or in a river on the

Sabbath. My dear sons, be careful not to take walks on the Sabbath outside a city wall or in a city without walls. My dear sons, be careful to pray in public because it is a *mitzva* often overlooked these days. My dear sons, be careful not to teach your children and your children's children foreign [studies?] and especially European languages, and do not let them study in [secular?] schools." Did he grow more conservative with age?

My great-grandmother Esther married David Brandeis, an *ilui*, a prodigy, according to family lore. Joseph, their oldest child, was born in 1878. Five years later, shortly after their second child, Sarah, was born something happened to David. One source says he drowned in the Sea of Galilee; another version has it that he studied too much and became mixed up, unbalanced. Whatever happened, Esther was left to bring up two children on her own. There was little a young woman could do to support herself in Tiberias during the 1880s, so others in her position returned to their parental home or lived with their in-laws. Esther, however, a forerunner of the liberated woman, refused to be a dependent. She tried to make a living by knitting sweaters and other garments, but there was little demand for her wares in the balmy winters of Tiberias and she found it difficult to provide for her two children. Meanwhile, Leah, one of her sisters, had married Moshe Elstein, a wealthy merchant who was living in Beirut. They could not have children and offered to raise Sarah, my mother's mother.

From Beirut to Jerusalem

Sarah Brandeis-Elstein

When Sarah Brandeis-Elstein arrived in Jerusalem in 1906, she was wearing a wide-brimmed hat with black feathers, as was the fashion in Beirut. Numerous bracelets adorned her arms and a small gold watch dangled from a chain around her neck. Attractive and urbane, her reputation slightly tarnished by divorce, she married my grandfather, Eliyahu Halevi Berman, a twice-widowed merchant with two sons almost as old as his new bride.

When Sarah first went to market, children ran after her and shouted: "Look at her! Look at that hat!" She soon gave up the latest creations of Beirut's milliners and settled for a plain kerchief, as was the local custom. Half a century later, after my grandfather died, she sold the house on Hayei Adam Street that he had built in the 1880s and moved to a nearby apartment. Helping to pack in anticipation of the move, I was sorting through piles of belongings when I came upon an old shoe box where, side-by-side, lay the baby locks of my uncle Moshe, Sarah's firstborn, and long black feathers from one of her old hats.

One of my earliest memories is of my grandparents sitting together every evening after supper at the dining room table. He would be peeling

General View of Beirut, 1898-1914
American Colony Collection, courtesy of the Library of Congress

an orange and offering it to her. (A diabetic, he was constantly urging the rest of us to eat what for him were forbidden fruit.) When she finished the orange he would take her hand and ask: "Did it taste good, my Sarahleh?" To me they seemed an idyllic, if ancient, couple. But back to the beginning ...

Sarah was four or five when she found herself in Beirut. Forlorn at first in the large metropolis, amidst the unaccustomed opulence of the Elsteins' house, she sorely missed her mother and brother. But her adoptive parents doted on her; it was said in the family that "she lived wrapped in cotton wool," sheltered and protected. Eventually the Elsteins won her over. She took their last name, and later, when her first son was born, she named him Moshe, for her uncle, and brought him to Beirut to visit.

*Moshe Elstein, Sarah's uncle who brought her up,
with Sarah's son, Moshe, on a visit to Beirut, 1908*

She named my mother, her second child, Leah. Since it is not customary among Ashkenazi Jews to name children after living relatives, an exception was made in this case, probably because the Elsteins were childless.

Moshe Elstein was an Orthodox Jew, but he was also a worldly man who traveled a lot, buying silk in Aleppo—on the ancient route of caravans from the East—and selling it in the West. He thought that Sarah should have an education beyond the prayer book and since there were no Jewish schools for girls in nineteenth-century Beirut, he sent her to a Catholic day school, run by French nuns. She did not eat there nor did she attend classes on Saturday, and she was exempt from religious instruction and church services. At home Sarah got to know many interesting people because her uncle was an early supporter of Zionism and meetings and discussions with like-minded individuals took place regularly in the Elsteins' drawing room.

Sarah remained a pious woman, yet glimmers of her time among the Catholics lingered well into my own childhood. Take Christmas, for example, an ordinary work day for Jews in the Holy Land, although some marked it by playing cards or dominoes—frivolous activities normally frowned upon—to show their low opinion of the man whose name would not cross their lips except as "he who had lost his way." Grandmother, on the other hand, would drag out one of her old school books and recite some version of the life of Jesus. By the time she reached the end she was always weeping, but since the book was in French, which I did not understand, it took me a long time to realize what the story was all about. It was especially confusing because sometimes she read aloud from another book dealing with the voyage of Christopher Columbus and the trials he faced just before reaching the New World. This she read in German and since I knew Yiddish I understood most of that saga. When the going got tough—for Christopher that is—Grandmother would shed tears once again, and for years, until I was seven or eight, I mistook Christopher for Christ, thinking they were one and the same.

When Sarah turned eighteen, a matchmaker was commissioned by the Elsteins to look for an appropriate bridegroom. I do not know much about her brief first marriage, not even her husband's last name, only that he was nicknamed Velveleh, or Wolf. Sarah moved to Haifa, to his parents' home, and in the beginning she was very happy. "He was young and handsome and we loved each other very much," she told me. "We were always laughing, and all we wanted to do was to be near each other." But Velveleh was the youngest son, the apple of his mother's eye, and it seems that it was too much for her to share him with another woman at such close quarters. And so, the family story goes, she began to spread rumors about Sarah's past, about her unorthodox education and her friendships with some of the young Zionists who frequented the Elsteins' house. When the gossip reached Beirut, it infuriated her uncle Moshe and he sent her a telegram: "Sarah, come home." He then dispatched Eliyahu Klinger, another uncle of Sarah's, to Haifa and together uncle and niece left for Beirut. According to Sarah she and Velveleh cried bitterly at their parting.

"How could you do it?" I asked her. "You loved him so. Why did you leave?"

"*Mein kind*—my child. You don't understand. Perhaps, if it had been my real father who had ordered me home, I might have disobeyed him. But I owed so much to *der Fetter* Elstein, to Uncle Elstein, who was so kind to me. It would have been unthinkable not to do as I was told."

Many years later I heard from my aunt Zahava who grew up in Haifa that Sarah's divorce was a *cause célèbre* in the city, where the former mother-in-law was considered to be a wicked woman. It was said that she was cursed because of her behavior; another one of her sons died young and destitute and left behind five small children whom she had to raise. Sarah never went back to Haifa. She stayed in Beirut, a young divorcée in a precarious social position. Before her marriage she mixed freely with the students who visited her uncle's house and was an active participant in events organized to raise money for various good causes. But now on such occasions she just sat at the door and sold tickets or else stayed home and perfected her embroidery. At times, she told me, she felt so trapped that she would rise at dawn and escape to a deserted beach nearby, where she would shed her outer garments behind a large rock, as she used to do when she was a child. Her aunt did not think that swimming was a suitable pastime for a young Jewish girl—and certainly not for a divorced woman—so Sarah did not own a bathing costume. She

IN THE LAND OF ISRAEL

*Cabinet portrait of my grandmother, Sarah Brandeis-Elstein,
which she sent to Eliyahu Berman, 1905*
Photograph by A. Noun, Beirut

would make sure no one was on the beach and in her bloomers dive into the balmy waters of the Bay of Beirut.

Meanwhile, her family was busily looking for another husband for Sarah. Her uncle Eliyahu Klinger—who had married Hinke, Esther's youngest sister—was a prosperous merchant and banker who often traveled on business from Safed to Jerusalem where he heard of a possible candidate, a most reliable man, a widower. Soon photographs were exchanged between the parties. I still have Sarah's picture, taken by "N.

Aoun, Photographe, Beyrouth, Syrie." Perhaps a bit plumper than is fashionable today, she looked quite appealing in a white dress with many strings of seed pearls around her neck. Her dark hair was piled high, a few tresses falling across her forehead. The photograph must have pleased Eliyahu Berman who came to Beirut to meet her, then married her and brought her to his house in Jerusalem.

⁂

With Sarah's departure for Jerusalem, my story shifts away from the Galilee, from the Ashkenazis and Epsteins. The history of the Bermans was easier to trace since I grew up among them, listening to stories about their early years in Jerusalem, familiar with most of the characters.

Entrance to Jerusalem through Jaffa Gate
Photograph by Bonfils, 1880s
Courtesy of the Berman Bakery

―――― *part two* ――――

Jerusalem

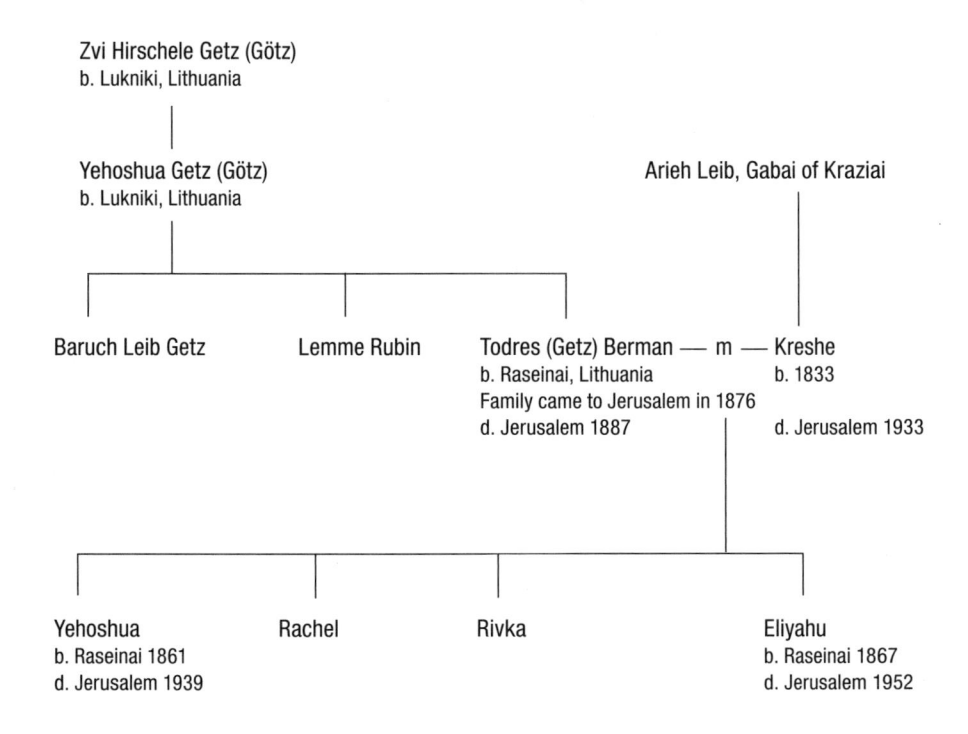

BERMAN FAMILY TREE I

Zvi Hirschele Getz (Götz)
b. Lukniki, Lithuania

Yehoshua Getz (Götz)
b. Lukniki, Lithuania

Arieh Leib, Gabai of Kraziai

Baruch Leib Getz

Lemme Rubin

Todres (Getz) Berman —— m —— Kreshe
b. Raseinai, Lithuania   b. 1833
Family came to Jerusalem in 1876
d. Jerusalem 1887   d. Jerusalem 1933

Yehoshua
b. Raseinai 1861
d. Jerusalem 1939

Rachel

Rivka

Eliyahu
b. Raseinai 1867
d. Jerusalem 1952

The Berman Family's Beginnings

The Bermans' Arrival in Palestine

My grandfather Eliyahu's parents, Todres (Theodore) and Kreshe Berman, arrived in Jerusalem in 1876. Todres's father, Yehoshua Halevi Getz, and his grandfather, Zvi Herschel Halevi Getz, who lived in Lucknick (now Lukniki), Lithuania, are said to have stemmed from rabbinical ancestry. (Every Jewish family claims to have had at least one famous rabbi in its past ...) Todres lived in Raseiniai, located some forty miles northwest of Kovno, today's Kaunas. There he married Kreshe, the daughter of Areih Leib the *gabai*—the director of the synagogue—of nearby Krozh, now Kraziai.

Todres was described as a God-fearing man, well versed in the Torah, who had devoted himself to the worship of the Almighty. But he was only "an average merchant," so it was Kreshe who operated the family's business in Lithuania, a store where housewares were sold. It was their lifelong dream to live in Eretz Israel and in 1876 they sold the business, realizing some two thousand rubles in addition to their travel expenses, and left for Jerusalem with their four children. Yehoshua, the oldest, was fifteen, Eliyahu was nine, and in between were two daughters, Rachel and Rivka.

Aviva Berman Harris, one of my second cousins, told me that since people sometimes called Todres *Getzeleh*, "little goat," which he resented, he changed the family's name to Berman shortly after arriving in Jerusalem because he admired a man called Shimon Berman who had arrived in Palestine in the early 1870s and tried to establish agricultural colonies there. It was said in the family that at some point Shimon helped Todres but it is not known how. Aviva also mentioned that in addition to Todres's desire to live in the Holy Land—which, in theory at least, every Jew hopes to do—Kreshe feared that their sons might be drafted into the army. In Russia, since 1827, Jewish boys over the age of twelve were often inducted into the army for twenty-five years and served under terrible conditions. Boys as young as eight were sometimes abducted from their families to serve as cadets. There was no way for them to observe the commandments to eat kosher food or not to work on Saturday, and they were usually lost to Judaism. When parts of Lithuania came under tsarist rule, a number of Jews left lest their sons be conscripted. But Kreshe and Todres only left in 1876, long after the law was passed, when their sons were fifteen and nine.

Could there have been other reasons for the family to leave? Raseiniai—also Rossieni, Raseyn, Rossyen, Rosienie, Raseina, Rossieeny—is an old city already mentioned in records from the thirteenth century. The city's Jewish community was among the oldest in Lithuania, and it became known as the "Jerusalem of Zamut," the latter being a region in northwest Lithuania, also known as Zemaitija. The city came under Russian rule in 1795, with the third partition of the Polish-Lithuanian Commonwealth. In the nineteenth century Raseiniai became a center of the *Haskala*, the Jewish Enlightenment, so Todres, who was strictly Orthodox, might have seen it as a danger to his children and perhaps that contributed to the family's move to Eretz Israel. When the Bermans left, about half of the city's population was Jewish.[19]

The family traveled to Odessa and spent about three months there before crossing the Black Sea to Constantinople, where they boarded

The Berman Family's Beginnings

Jaffa from the Sea, 1890-1900
Detroit Publishing Co., courtesy of the Library of Congress

another boat and continued to Jaffa. Large vessels could not enter the rock-strewn harbor and all steamers had to drop anchor about a mile out of the city. Over the centuries hundreds of passengers—pilgrims, immigrants, tourists—wrote about their first glimpse of the Holy Land which usually filled them with great joy; a few described the trauma of disembarkation at Jaffa. William Makepeace Thackeray, who landed in Jaffa in 1844, wrote that when his rowboat approached the shore "hideous brutes in brown skins and the briefest of shirts" waded over to the boat, grinning and shouting in Arabic for everyone to mount their shoulders, and the ladies "were obliged to submit; and, trembling, were . . . carried through the shallows and flung up to a ledge before the city gate, where crowds more of dark people were swarming."[20]

Transportation by donkey
Detroit Publishing Co., courtesy of the Library of Congress

Transportation throughout the country, for both passengers and goods, was makeshift, provided by horse, donkey, camel, or mule. An ingenious contraption made of two crates tied together, one on either side of the animal, carried small children, one or two deposited into each crate; rocks were used to correct any imbalance. The journey from Jaffa to Jerusalem—a distance of some forty-five miles and an elevation of about two thousand five hundred feet—along the unpaved road took a day-and-a-half. Travelers usually spent the night in Ramla or at the khan, the inn, at Bab el-Wad—the Gate of the Valley—where the Shphela, the coastal plain, ends and the Judean hills begin. At the khan, the animals slept on the first floor, the passengers on the second. Kreshe and Todres Berman's arrival in 1876 could not have been much different from that experienced by thousands of other passengers.

When the Bermans finally reached the Holy City, Todres went off to the Etz Haim Yeshiva at the Hurva Synagogue, where he dedicated himself to studying the Torah. While he was securing himself and his family a safe place in heaven, Kreshe was left to deal with earthly matters such as providing food for their four children. Todres was not too concerned. "God will provide," he said. After all, the Almighty would not bring them all the way to Jerusalem to let them starve there. Being somewhat more practical, Kreshe soon opened a small grocery store on the Street of the Jews in the Old City, just across from the Hurva. In fairness to Todres, it should be added that Etz Haim was the city's major yeshiva of the Perushim, or Mitnagdim—that is Ashkenazi Jews who were not Hasidim—and it granted small stipends to its scholars. But the independent-minded Kreshe wanted something better for her children.

At first the family lived in the Muslim Quarter, near the synagogue of Kolel Reisin on Hebron Street that runs parallel to Bab el-Silseleh, between the Three Covered Bazaars and the Temple Mount. Chaim Hamburger, a family friend, wrote about the location. In 1876, when he used to study with his uncle Pinhas—who lived in the same courtyard on Hebron Street as did Todres Berman—Chaim befriended Todres's sons, Yehoshua and Eliyahu.[21] Shortly thereafter the Bermans moved to the Street of the Jews, closer to the store.

Beginning in the late 1970s and for the next couple of decades, I interviewed many Bermans: my mother's siblings, that is Eliyahu and Sarah's children and their spouses; descendents of Eliyahu's brother, Yehoshua Berman: Zahava Berman, the widow of his son Baruch, and their daughter Aviva Berman Harris; Yehoshua's son Arieh; and Rachel Ben-Tovim Gretz, the daughter of Rashke, Yehoshua's oldest child. I also got information from some of my first and second cousins.

NINETEENTH-CENTURY JERUSALEM

Jerusalem was a small city of about 22,000 inhabitants when the Bermans arrived there in 1876: 11,000 Jews, 4,500 Christians, and 6,500 Muslims. Still, it was a much more livable place than it had been at the beginning of

Aerial photo of Jerusalem: Temple area from the north showing Siloam in the distance, 1931
Courtesy of the Library of Congress

the century. In 1800—when one million people lived in London and one-and-a-half million in Tokyo—the total population of the Holy City numbered 9,000 (2,250 Jews, 2,750 Christians, and 4,000 Muslims). They all dwelt within the confines of the Old City's wall, an area of about a third of a square mile (eight hundred dunams). "A fast walker could go outside the walls of Jerusalem and walk entirely around the city in one hour. I do not know how else to make one understand how small it is," wrote the disillusioned Mark Twain in *The Innocents Abroad* after his 1867 visit.

In the late 1530s, some twenty years after the city and the country came under Ottoman rule, Sultan Suleiman the Magnificent rebuilt the wall that still surrounds the Old City. (It was built along the lines of Emperor Hadrian's second-century wall that, in turn, had incorporated remains of earlier fortifications from the First Temple, Hasmonaean, and Herodian periods.) But after Suleiman, the Ottomans neglected Jerusalem. They forbade new construction or even repairs of non-Muslim holy places. Greedy officials imposed high taxes and in the absence of commerce and industry, chronic poverty prevailed. There was no doctor in the city until 1838; malaria, trachoma, and stomach ailments were treated by quinine, silver nitrate, and castor oil, respectively. Women in labor were given a key to a saint's grave to put under their pillows. Lepers sat by Zion Gate and begged. "No gas, no oil, no torch, no wax lights up the streets and archways of Jerusalem by night," wrote William Hepworth Dixon, an Englishman who toured the city in 1866. Raids by marauding Bedouin were so common that the city gates were locked half an hour after sundown. Late travelers spent the night outside the gates and in an emergency, if someone had to leave the city unexpectedly, he would be lowered by rope over the wall. In the markets rotten fruit, camel dung, and an occasional dead cat floated in open sewers. When too much garbage blocked the streets, the city gates were left open for one night so that the jackals could come and scavenge. Within the squalid city, the overcrowded Jewish Quarter was dirtiest of all.

Todres Berman, my great-grandfather spent his days at the Hurva Synagogue. *Hurva* means "ruin" in Hebrew, and the name goes back in the days of Rabbi Yehuda Hasid who left for Jerusalem in 1700, filled with messianic fervor, and accompanied by many disciples—the number varies with the sources. As the group traveled through Eastern Europe, Jews there promised to support the endeavor. Once in Jerusalem they settled in a courtyard that had been purchased for them earlier by some of Rabbi Yehuda's supporters with money borrowed from their Muslim neighbors, counting on future donations from abroad to repay the loan.

Unfortunately, Yehuda Hasid died three days after his arrival in the Promised Land. Without his name and prestige the money pledged in Europe never arrived and the debt kept growing until the Muslims lost patience. The second Saturday in November of 1720, was *Shabbat Lech*

In the Land of Israel

The Hurva Synagogue, 1934-1939
Courtesy of the Library of Congress

Lecha, named after the Torah portion for that week, which began with God telling Abraham "Get thee out ..." A group of Arabs broke into the small Ashkenazi synagogue that had been built in the courtyard, tore up the Torah scrolls and later burned the building. The remains became known as "The Ruin—the *hurva*—of Rabbi Yehuda Hasid." The authorities then banned Ashkenazi Jews from the city—since they were all regarded as responsible for the debt—and most resettled in Safed and Tiberias. If one wanted to visit Jerusalem, he would don Oriental garb and try to pass for a Sephardi.

Life took a turn for the better for all Jerusalemites over a century later when, in December 1831, the city surrendered to the armies of Ibrahim Pasha, the son of the Egyptian ruler Mohammed Ali who had rebelled against the Ottomans. As previously mentioned, the Egyptians occupied Palestine for the next nine years and brought about many changes. They permitted repairs to churches and synagogues and made the roads safer, so pilgrimage increased. They allowed England to open a consulate in Jerusalem and let the London Society for Promoting Christianity Amongst the Jews—a missionary organization founded in England in 1809 and in Jerusalem in 1834—establish the first infirmary in the Holy City in 1838, complete with a dispensary and a European-trained doctor. This alarmed Jews and non-Protestant Christians alike because they worried that in extreme cases their co-religionists might be tempted to visit the infirmary and thus come under the influence of the missionaries. So in 1842 the philanthropist Moses Montefiore sent a Jewish doctor, Simon Fraenkel, to Jerusalem to dispense drugs and medical advice and, in the 1850s, two Jewish hospitals were founded in the Old City, the Rothschild Hospital and Bikkur Holim.[22] Several Christian denominations founded clinics and hospitals as well, and followed with schools and orphanages. The construction of new facilities meant additional jobs for Jerusalemites, and thus, as the result of the competition among the various religions, the quality of life in the city improved.

When Jerusalem returned to Ottoman hands in 1840, the clock could

The Jewish Quarter of Jerusalem with two synagogues, c. 1900
Taken from a stereograph by Underwood & Underwood
Courtesy of the Library of Congress

not be turned back. The British, for example, were allowed to build a small chapel for the use of the consul, a chapel that somehow grew into the impressive Christ Church, the earliest Protestant church in the Middle East. The person sent to serve as the first Anglican bishop to Jerusalem was a converted Jew, Michael Solomon Alexander. He arrived in January 1842 with his wife and six children on *Devastation*, a Royal Navy frigate, in time to lay the cornerstone for the church but died before the building was completed. (It was common practice among missionary societies to send converts as apostles to Jewish communities in the mistaken belief that it would be easier for them to make other Jews "see the light." Jews generally treated converts with contempt, and if someone in an Orthodox family converted, he or she was considered dead.) Alexander was soon replaced and in order not to be outdone by the Protestants, both the Greek Orthodox and Latin patriarchs moved to the Holy City, leaving behind the greener pastures of Constantinople where their predecessors used to reside. By 1860, some twenty years after the inauguration of the British consulate, every major European power as well as the United States had diplomatic missions in the city. More and more visitors arrived—tourists, archaeologists, scientific investigators, writers, painters, photographers—which benefitted the city.

The number of residents grew as well, especially the number of Jews, after a law was passed canceling old debts of the Ashkenazim, and the Qadi of Jerusalem, the supreme Muslim judge, declared that the courtyard of the Hurva Synagogue belonged to the Jews. The synagogue was rebuilt—between 1857 and 1864—only to be destroyed by the Jordanians in 1948, after the surrender of the Jewish Quarter. (It was rebuilt once again in 2010.)

Ashkenazim began to resettle in Jerusalem. Many arrived from Safed and Tiberias after the 1837 earthquake. Most newcomers moved into the Jewish Quarter—the smallest of the Old City's quarters, the others being the Muslim, Armenian, and Christian quarters—where most houses belonged to Muslims since Jews were not allowed to own real estate. Between 1800 and 1860 the Quarter's population quadrupled and living conditions became unbearable. The worst problem was the shortage of water. The main source of water was rain collected from rooftops into the cisterns that were an integral part of every courtyard, usually shared by several families. By the end of the rainless summers the water would be very low and it was often contaminated, the source of intestinal ailments and a breeding ground for the Anopheles mosquito, the carrier of malaria. The Jewish Quarter was also the poorest in the city since most Ashkenazi Jews did not work but subsisted on the meager quotas of the *haluka*, the money sent by their brethren abroad. In the 1860s the Quarter's overcrowded conditions finally forced some residents to move outside the Old City and establish new neighborhoods; a number of Christian institutions began to appear outside the wall, as did private Muslim residences.

Some ten years after their 1876 arrival in Jerusalem, the Bermans too were ready to leave the Jewish Quarter for the new city.

The Business and the Family

THERE ARE SEVERAL VERSIONS within the Berman family as to why Kreshe went into the business of baking bread. One is that while still in Lithuania she planned to open a store in Jerusalem but that the crockery she had carried with her broke during the arduous journey and she had no stock with which to launch a new business. Another story is that the family's money was stolen somewhere along the way. The third version, recounted below, is based in part on interviews with family members but mostly on an article which appeared in a 1930 issue of *Mignazei Yerushalayim*, "From the Jerusalem Treasury," published to celebrate a half century of contributions made by Yehoshua Berman and his mother and brother to the development of industry in Jerusalem. (Kreshe was still alive when the piece came out and she must have provided much of the information in it.) According to the article, Kreshe's grocery store did not do well because she was not familiar with the way business was conducted in the Holy City, and the two thousand rubles she had brought from Lithuania were soon gone.

In an effort to drum up trade, Kreshe began to bake honey cakes, *honig lekah*, and in order to reach new customers, she sometimes stood near Jaffa Gate or by the Lions' Gate, on the Via Dolorosa, and offered her goods to pilgrims on their way to the Church of the Holy Sepulchre. Thousands of pilgrims, many of them Russian, arrived in Jerusalem each year before Christmas and stayed there until after Easter. One day a pilgrim said to her: "Babushka, your cakes are very good but what I really long for is some black Russian bread." Kreshe took the pilgrim's wish seriously but the local grain, which was quite inferior, was neither dark enough nor dense enough to produce the right texture. So she began to experiment and eventually succeeded in creating a rich dark bread by adding to the dough a paste made from the fruit of the carob tree. Russian pilgrims snatched up the bread and Kreshe could hardly keep up with the demand. She began by baking two *tavalach*—two trays—of bread a day then four and when she reached six, she got her son Yehoshua to leave the yeshiva and help her. But after Easter, when the pilgrims went home, she was left with few customers. Yehoshua then became a door-to-door salesman and tried to persuade the local housewives to buy ready-made bread.

Baking one's own bread was a major production. Grain supplies for a whole year had to be purchased in late summer, after the harvest, when *falaheen* from the outskirts of Jerusalem and from Hebron and beyond brought wheat and other produce to the grain market; once purchased, the supplies had to be stored at home in tin-lined wooden boxes, to keep out the mice. Every month women equipped with large sieves came to each courtyard to sift a month's supply of wheat, removing from it small stones and other impurities. The wheat was taken to be ground at one of four flour mills in the city, owned and operated by Arabs; then the women with the sieves returned to sift the flour while other women supplied yeast. In those days, it was the man in the Jewish household who did most of the shopping, but it was the woman who, three evenings a week, had to knead dough and let it rise overnight, shape it into loaves early in the morning and then wait for the delivery boys who took the loaves to a *furnus*, or furnace, several of which were owned by Sephardim and located in the Jewish Quarter. The same boys returned the baked loaves later in the day, and, although each housewife had a special way of marking her loaves, sometimes they got mixed up and if that happened

The Business and the Family

on a Friday to the *hallot* prepared for the Sabbath, chaos ensued since each woman wanted to show off her own handiwork.

Either because baking bread was such a time-consuming task, or because Yehoshua was such a good salesman, the family was soon operating the first modern bakery in the country. Within a couple of years Kreshe sent Yehoshua to Odessa, where, according to cousin Aviva, he trained for a while with a baker called Weinstein. When he returned he brought back samples of high-quality flour and soon the Bermans were importing flour, grains, sugar, and legumes from Russia and other European countries, both for their own use in the bakery and to sell to others. Goods arrived by boat and were unloaded at the port of Jaffa and from there, by camel, continued to Jerusalem. Arieh Berman, one of Yehoshua's sons, told me that it was a risky business because the camel drivers often removed flour or grain from the sacks at night and substituted sand and gravel. Still, being the only commercial bakery in the city until the end of the nineteenth century, the business did well. Its major customers were hospitals, orphanages, and other charitable institutions, in addition to the local housewives.

Kreshe was determined that her sons engage in gainful occupations, since her husband spent his life studying while she was forced to support the family. Yehoshua was content to work alongside his mother but Eliyahu was not interested in business. He was a bit of a dreamer, a young man with artistic tendencies that were frowned upon by his older brother. My grandfather once told me that when he was a teenager he grew geraniums in tin cans on the roof of their house. Between the prevailing crowded conditions in the Jewish Quarter and the chronic water shortage in the city, it was a miracle that any flower survived. Yehoshua, however, thought it was disgraceful for a young man to waste his time on such frivolities and one day simply tossed Eliyahu's flower containers off the roof.

In 1882, the Bermans opened the first Jewish store outside the Old City, just north of Jaffa Gate, where newly built shops had stood empty

In the Land of Israel

*Grinding stones from the old Berman flour mill
now standing near Hutzot Hayotzer*

for a long time because people were afraid to move beyond the protection of the wall. (It is possible that for a number of years the store was also used for baking bread. If one walks north out of Jaffa Gate, along the Old City wall, one can still see burn marks on the second tower protruding from the wall—just about where the Latin Patriarchate is located on the other side, within the Old City. My second cousin Isaac "Izzy" Berman told me that his father, Arieh, showed him the spot that he remembered from his childhood.) In 1886, Yehoshua purchased "a ruin near the stores by the Temple Mount" and built a motorized flour mill that operated on kerosene, the first such mill owned by an Ashkenazi Jew. A few years later the Bermans moved the mill to the Valley of Hinnom just west of Jaffa gate, to a neighborhood then known as Jorat el-Anab, "the Pit of the Jujube Trees," populated by poor Sephardi Jews. The Ladino-speaking Sephardim knew Yehoshua as *la barba blanca*, the "white beard." The mill switched to steam power in the 1890s and was considered a technical marvel. Two of the mill's grinding stones can still be seen in the Valley of Hinnom, next to Hutzot Hayotzer. I walk by them every time I am in Jerusalem.

Rather than work in the bakery, my grandfather Eliyahu tried his hand at carpentry and opened a small workshop in Nahlat Shivah, a Jewish neighborhood established in 1869 on Jaffa Road, not too far from the Old City. A contemporary writer described Eliyahu as "an honest, loyal person, sensible and good natured, with sterling qualities as a merchant and a trustworthy man." Perhaps his qualities were too sterling. His venture was not very profitable and, at some point after Todres died, Eliyahu joined Yehoshua—Joshua in English—in the family business.

The brothers founded the firm of "J.&E." Berman—or "Y.&E." in Hebrew—and in the late 1880s acquired land near Mea She'arim, north of the Old City, where they built a new bakery and several family residences. The bakery stood at one end of the large lot, with a spacious apartment on the second story where Kreshe lived with Yehoshua and his family after her husband died. Next to the bakery was a piece of land that the family later donated for the construction of a small synagogue. Across a narrow alley the Bermans built two other houses, one for their sister Rivka and her husband Arieh Levy, and one for Eliyahu. In 1902 a much larger "perfected modern bakery," as one reporter proclaimed, replaced the old one, with a warehouse and an enclosed courtyard for the donkeys, horses, and carriages used to distribute the bread. I grew up in the house that Eliyahu built and my childhood revolved around the bakery, the family's business.

Several Jewish neighborhoods had been established outside the Old City since 1860, but relatively few private houses were built beyond the wall for lack of security. The land that the Bermans purchased abutted the northwest corner of Mea She'arim, a neighborhood dating to 1874. It was typical of Jewish communal construction from that period, consisting of long blocks of attached townhouses built around a central courtyard that all entries faced. The street facades were doorless and at night, when the gates were locked, no one could enter or leave. After dark, gangs of Bedouin and thieves ruled, along with stray wolves, howling jackals, and packs of wild dogs. Over a hundred families lived in Mea She'arim when the Bermans moved next door. At that time the populace—which at present is among the most extreme ultra-Orthodox in the city—was more diverse. The neighborhood, which featured many shops and a large open-air market, was one of the first in the city to be illuminated by kerosene streetlights. Periodically fashion shows took place there, as did magic lantern presentations—forerunners of slide shows—and for a brief period the area was known as the "Paris of the Orient." (For anyone familiar with the area today, this is hard to believe!) Another neighborhood just across the street from my grandfather's house was Batei Moshe Wittenberg, two long rows of one-story townhouses with red-tiled roofs. Built in 1886, it was named for the donor, a childless merchant from Vitebsk, who wanted to provide housing for poor Jews.

In 1883 Yehoshua Berman married Sarah Haskel of Vilkovishk,

Lithuania—the eldest of four sisters—a marriage that eventually resulted in ten children, five sons and five daughters. When Eliyahu turned twenty in 1887 he married Miriam, one of Sarah's younger sisters, a beautiful woman whom he loved. Tragically, she died soon after she gave birth to twin boys; one of the twins died as well.

Life became very difficult for the grieving young widower since it was against Jewish custom to have a woman, an outsider, serve as a live-in housekeeper for a single man, even for the purpose of caring for a baby. A family council soon decided that Eliyahu should marry Rachel, Haskel sister number three. After all, who could better provide for Meir, the surviving orphaned baby, than an aunt, his mother's flesh and blood? In due time Rachel, who was also a beauty, bore her own son, Zalman. More sophisticated than her sisters, she was considered rather extravagant by the family since she used to hire a carriage every afternoon and ride with the children to Motza, a village some four miles away. But she too took to bed—I am not sure what ailed her—and there she stayed for a number of years until she died, when Zalman was eleven. At that point, after the appropriate mourning period, it was suggested that Eliyahu marry Sheinke, Haskel sister number four, who was still *tsum haben*, or "available." But he said no, to the consternation of the "other side" (which is how Yehoshua, his wife, and their descendants were defined by Eliyahu's children, to stress the difference between the two sides of the familiy).

It was then that Eliyahu married my Tiberias-born and Beirut-bred grandmother, Sarah Brandeis-Elstein. She was not well received by her new relations who still resented Eliyahu's refusal to wed the last Haskel sister. "I was not so happy when I first married your grandfather," Sarah told me when I was a very young woman going through a difficult period in my own life. "He was almost forty and he had not been with a woman for a long time. In addition, some members of his family were not very nice to me," she added in what was at best an understatement. "But once your uncle Moshe was born I was much more content and I did not care anymore about the attitude of my sisters-in-law."

My grandparents, Sarah and Eliyahu Berman, Jerusalem, 1907

It is not hard to picture Sarah's early life in Jerusalem. She was twenty-three, her two stepsons sixteen and thirteen. She had no relatives of her own in the city. Her mother and brother were living in Tiberias, her adoptive parents were in Beirut, the rest of her aunts, uncles, and many cousins were in Safed and Tiberias. Her new husband used to leave for the bakery when it was still dark, come home for a quick lunch and return to work until after sunset. Her eldest sister-in-law, Yehoshua's wife, was the bereaved sibling of Miriam and Rachel, Eliyahu's first and second wives, and Sheinke, the one he did not marry, was still around. (Sheinke eventually married one Avraham Baer, a handsome, ultra-Orthodox man from nearby Mea She'arim.) Eliyahu's sister Rivka who lived next door used every opportunity to criticize Sarah.

The family was doing well financially. Yehoshua went to Russia so

The Business and the Family

BERMAN FAMILY TREE II

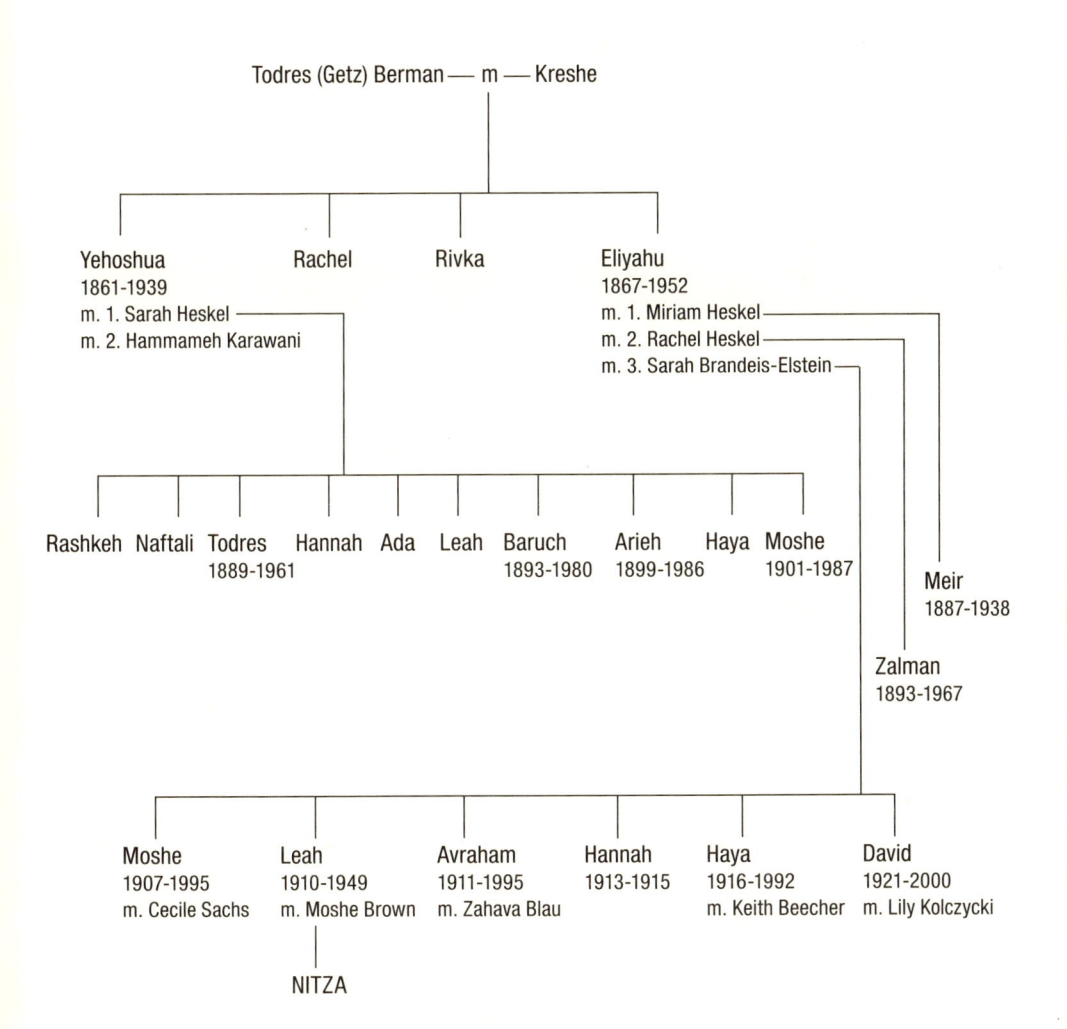

Todres (Getz) Berman — m — Kreshe

- Yehoshua
1861-1939
m. 1. Sarah Heskel
m. 2. Hammameh Karawani
- Rachel
- Rivka
- Eliyahu
1867-1952
m. 1. Miriam Heskel
m. 2. Rachel Heskel
m. 3. Sarah Brandeis-Elstein

Children: Rashkeh, Naftali, Todres (1889-1961), Hannah, Ada, Leah, Baruch (1893-1980), Arieh (1899-1986), Haya, Moshe (1901-1987)

Meir 1887-1938

Zalman 1893-1967

- Moshe 1907-1995 m. Cecile Sachs
- Leah 1910-1949 m. Moshe Brown
  - NITZA
- Avraham 1911-1995 m. Zahava Blau
- Hannah 1913-1915
- Haya 1916-1992 m. Keith Beecher
- David 1921-2000 m. Lily Kolczycki

77

often that he became known as *der Odesser beker*, the baker from Odessa. Eliyahu began to travel as well. The brothers purchased new machinery in Europe and continued to upgrade and modernize the equipment in the bakery and the flour mill. Eliyahu kept the books and was in charge of correspondence. He could look at a column of figures and total it instantly in his head—a feat that never ceased to amaze me when I watched him doing it—and he had a perfectly beautiful handwriting. When he wrote in Hebrew, he would begin the letter with the words *Yerushalayim, po, ir hakodesh*, "Jerusalem, here, the Holy City," and denote the date by naming the *parasha*, the portion of the Torah read in the synagogue that week, followed by the Jewish calendar year. As the business expanded he had to learn to write in English in order to correspond with suppliers abroad. An English missionary, a woman, lived nearby in a small house, now gone, near the B'nai B'rith Library where Beitar, the Revisionists' youth movement, was located in the 1940s. Eliyahu used to sneak surreptitiously into her house at night to study. Any association with a missionary, and a woman to boot would have scandalized Orthodox Jerusalem! Eliyahu had a good ear for languages. Since Yiddish, the main language used by Ashkenazi Jews, is based on dialects of Middle High German from the Rhineland, he understood German. I do not know whether he spoke Turkish, but he was fluent in Hebrew and Arabic and he remembered some Russian from his early childhood in Lithuania. It was a Russian pilgrim who was responsible for the change in Kreshe's fortunes, and the Berman Bakery continued to provide bread and other foodstuffs to some twelve thousand Russian pilgrims who used to descend upon the city annually between Christmas and Easter until the onset of World War I. Once a year, my uncle Moshe told me, Eliyahu used to meet with the archimandrite, the local head of the Russian Orthodox Church, to make the proper arrangements.

One of the hopes of Zionism was that Jews in Eretz Israel would learn to till the land and participate in other occupations that required physical labor. *Avoda ivrit*, "Hebrew" labor, was the term used, rather than

Jewish labor, as if to emphasize the contrast with the stereotypical image of European Jews who were limited by law to only a few professions—tradesmen, moneylenders, saloonkeepers. Although Arab labor in Jerusalem was cheaper, the Bermans were sympathetic to the Zionist cause and, by the beginning of the twentieth century, were employing over fifty Jewish workers. (It is interesting to note that some Jews thought it might be better to employ Arabs as well and provide poor laborers with an income that might lessen their hostility to Jews.) In 1902 the Bermans built a brick-making factory near the bakery that functioned until World War I, and they continued to operate the mill and the store outside Jaffa Gate. After her sons took over running the bakery, Kreshe remained in charge of the store, selling bread, flour, yeast, and legumes. There was a big storage room behind the shop adjacent to the Old City Wall. Yeast was prepared in a smaller room where a large water jar stood, covered by a wooden lid with a pewter measuring cup on top. Kreshe—who lived to be a hundred—told one of her great-granddaughters, Ayala Zacks-Abramov, that she once found a large black snake wrapped around the jar and intuitively knew it was bringing luck to the family, so she left it alone. A while later, the jar was smashed by the snake who sensed that the water had become contaminated. Kreshe replaced the jar with a new one, and from then on the snake acted as the guardian of the water.

Moshe, Sarah's first son and Eliyahu's third, was born in 1907 and was named for Sarah's uncle. When the baby was one year old Sarah took him to Beirut to visit the Elsteins and the occasion was commemorated by a photograph taken in one of the city's studios (see p. 49). It portrays the two Moshes. The older one, with a white beard and mustache, is in a dark suit, his head covered by a tarbush, a fez. In his lap is baby Moshe wearing a short cotton dress with white shoes and socks. Three years later, when my mother was born, she was named Leah, for Sarah's aunt. She was Eliyahu's first daughter and he spoiled her shamelessly. Avraham followed in 1911, Hannah two years later.

Sarah Berman and her son Moshe, Beirut, 1908

Life in the house became very hectic with four children under ten. Moshe, always thoughtful and considerate, seems to have stayed out of trouble but Leah, fascinated by and undoubtedly jealous of baby Avraham, would not leave him alone. Once she turned his pram upside-down while he was in it; another time she shoved a pacifier down his throat and he almost choked. A few years later Avraham managed all by himself to push a carob seed up his nose and, despite the discomfort, was afraid to mention it to anyone. Ultimately a foul odor revealed his secret and he was rushed to the Shaare Zedek Hospital for surgery. Hannah, an exceptionally beautiful baby, was treated by her older siblings as if she

My uncles Avraham and Moshe (left and middle) with my mother, 1913
Photograph by M. Savides

were a doll. Once they even placed her on a shelf in a glass cabinet where knickknacks were displayed until Sarah rescued her. Hannah's tale is a sad one, since she died at age two, after a brief illness. Her tiny body was carried to the cemetery on a small wooden plank, a sight her siblings never forgot. A few days earlier she had been playing with them on top of the large stone that covered the mouth of the water cistern in the yard. It seems unlikely that there was any connection between her catching cold and sitting over the cistern, but the older children—who were frequently told not to play there—always felt uneasy about it. (My uncle Avraham's eyes filled with tears as he told me the story in the 1980s.)

By late summer, when the cisterns were running low, many families tried to leave the city for fear of disease. Sarah would have liked to go to the seaside, but she bowed to the long-established Berman tradition and went with the children to Hebron where the air was cooler and the water purer. Eliyahu used to rent a house from a local family and then hire two carriages to transport kin, kit and caboodle—children, clothes, bed linen, pots and pans. It was too hot to travel during the day so the family would set out at sundown; the journey, which included several breaks, took almost the whole night. They usually stopped along the way for a late supper: hard-boiled eggs, cucumbers, tomatoes, cheeses, olives, and many different kinds of bread. The children were treated to lemonade while Eliyahu sipped a little arak, a drink similar to ouzo. Hebron was famous for its grapes and in the summer many vineyard owners slept in watchmen's towers to guard the ripening fruit. Grandfather knew some of the Arab landlords who called him *Hawaja* Eli, Mister Eli, and toward morning, as the carriages were passing by rows of vines, the Bermans were often invited to stop and visit and were offered Turkish coffee. A day or so after the family settled into its quarters, Eliyahu would return on horseback to Jerusalem and come out again on Fridays to spend the Sabbath with his family. My mother often reminisced about those summers.

I found a Hebron-related vignette about Eliyahu in *Sefer Sheloshah Olamot*, "The Book of Three Worlds," the memoirs of his friend Chaim Hamburger.[23] The famous Hasidic rabbi Shneur Zalman of Lublin, *der Lubliner rebbe*, who had moved to Palestine in 1892, was spending some time in Hebron. The sage's digestive system was very delicate and he subsisted mainly on hard white rolls that were a specialty of the Bermans, baked in a slow, covered oven. Inexplicably, the rabbi ran out of rolls one day so a messenger was dispatched to Jerusalem. Riding over the mountains he arrived at Hamburger's house at ten o'clock at night and together they rushed to wake up my grandfather and seek his help. Eliyahu took them to the bakery, saw to it that a fresh batch of dough was mixed and waited for it to rise. Once the rolls were baked, he carefully wrapped them up in paper and added a couple of loaves of bread for the *rebbetzen*, the rabbi's wife. He refused to be paid for the rolls: "I will not take money from the Rabbi of Lublin," he said. "It is a great honor for me to be able to fulfill his wish." From 1898 until his death four years later, the rabbi lived in a courtyard near the Berman Bakery.

In late October 1898, Theodor Herzl, the "father of modern Zionism," traveled to Palestine in order to meet the German emperor, Kaiser Wilhelm II, who was visiting there. Herzl hoped that the Kaiser, who had shown some sympathy for Herzl's ideas, would recommend the Zionist Organization to Abdul Hamid II, the Turkish Sultan. However, the meeting in Jerusalem on November 2 was not a success since the Kaiser had changed his mind. Herzl had called upon the Kaiser in his tent encampment on the Street of the Prophets, a few blocks away from our house. I often wonder whether anyone in my family caught a glimpse of the man who dared to think of establishing a modern, independent Jewish state: "If you will, it is no legend."

Between the Old and the New

The phrase "old and new Yishuv" refers to the Jews of Eretz Israel between 1881, when the first Zionist group left Russia for the Promised Land, and 1914, the onset of World War I. Yishuv here means population, and the "old" were mostly the Ashkenazi Jews who dedicated their lives to study and worship, while awaiting the arrival of the Messiah, and Sephardi Jews—Jews from Spain and also from North Africa and the Middle East. The "new" were the Zionists, the secular nationalists who came to reclaim the ancient land through their own labor, and who hoped to modernize both Jewish culture and the Hebrew language. The old Yishuv was suspicious of the newcomers' secular ways, while the latter viewed the unproductive lifestyle of the old Yishuv and its dependence on charity with a certain disdain. But the line separating the old

Dedication of a workers' housing facility in Motza, 1885
Among the dignitaries present: standing first on the left is Shimon Rokach; David Yellin is third; Yehoshua Press, fourth; Ephraim Cohn-Reiss, fifth; Yoseph Meyuhas, ninth; Yehoshua Berman, tenth followed by Arieh Levy, Yehezkiel Blum, and Eliyahu Berman, and Meyuhas's son. Yehoshua Yellin, is by the tree on the far right.

and the new was really not very clear. On all fronts, social, economic, and cultural, some Jews from the old Yishuv had begun to break out of the traditional mold before the Zionists' arrival. While still observing the commandments, they were open to new ideas and wanted to support themselves and get away from the politics of the *haluka*. They established agricultural settlements, opened banks and other commercial ventures; they founded hospitals, secular schools, a national library, and several Hebrew newspapers. In Jerusalem, where most Jews lived, they began to move out of the Old City into new neighborhoods that they had built.[24]

Kreshe and her sons were among those who bridged the old Yishuv and the new one; today we would call them modern-Orthodox, observant Jews who were not fanatic and tolerated those who practiced Judaism in their own way. Kreshe, by refusing to rely on the *haluka*, eventually became an entrepreneur who established the first commercial bakery in the country and opened the first Jewish-owned store outside the Old City. Interested in the efforts to modernize their society from within, the Bermans supported many civic causes. For example when, in 1895, a new agricultural settlement was established through B'nai B'rith in Motza, not far from Jerusalem, Yehoshua, Eliyahu, and their two brothers-in-law, Yehezkiel Blum and Arieh Levy, were among the dignitaries present at the dedication of a new facility, built to house farm workers. A photograph taken on that occasion shows all four with mustaches and beards; Yehezkiel had on a European-style hat while Yehoshua, Arieh, and Eliyahu wore tarbushes as was the local custom.

The Bermans were not *Maskilim*—proponents of the Enlightenment—but they supported secular education. Eliyahu was determined that his children have all the opportunities he had missed, since his only formal schooling was in *hader* and yeshiva. "*Tilmedu, tilmedu. Lemi sheyesh melacha yesh melucha,*" he would urge the children. "Study, study. Whoever has a trade [a profession] has a kingdom." He wanted them to understand math and science, history and geography. He was also intent that they learn to speak Hebrew fluently; the children reached school age at the time when the battle for reviving the language was raging in Jerusalem.

❦

Eliezer Ben-Yehuda is credited with the rebirth of Hebrew as a living, spoken language—a near miracle. Throughout the generations, almost all Jewish men knew some Hebrew, the language of the Bible and the daily prayers, and even some women were taught enough to be able to follow the *siddur*, the prayer book. Commentators, poets, and philosophers continued to write in Hebrew throughout two thousand years in the Diaspora, and ordinary Jews living in different parts of the world corresponded with each other in Hebrew since it was the one language

Eliezer Ben-Yehuda at his desk, c. 1912

they all had in common. In their daily conversation, most Ashkenazim used Yiddish while Sephardim spoke Ladino, so when they met they were forced to use Hebrew to communicate. They could understand each other even though their pronunciation varied and their vocabulary was archaic. Ben-Yehuda is known as the father of modern Hebrew because he turned it into the vernacular of his people, spoken on the street, in kindergarten, used in schools to teach every subject, in scientific research, in the media, in politics, and in all other walks of life. When he first arrived in Palestine, in 1881, he was determined to speak nothing but Hebrew so when his first child was born he had to coin many new words: bicycle, doll, jam, towel. Until then gloves were "houses for hands" and a clock was an "hours indicator." He also insisted that modern Hebrew use the Sephardi, rather than Ashkenazi, pronunciation which he found more melodious and thought it was probably the way Hebrew sounded in ancient times.[25] Ben-Yehuda's efforts met with fierce opposition from ultra-Orthodox

Jews who objected to the secularization of the holy tongue. It was meant, they said, to be used in prayer and study alone. They denounced Ben-Yehuda to the Ottoman authorities who were suspicious of him to begin with, fearing any new ideas that hinted at nationalism, and he was jailed for a while. Yet in the end, victory was his.

At the turn of the nineteenth century Ben-Yehuda lived a couple of blocks away from my grandparents' house, on Ethiopia Street, where numerous leaders of the Jewish community resided—politicians, teachers, the intelligentsia. (Named for the large Ethiopian church built there in the 1880s, it is still one of the most charming streets in the city with elegant stone houses and hidden gardens.) A number of Jewish educational institutions were located there as well: the Teachers Seminary, Bezalel Art School, and for a while, Laeml and Tahkemoni, separate schools for girls and boys. The American Institute of Archaeology (later part of ASOR), established to study biblical archaeology, was also there between 1906 and the end of World War I. The presence of so many young people on the street, especially art students, lent it a certain Bohemian air and it was dubbed the Latin Quarter.

Various family members took part in the battle for the Hebrew language. Arieh Levy and Yehezkiel Blum, Eliyahu and Yehoshua's brothers-in-law, were involved in establishing the first Hebrew nursery schools in Jerusalem, beginning in 1903. They worked with leaders of the old Yishuv who were trying to change it from within, such as David Yellin, Ephraim Cohn-Reiss, and Yeshayahu Press. The nursery schools were supported by the B'nai B'rith Lodge which Blum and Levy helped found in 1888, and where Eliyahu and Yehoshua were members. (The organization, which originated in the United States in 1843, encompassed Jewish interests as well as those of the outside community.) In 1910 my uncle Moshe began to attend a nursery school that was located a block away from our house, at the top of Hayei Adam Street, opposite the Straus Health Center—as yet to be built. His siblings followed. From then on the children spoke Hebrew among themselves and with their father, but they continued to use Yiddish with Sarah whose Hebrew remained weak. As part of their secular upbringing, the boys were not made to cover their heads, even though their father always wore a *kippa* inside the house and a hat—or until 1918 a tarbush—outside.

The road to the family's secularization started with Kreshe's determination that her sons earn a living and not spend all their time studying the Torah, which usually meant depending on charity. Eliyahu was equally determined that his children—his daughters as well as his sons—get the secular modern education he had missed. He sent them all to schools which were not dominated by religion and encouraged them to become part of the new Yishuv. Eventually he would give them the opportunity to study abroad.

It was my uncle Moshe who retained the clearest memories of pre-World War I Jerusalem, of the city at the twilight of the Ottoman period. He often went with his father to the family's store outside Jaffa Gate, he told me, and Eliyahu would treat him to an ice cream on the balcony of a nearby hotel, perhaps the Howard or the Fast. They would then enter the Old City and pass by the clock tower that was built over the gate in 1907 in honor of the thirtieth anniversary of the rule of Sultan Abdul Hamid. Moshe, who was born that year, recalled the clock with special fondness since it had four faces, two showing European time, the others Eastern time. (The latter, I am told, was used locally to measure the time between sunrise and sunset, rather than the twenty-four hours daily cycle. The clock and a nearby ornate Turkish *sabil*, a water fountain, were later removed by the British who considered their architectural style too flamboyant and out of character with the Old City wall and the adjacent citadel, popularly—and incorrectly—known as the Tower of David.) Eliyahu and Moshe would amble past legions of shoeshine boys with glittering wood-and-brass boxes and go into the arcade of the New Grand Hotel where Eliyahu would get his tarbush pressed. On the way back they sometimes stopped at the small public garden, a novel concept

The Business and the Family

Yehoshua Berman's family, c. 1905
Back row: Hannah, Todres, Baruch, Rashkeh and her husband,
Shmuel Ben-Tovim, and the twins, Leah and Ada.
Front row: Moshe, Kreshe and her son Yehoshua, Arieh,
Yehoshua's wife, Sarah, and Haya

in arid Jerusalem, planted in the 1890s by Mayor Salim al-Husseini in an empty field by the Russian Compound, a space formerly occupied by camels, donkeys, and garbage. Moshe, who later became a connoisseur of classical music, considered it a lucky occasion if they caught a performance by the Turkish military band which played in the garden twice a week, although not everyone appreciated it: "Oriental squeaks and shrieks, irrelevant beating of drums and cymbals," wrote one visitor to the city. Cutting through the Compound, in the shadow of the Cathedral of St. Trinity, father and son would often be greeted by officials of the Russian Church whom Eliyahu knew through his arrangements to supply bread to the pilgrims. Happy, if exhausted, Moshe would continue with his father down the Street of the Prophets, sometimes called Hospital Street or the Street of the Consuls for the many hospitals built along its course during the late nineteenth century and for the foreign legations which stood there. Walking along the street one could sometimes catch a glimpse of a *kawwass*, an official escort nominated by the Ottoman authorities to accompany consuls, religious leaders, and other dignitaries. The *kawwass*, dressed in a colorful embroidered uniform and carrying a tall cane with a silver cap, would march ahead of his master, banging on the pavement and loudly announcing the VIP's progress.

In 1908 the Young Turks in Constantinople rose against Abdul Hamid, the aging sultan, and demanded that he implement the constitution he had promised thirty years earlier. Intoxicated by the prospect of more freedom, people throughout the Ottoman Empire celebrated. Thousands gathered in Jerusalem and danced in the streets, Jews and Arabs together. But the new ruling party—which soon deposed the sultan with the help of the army—was nationalistic rather than liberal and it tried to ottomanize the minorities in the Empire and form a single nation-state out of some thirty million people. Disappointed by the lack of progress on the political front and by the enduring corruption in the government, the non-Turkish Muslims—Arabs, Kurds, Albanians, Macedonians—became restive. So did the Christians in the Balkans. Foreign powers—Austria, Bulgaria, Italy—saw a chance to seize territory from the weakened Empire, and by the end of 1913, after two Balkan wars, the Ottomans had lost most of their European possessions.

Meanwhile, the shadow of another war was on the horizon, a war that would forever change the Middle East, Palestine, and Jerusalem.

THE GREAT WAR

THE GREAT WAR BEGINS

At the end of October 1914, Turkey joined the Central Powers in a war that eventually brought to an end four hundred years of Ottoman rule in Palestine. During the war Turkey and its allies used the country as a base from which to launch attacks against Egypt, especially the Suez Canal. Local farmers, Jews and Arabs alike, had to supply food to the Turkish and German troops in addition to paying heavy taxes. The government routinely confiscated livestock, grains, and other agricultural products, ravaging the countryside. Food became even scarcer when, in March 1915, locusts devoured the meager crops that had escaped the authorities, while a British naval blockade prevented imported supplies from reaching the country. Hunger and starvation prevailed, and as the war progressed, rich and poor alike stood in line at soup kitchens set up by charitable organizations. Contagious diseases, often spread by the presence of troops, further ravaged the civilian population. An epidemic of the dreaded spotted typhus, transmitted through lice, occurred late in 1915, followed by outbreaks of cholera and the ubiquitous malaria.

Conscription was another calamity. As soon as war was declared, all men of Turkish nationality under age forty-five were drafted into the army. The special privileges, granted to the Christian and Jewish minorities during the nineteenth century by the Capitulations, were abolished on the eve of the war and members of those communities could no longer escape the draft by paying a special tax. Yet the Turks did not trust their non-Muslim subjects enough to let them carry arms, and instead forced them into labor corps where, under intolerable conditions, they paved roads, quarried stones, and lived on very little food in vermin-infested barracks. Those accused of avoiding the draft often had their feet lashed—a traditional form of punishment—even before their cases were heard by the military court. Turkish cruelty intensified as the war dragged on and people were arrested on mere suspicion of sympathizing with the Allies. Public executions took place in Jerusalem, at Damascus Gate, where the bodies were left hanging to serve as a lesson. The city was under martial law and no one was allowed to move around between sundown and sunrise.

Many Jews in Palestine were foreign nationals, an advantageous position that allowed them to claim the protection of their respective consuls rather than depend on Ottoman bureaucracy. But with the abolishment of the Capitulations and the onset of war, they found themselves enemy subjects. On December 17, 1914, Jamal Pasha, the governor and military commander of Syria, including Palestine, ordered that all Jews who were nationals of enemy countries be immediately expelled. Seven hundred Russian Jews were shipped from Jaffa to Alexandria before the order was rescinded under pressure from diplomatic representatives in Constantinople. This act had caused such panic that within one month several thousand Jews had fled the country. The Turks, beginning with Jamal Pasha, believed that most Jews secretly hoped for their defeat, and they were especially leery of the Zionists and of anything that smacked of nationalism. During the course of the war, the Turks closed Hebrew schools, outlawed the Zionist flag as well as pictures of Theodor Herzl, and stamps issued by the Jewish National Fund. They deported many Zionist leaders including David Ben-Gurion and Izhak Ben-Zvi who later

The Great War

become Israel's first prime minister and second president, respectively. Some of the exiles settled in refugee camps in Egypt and tried to join the war effort on the side of the British; among them were Vladimir (Ze'ev) Jabotinsky, a journalist from Russia and the father of the Revisionist Movement, and the one-armed Joseph Trumpeldor, a former officer in the Russian army who later joined Tel Hai, a farming community in the Galilee. Eventually the British allowed the Jews to form the Zion Mule Corps, a transportation unit whose five hundred volunteers helped supply the Allied soldiers in the trenches of the ill-fated Gallipoli campaign.

All the inhabitants of Palestine suffered greatly during the war, but the Ashkenazi Jews within the old Yishuv were the most vulnerable because the war brought to a halt the flow of money sent to them by Jews abroad on which many depended. At the beginning of the war some funds, food, and medical supplies arrived from the United States, mostly from the Jewish community, transported by the United States Navy with the help of the State Department and Henry Morgenthau, the American minister to Constantinople. Some assistance continued to trickle in even after the United States entered the war, and help also came through the representatives of two allies of the Turks, Austria and Germany. Many Jews were either citizens of Austria or under its protection and they received money through Vienna, while the Germans often intervened on the political front, pressuring the Turks to cancel deportation orders. Yet deportation and emigration continued.

The Bermans, though they were Turkish citizens, fared somewhat better than the rest of the population since they always had bread. Nevertheless, those were difficult years. The Turks sent Zalman, Eliyahu's son from his second marriage, to an officers' training school. Upon graduation, since he knew English, the Turks assigned him to work for the censor in Damascus. Eventually he came down with typhus and my grandfather rushed to Syria where, by bribing the right people, he managed to get Zalman out. They returned to Jerusalem on a military train filled with unwashed, battle-fatigued troops and it took them several days after they got home to get rid of the lice they picked up on the voyage. It took Zalman even longer to regain his health.

Eliyahu's nephew Baruch Berman, one of Yehoshua's sons who had been studying in Germany when the war broke out, was recalled and drafted. He was then assigned to accompany a German major who was surveying the remaining woods in the country. (Coal was not available during the war and the Turks, who used wood to power their trains, destroyed the country's scant woodlands, including the few remaining clusters of ancient oaks.) As they crisscrossed the land Baruch began to suspect that the major was spying on the Jewish community and wanted no part in it. He deserted from the army and spent the rest of the war hiding in a hut in Petach Tikva, in an orange grove that the Bermans owned, where it was easier to avoid the Turkish military police. A sister and a couple of brothers joined him there since food was more abundant in the countryside. I heard many stories about the war from Baruch's widow, Zahava. Some of the information also appears in her autobiography.[26]

A major change took place in Eliyahu and Sarah's household during the war. Esther Ashkenazi Brandeis, Sarah's mother, who used to live in Tiberias with her son Joseph and his family, refused to join them when they emigrated to Argentina to escape the hardships brought on by the war. Esther moved to Jerusalem, to her daughter's house, but it was hard for her to accept the fact that she had become dependent on her son-in-law and their relations were strained. Another event that occurred in 1916 was the arrival of Eliyahu and Sarah's third daughter. She was named Haya, for Esther's mother.

Near the end of the war the Turks confiscated the Berman Bakery and used it exclusively to provide their troops with bread. The family survived by continuing to operate the flour mill in the Valley of Hinnom. By then supplies were so scarce that even Turkish soldiers were starving and many deserted. My mother, seven years old at the time, remembered them knocking on the door and begging for bread, *ek mak, ek mak*.

The Great War

By the spring of 1917, the battlefront loomed closer and the Turks became desperate. Their attack on the Suez Canal in September 1916 had failed and now the British, who had occupied Rafah, were planning to assault Gaza, advancing from south to north. The Turks ordered the evacuation of all civilians from the town. The shortage of food and other materials caused prices to skyrocket and inflation was rampant. The Turkish currency lost much of its value and paper money was worth only one eighth of its official rate. It was then that the authorities accused Jerusalem's Jewish merchants of irregularities in foreign currency exchange and, without trial or proof, decided to deport two merchants to Turkey, to set an example. Lots were cast and my grandfather Eliyahu and another merchant, a member of the Hamburger family, were the "winners."

Sarah could not stand by passively and accept the disaster that befell her family. Aware that many deportees died in exile, she decided to go and see Jamal Pasha, despite his reputation as a Jew-hater, and beg him for a pardon. She put on a fine dress and one of her old Beirut hats and walked up the long road to Mount Scopus, to Jamal Pasha's headquarters, located at Augusta Victoria—the hospice built by Kaiser Wilhelm II and named for his wife. But the pasha's attendants refused to let her in and she never got to make her plea. Eliyahu was destined to leave for Turkey at the end of March, a few days before Passover.

On the same day, just before the holiday, the Turks ordered the deportation of all civilians in Jaffa and Tel Aviv. When the news reached Jerusalem Esther Kaminitz, wife of the educator Ephraim Cohn-Reiss, somehow persuaded a German officer to lend her a military truck. She then loaded it with bread donated by the Berman brothers—despite their despondency over Eliyahu's imminent departure—and she hastened to the coast to distribute the bread among the deportees.[27] (The decree affected some ten thousand Jews. The Turks were less strict with their Muslim subjects.)

Before leaving for a fate unknown, Eliyahu handed Sarah a jar full

One of the coins Eliyahu gave Sarah before he was exiled to Turkey, 1917, now in my possession

of gold coins. "I don't want you to starve or to have to depend on anyone," he said and together they buried the jar under the floor. Then he left, and Sarah feared that she would never see him again. Rumors persisted throughout the spring that Jamal Pasha was plotting to evacuate the civilian population of Jerusalem supposedly for military reasons, a plot thwarted with the help of foreign diplomats. Sarah decided to send Moshe, her ten-year old son, to the Klingers, her aunt and uncle in Safed, to have one less child to worry about while her husband was gone. (Moshe and his friends used to loiter by a German army camp, not far from my grandparents' house, to watch the slaughter of cows which were first hit over the head with a large hammer.)

Going to Safed was an unforgettable adventure that Moshe thoroughly enjoyed, war or no war. Accompanied by a family friend, he traveled to Haifa on a German-made truck of the kind used by the Turkish army. From there they continued by train to Zemach, near Tiberias, where they were met by Todres Epstein, a cousin of Baba Esther's, who owned a nearby flour mill. He took Moshe to Tiberias and from there they went up to Safed by diligence, a carriage drawn by four horses, not by the usual two, Moshe stressed when he told me the story, his eyes gleaming.

The Great War

My grandfather Eliyahu Berman, c. 1918

For years the steep road between Tiberias and Safed could barely accommodate a single horse and the trip, usually made by donkey or mule, took six hours. So going there by carriage was a great improvement, even though at several points the passengers had to get off and help push. When darkness fell, Moshe added, a full moon rose over the Sea of Galilee, turning its waters silver. It was the most beautiful sight he had ever seen.

Eliyahu meanwhile was taken to Turkey, to Adana in the south, then sent to a place known as the Turkish "Devil's Island," a dreaded penal settlement. He soon came down with pneumonia and would have surely died had he not been moved to a hotel run by a Jewish family where a man called Weingarten helped him. Eventually, the Turkish physician who was treating my grandfather agreed, in exchange for the appropriate remuneration, to supply Eliyahu with false documents that enabled him to go back to Jerusalem. He arrived there on December 7, 1917, eight months after he was deported. Upon his return, Sarah dug up the jar and gave it back to him. She did not touch the money while he was away, but once he was back she set aside half a dozen gold coins and many years later gave one to each of her children. I am looking at one of those coins as I write, a United States five dollar gold piece minted in 1880, with an American eagle on one side, and on the other a woman's head inscribed "Liberty" (see p. 96).

The Surrender of the Holy City

Saturday, December 8, 1917, dawned bright and sunny, according to the memoirs of numerous Jerusalemites. Several friends and relatives who had heard of Eliyahu's safe return came to congratulate him. Some might have whispered that the road leading east of the city was full of retreating troops and vehicles, a chaotic scene. That night the weather changed dramatically and a storm raged over the city—thunder and lightning and howling winds. Yet even the roar of the elements could not disguise the sound of cannon fire over the Judean hills. When Sunday arrived, after what was a sleepless night for many, the clouds were gone and so—after four hundred years—were the Turks.

In the recounting of events, the surrender of the Holy City to the British took on a mythical aura. It was said that the local authorities had made seven attempts to capitulate, a good biblical number. It seems that before leaving Jerusalem, the Turkish governor deposited an official letter of surrender with the city's Arab mayor, Hussein Salim al-Husseini. In her memoirs, *Our Jerusalem*, Bertha Spafford Vester—whose parents established the American Colony in 1881 to help Jerusalem's poor—wrote that the mayor stopped at the Colony on Sunday morning to bring the news of the Turkish retreat. He was on his way to find the British army, reportedly camping on the outskirts of the city, to hand over the Turkish governor's letter. The Spaffords warned the mayor not to leave without a white flag and one was soon fashioned by tearing a Colony hospital sheet in two.[28] The mayor then departed to continue his search, accompanied by a crowd of civilians eager to be part of a great historic moment. There are many versions of Husseini's attempts to persuade different members of the British armed forces he encountered to accept the letter of surrender but they all refused to take on such a weighty responsibility. But eventually the letter reached a British major general, J. S. M. Shea. The formal surrender was to take place at an official ceremony two days later.[29]

Hundreds of residents—Jews, Christians, and Muslims alike—came out to welcome the city's liberators. A Jewish soldier serving in the British army brought the news of the Balfour Declaration which was issued on the second day of November but had not yet reached the embattled city: "His Majesty's Government view with favour the establishment in Palestine of a national home for the Jewish people . . ." By coincidence—or maybe not—the first candle of Hanukka was lit that night, the twenty-fourth day of Kislev, celebrating freedom from tyranny two millennia earlier.

On December 11, General Sir Edmund Allenby, commander of the Allied forces—mostly Englishmen, Scots, Australians, New Zealanders, and a few French and Italian soldiers—formally entered the Old City and accepted the surrender of Jerusalem on the steps of the Tower of David. Among the dignitaries accompanying Allenby was Major Thomas Edward Lawrence, better known as Lawrence of Arabia, champion of Arab nationalism. (The ceremony at Jaffa Gate was "the supreme moment of the war," he wrote in *Seven Pillars of Wisdom*.) Some seven centuries after the Crusaders lost Jerusalem to Saladin, the city's Christian population and most of the Western world hailed the rescue of the Holy

IN THE LAND OF ISRAEL

General Allenby's entrance into Jerusalem
Photograph by Underwood & Underwood
Frank and Frances Carpenter Collection
Courtesy of the Library of Congress

City from the "Mohammedan yoke." Muslims claimed that they knew from the moment Allenby entered the battle that he would be victorious. After all his name, Al-Naby, means "The Prophet" in Arabic.

Leah, Eliyahu's oldest daughter, was glad to have her father back. She got caught up in the general excitement as the family watched Allenby's forces enter the city. But shortly thereafter, when Sir Ronald Storrs became military governor of Jerusalem and moved to a house on the Street of the Prophets—only a few hundred yards away from the Bermans' house—tragedy struck. Fido, Leah's beloved dog, had developed a skin rash during the war, at a time when there were no drugs available for humans, let alone dogs. The new administration could not solve all problems and, in the absence of salves, Fido continued to scratch and yowl all night long. The governor could not sleep. When the culprit was identified and his condition pronounced incurable, it was ordered that he be destroyed. The task fell to Arieh, one of Leah's older cousins, who shot Fido in the basement, putting him out of his misery. My mother never forgave Storrs.

It was rumored that the Turks had planned to dynamite all the flour mills in the city before their retreat but fortunately that did not happen and the Bermans' mill survived. But the bakery was in shambles. The troops who had confiscated it near the end of the war removed everything they could carry, even ovens, as they pulled out of Jerusalem. The war "to end all wars" was over. It was time to rebuild—the bakery, the city, and the country.

In the Aftermath of the War

The Early Days of the British Mandate

During the Ottoman period, despite some instances of ethnic riots when Arabs attacked Jewish communities, the two peoples coexisted in relative harmony. For a long time the number of Jews in Palestine was so small that the Arabs did not feel threatened by their presence, but this began to change in the last decades of the nineteenth century, especially after the arrival of the Zionist pioneers in the 1880s, representing a new, more assertive kind of Jew.

The revolt of the Young Turks in 1908 gave rise to nationalism among the different communities living in the Ottoman Empire. The Young Turks' attempt to mold all the different people into one nation-state, loosely based on Western ideas, further alienated the Arabs who longed for the past when they were the leaders of the Muslim world, rather than the non-Arab Turks. At first the Palestinian Arabs were not involved in the Damascus-based Pan-Arabism movement, but they became concerned by both the growth of the old Yishuv and the continuous Zionist immigration. As early as 1891, they began to demand that the Ottoman government halt immigration and ban the sale of land to Jews.

Few of the early Zionist leaders were concerned about the fact that the land they wished to resettle was not devoid of people. When the subject of the Arabs in Palestine arose, it was generally assumed that the prosperity the Jews hoped to bring to the country would benefit all, Arabs included, and that the two peoples could live peacefully side-by-side. The Zionists were also preoccupied by internal disagreements and opposition from the ultra-Orthodox, in addition to their constant struggle to raise funds to support the pioneering efforts in Eretz Israel.

The 1917 Balfour Declaration with its promise of a Jewish national home heightened Arab anxiety even though the British military administration in Palestine had little sympathy for the Declaration or for any other Zionist aspirations. In 1918, when the Zionist Commission arrived in Jerusalem—consisting of Jewish representatives from Europe and the United States and headed by Dr. Chaim Weizmann—it faced many difficulties in dealing with the military administration despite the fact that the government in London had sanctioned the Commission.

Early in 1919, Weizmann—credited for securing the Balfour Declaration—met in Paris with Emir Faisal, the son of Hussein, King of Hejaz. Faisal played a crucial part in the Arab Revolt against the Turks during the war and was the leader of the Arab delegation to the Paris Peace Conference. Weizmann and Faisal signed an agreement to collaborate "in the development of the Arab State and Palestine" with the boundaries to be determined after the Peace Conference. (The Arab State—which was to stretch approximately from the Arabian Peninsula to Persia—was the condition set by Hussein for agreeing to help the British fight against the Turks.) Faisal and Weizmann planned to carry into effect the Balfour Declaration—"the British Government's Declaration of the 2nd of November, 1917"—and to encourage "the immigration of Jews into Palestine on a large scale." But, at the end of the Peace Conference the independent Arab State that Faisal and his father Hussien had hoped for was not established and the agreement with Weizmann did not materialize.

On March 1, 1920, Arabs attacked Tel Hai, a small settlement in the

Galilee, at the northern tip of the country, and killed six Jews. Among them was the legendary Joseph Trumpeldor, the former Russian officer who had settled in Eretz Israel and was exiled by the Turks during World War I. His alleged last words—part of the mythology surrounding the birth of the State of Israel—are reported to have been: "It is good to die for our country." A month later, in early April, three holidays were due to fall within one week: Passover, the Greek Orthodox Easter, and the Muslim festival of Nebi Musa. In Jerusalem the latter was traditionally celebrated with a colorful procession—"drums pound, cymbals clash, fifes squeak, guns fire" wrote a visitor in 1875—which began at the Lions' Gate and continued to the tomb of Moses which according to Islamic tradition is located near Jericho. Easter always brought thousands of Christian pilgrims to Jerusalem, so whenever it coincided with Nebi Musa, many Muslims arrived there as well to make sure that the Christian presence did not dominate the city. Aware of the potential for trouble on such occasions, the Ottomans used to deploy a large number of soldiers to keep the revelers under control, but in 1920, the British military authorities did not seem alarmed. Leaders of the Yishuv—forewarned by events in the Galilee—worried that if large crowds gathered in the Holy City, riots might break out and engulf the Jewish community. But when they expressed their concern to the British authorities, they were assured that the situation was well in hand.

What started the riots was never officially established, but it is clear that after listening to a number of inflammatory anti-Zionist speakers, an Arab mob attacked and looted the Jewish Quarter. The riots continued for three days, from April 4 to 7, while British troops barely intervened and by the time they were over, five Jews had been killed and over two hundred wounded. When a British court of inquiry was convened, it blamed Military Governor Storrs for his overconfidence, for thinking his small police force capable of keeping the peace. Two Muslim leaders, who by then had fled the city, were sentenced in absentia to ten years in prison for inciting the crowds; one was Haj Amin al-Husseini, a member of the powerful family that had supplied thirteen mayors to Jerusalem in the previous five decades. The incumbent mayor, Musa Kazem al-Husseini, was dismissed and Raghib al-Nashishibi, member of a rival family, took his place. The court concluded that the troubles really began with the Balfour Declaration. The riots made the Jewish community realize that it needed to take steps to increase its own security.

From April 19 to 26, 1920, the representatives of the Allied Powers of World War I met in San Remo, Italy, at the Peace Conference to determine the mandates for administrating former Ottoman-ruled lands. On April 24, they granted Britain the Mandate over Palestine with the understanding that a national home for the Jewish people be established there, without prejudicing the rights of existing non-Jewish communities in the country. Herbert Samuel, a Jew and an early supporter of Zionism, was appointed as the country's first high commissioner. When he arrived in Jerusalem on June 30, he signed a receipt: "Received from Major General Sir Louis Bols, one Palestine, complete." Bols was the Chief Administrator for Palestine. A week later Samuel met with representatives of the Jewish community to whom he brought greetings from King George which included the promise made in the Balfour Declaration, regarding the establishment of a national home for the Jewish people.[30] (It is nearly impossible to get accurate population numbers for the country at the time. A 1922 census taken by the British, listed some 590,000 Muslims, 84,000 Jews, 73,000 Christians and 9,500 "Others." The census included British army personnel and civil administrators as well as other foreigners.[31])

In April 1921 Samuel pardoned Haj Amin al-Husseini who returned from Jordan and shortly thereafter became Grand Mufti of Jerusalem, the legal adviser on Quranic law. Soon he also became head of the Supreme Muslim Council that directed all religious courts, schools, and the *waqf*—property left for the benefit of religious institutions. Though mild in manner, Husseini was a preacher of hatred against the Mandate and especially against Zionism. Further riots occurred in May 1921. Forty-seven Jews were killed as were forty-eight Arabs, most of the latter shot by British troops trying to contain the rioters.

Samuel's appointments to the new civil administration were considered fair by both sides. He began with an open-door policy on immigration, but under Arab pressure and alarmed by the large influx of Jews—37,000 were to arrive between 1919 and 1923—he temporarily halted it. When it was renewed, it was limited to what the British perceived as the country's "economic capacity" to absorb newcomers. Winston Churchill, then Colonial Secretary, visited the country in March of 1921 and agreed to place Transjordan—until then considered part of Palestine—under the rule of Emir Abdullah Ibn Hussein, brother of Faisal. In 1922, Churchill's White Paper was an "interpretation" of the Balfour Declaration and it stated that Britain would continue to support a Jewish national home in Palestine (excluding Transjordan), but that "a Jewish nationality" would not be imposed on the country's other inhabitants. After some hesitation, the Zionist Organization accepted the paper. It was approved by the House of Commons and the League of Nations, but was rejected by the Arabs.

Back to Normal

After the war, as soon as it was possible to travel abroad, both Yehoshua and Eliyahu Berman embarked on purchasing missions to replace what the retreating Turkish army had plundered. They brought back the latest Europe had to offer, from new ovens to mechanized kneading arms. And since there was still no central power supply in Jerusalem, they also acquired a generator that provided electricity to the bakery and to the Bermans' private houses that were among the first in the city to enjoy such luxury.

Family life was also settling into a routine as the older children went back to school. For a while, during the war, Moshe attended the

Tahkemoni boys' school, founded in 1916, which eventually moved from Ethiopia Street to Makor Baruch. Later Eliyahu enrolled him in the Hebrew Gymnasium, Hagymnasia Haivrit—popularly known as the Gymnasia—established in 1909, the first school in Jerusalem where Hebrew was the sole language of instruction. Until then, with the exception of the professional Teachers Seminary and the Commercial School, there were no schools in the city where all subjects were taught in Hebrew, although the language was part of the curriculum in several other learning establishments. In those days many older boys went to *yeshivot*, others to schools founded by Jewish organizations from abroad where French or German predominated, as they did at the Evelina de Rothschild School and the Laeml School for Girls. A few Jewish children went to schools run by missionaries.

The Gymnasia was to play a major part in the education of many Jerusalemites, including the Bermans. When it first opened, it occupied a small building in Zichron Moshe; the total enrollment was two dozen students. The school struggled with financial problems and with strong opposition from the ultra-Orthodox. Teachers lacked experience—and textbooks—in Hebrew, yet the curriculum was very ambitious: Bible, Talmud, Hebrew, mathematics—including algebra and geometry—natural sciences, physics and chemistry, history, geography, drawing, and penmanship. Several foreign languages were offered as well, including French, Arabic, Turkish, and Latin. For reasons of accreditation, so that universities abroad would recognize its graduates, the school was under the patronage of the French Government. During the war, when many Jews suddenly found themselves citizens of enemy states and had to leave the country, the Gymnasia lost both students and supporters. Using the school's French connection as a pretext, the Ottoman authorities soon closed it and confiscated everything in the building. For a while, studies continued surreptitiously at the Bezalel Art School but in 1916 the Gymnasia shut down completely. Some seniors were sent to Gymnasia Herzeliya in Tel Aviv so they could graduate.

The school reopened after the war, in 1919. A photograph taken that year appears in a volume published to celebrate the Gymnasia's 50th anniversary and there, sitting on the far right is Little Moshe, as Yehoshua Berman's youngest son was known in the family to differentiate him from Big Moshe, Eliyahu's son, who was about five feet four but was still taller than his cousin. Big Moshe transferred to the Gymnasia in 1921, and at first found the experience rather traumatic. The future engineer, arriving unprepared from Tahkemoni, got a failing grade in math from Dr. Pesach Hevroni but he soon recovered and to his last days praised the institute's teachers. In awe he recalled one assignment given by the writer Aharon Avraham Kabak, to compare the treatment of Weltschmerz in Ecclesiastes, Job, and Byron! In the Jerusalem City Archives, I found a receipt in Hebrew, signed by Shlomo Schiller, the Gymnasia's first principal: "Shvat 14, 1921. Received from Mr. Eliyahu Berman, tuition for his son Moshe, student in the fourth grade [eighth grade in the USA], the second installment for 1921, a total of two hundred Egyptian piasters." (One hundred piasters, or one pound, was worth $5. See Endnote 6.) By then the school had moved to a spacious house in the Bukharian Quarter and Moshe had to walk a long way to reach it, through muddy, rock-strewn fields.

In 1929 the Gymnasia built new quarters in Rehavia, one of the city's more elegant neighborhoods, where it is still located (and is often referred to as Gymnasia Rehavia). Eventually, in addition to my uncles Moshe and Avraham Berman, my father, Moshe Brown, and his brother Eliyahu, some of my first and second cousins, as well as I were graduated from the Gymnasia. Leah and Haya, Eliyahu's daughters, went to the Laeml School for Girls which was founded in 1856 in the Old City under the auspices of Austrian Jews; half a century later it moved to a new building, just a few blocks away from the Bermans' house. In the Jerusalem City Archives are three receipts made out to Eliyahu Berman from "Beit Sefer Lebanot A (Laeml), Zichron Moshe, Jerusalem." One is from April 1921, for three hundred Egyptian piasters, tuition for his daughter Haya for the spring

*A receipt from the Laeml School, 1922,
for four hundred piasters—or Egyptian grushim*
Courtesy of the Jerusalem City Archives

semester. The others are from 1922, for four hundred piasters each—tuition for Leah and Haya for two terms each. A discount was evidently called for when two children were at school at the same time.

⚜

The years between 1920 and 1932 presented a period of growth for the Jewish community. Some 174,610 Jews were registered in the country when the first scientific census of the whole population was taken there in 1932. Their number had more than tripled since the end of World War I. New settlements were built, industry kept expanding, and additional communal institutions were established, creating the foundation for Jewish self-governing in the future. Most important was the creation of the Elected Assembly that in turn appointed the National Council, or Vaad Leumi, whom the British recognized as authorized to deal with civic issues within the Yishuv, as both the old timers and newcomers were now called. Great strides were made on the educational front: In

1925 the Technion was inaugurated in Haifa and the Hebrew University opened in Jerusalem with a ceremony attended by Lord Balfour and other international dignitaries; the Board of Governors included Albert Einstein, Sigmund Freud, Martin Buber, and James Rothschild. By then Hebrew had become the daily vernacular of schools, newspapers, literature, and the theater.

The Family Firm

In *Kol Yerushalayim*, a 1921 city directory, Yehoshua and Eliyahu Berman were listed as "Merchants." At that point they owned the bakery, a flour mill, the store near Jaffa Gate, and the orange grove in Petach Tikva. Although my entire childhood was spent next door to the bakery, I did not appreciate the scope of the firm until many years later. And here I must make a detour.

In the early 1980s, while looking in the Jerusalem City Archives for old photographs for another project I was working on, I was informed that the Archives held some material from the Berman Bakery. But it was only in October of 2001 that I finally got back to the Archives, located in the basement of City Hall. I spent many hours there leafing through hundreds and hundreds of old documents, taking notes and struggling with a temperamental photocopier.

I had assumed that someone with great foresight—a family member or a wise employee—decided to deposit outdated papers at the Archives. But it turned out that in 1965, when the bakery moved to Givat Shaul after eight decades next to Mea She'arim, inactive files were left in the old offices. Two years later, vandals broke into the empty premises and tossed out thousands of documents—letters, invoices, receipts. According to the Archives' card catalog, a passerby—*over vashav* in Hebrew—gathered three cartons full of papers and brought them to the Archives. He did not even leave his name. Most of the documents were in their original folders, sorted alphabetically and by the year, from 1920 through 1922, and

In the Aftermath of the War

then again from 1930 through 1933. It was sad to realize that most of the records of an institution which formally began in 1879 were gone because what was lost is more than the story of a family business: what happened in the bakery reflected general events in the country—economic development, the changing political situation, even global occurrences. A few personal notes survived among the business letters, ephemeral traces of a family's past.

༄

The documents indicate that by 1920, only two years after the end of the war, the Bermans were thriving, upgrading equipment at the bakery, exporting oranges, dealing with flour mills all over the world. A statement from the Pardess Association, *pardess* meaning citrus grove, shows that the Bermans were selling oranges in England, Egypt, Turkey, and Syria for a total of 111,400 Egyptian piasters, about $5,570. (See Endnote 6 to calculate current value.) About half of that sum was spent on annual expenses such as guards, storage fees, chemical fertilizer, and office overhead. The Bermans were early customers of the Anglo-Palestine Bank that had branches in London, Beirut, and half a dozen cities in Palestine; the family also opened direct credit lines with many different companies. The folders from 1920 contain dozens of letters from agents, brokers, and commissioners in the port cities of Alexandria, Jaffa, and Port Said regarding flour shipments from distant lands, from Australia to the United States.

New stationery, in Hebrew and English, proclaimed: "J.&E. Berman, Jerusalem, Palestine. Bakers-Millers and Importers of Flours. Established 1879." By 1921 the business had a more formal address, "Post Office Box 36, Jerusalem," evidence of a centralized postal system run with British efficiency. And while the bakery was billed for a trunk call made in July 1921 from the General Post Office, one year later the firm's letterhead included two telephone numbers, 131 and 179, as well as a "Telegram-address JEBER." In the days when every word counted, acronyms were used to avoid having to write—and pay for—the full address.

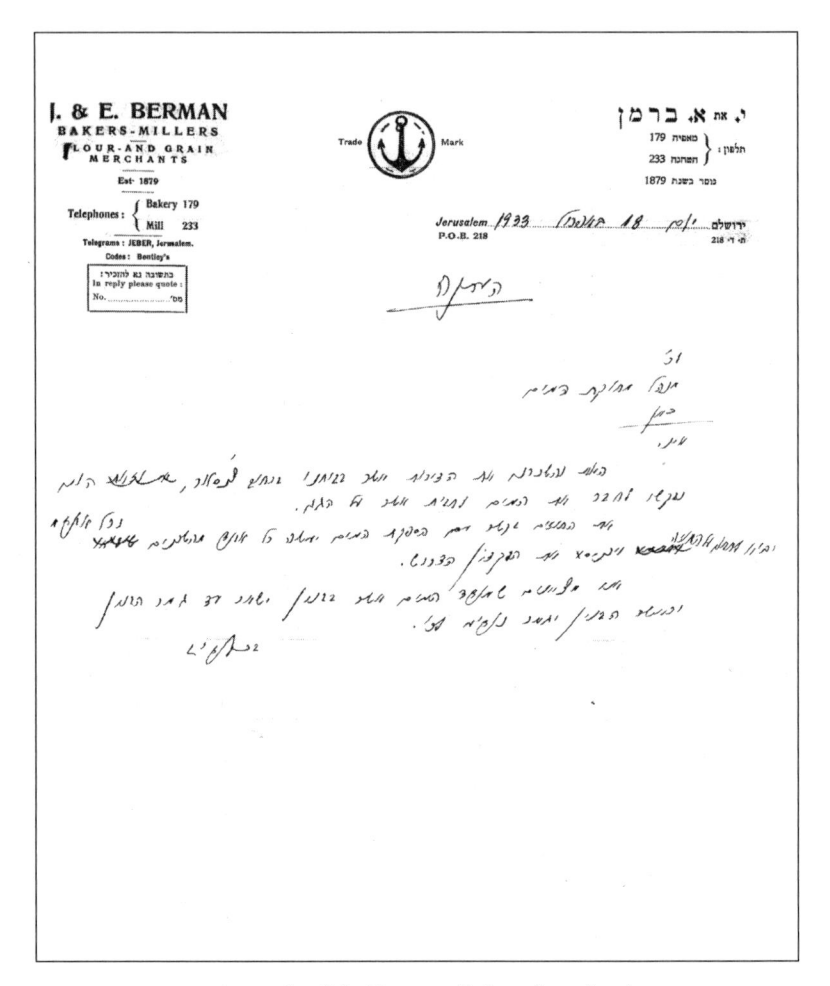

A sample of the Berman Bakery letterhead
Courtesy of the Jerusalem City Archives

    The Bermans worked mostly through brokers but they also dealt directly with some mills. The Kehlor Flour Mills in St. Louis sent them about twelve hundred pounds worth of Star Flour. It was transported by the Pennsylvania Railroad to New York, and from there, via the *Knowsley Hall*, an American Mediterranean Levantine steamer, to Alexandria, Egypt, and again by rail to Jerusalem. Semolina and other flours "of

In the Aftermath of the War

various grades" arrived from Marseilles. J. Gouldin in Alexandria billed the bakery for three hundred sacks of Farine Chinoise shipped by the Green Battleship. Shoumill, the Eastern Trading Company in Cairo, offered flour from both America and Australia. The Bermans exchanged letters with the Marine Insurance Co, Ltd. in London regarding flour shipments, and with Lloyd Triestino, Societa di Navigazione a Vapore, to arrange for the transportation and insurance of machinery. Some letters were written on heavy stationary, with engraved pictures of factories, flour mills, medals. My favorite one is from London Roneo Ltd., manufacturers of office equipment: a sprawling factory is depicted at the top of the page as well as the retail store where the goods were sold, and the company's private shipping wharf. By the time the main address and all the branches and agencies were listed, less than half a page was left for the body of the letter.

Prices in the 1920 through 1922 files were quoted in British pounds sterling or in Egyptian piasters. The correspondence was in English, German, French, Hebrew, with a few letters in Yiddish. With time, typewritten letters began to replace handwritten ones. Most of the incoming mail was addressed to "J.&E. Berman, Jerusalem." Sometimes the words "Bakers" or "Flour Merchants" were added; one letter was simply sent to "The Largest Bakery in Jerusalem." Only a few unsigned copies of the Bermans' outgoing letters are in the Archives, written in either Hebrew or English.

Two incoming letters were addressed to my grandfather by Moshe Elstein, my grandmother's uncle who had brought her up in Beirut. They were written in Hebrew, not in Yiddish, the language the two men used when Eliyahu first met Sarah, at the beginning of the century. One letter, from 1921, was merely a note about some letters of credit. The second, dated October 29, 1922, notified Eliyahu that Moshe was sending him nineteen bonds, purchased from Credit Foncier Egyptien in the years 1886, 1903, and 1911 and due to mature on May 1, 1923, plus another bond, "Unified Debt of Egypt, No. 014,306." He signed his letters: "And I

Letter from the Roneo office supplies company in England

am your friend and uncle." Moshe's letterhead, "Post Office Box 78, Jaffa-Tel Aviv," indicates that he had left Beirut where he had lived for many years. He sent warmest regards to his niece Sarah but did not mention his wife, Leah, so I presume she was dead by then. I cannot tell whether the bonds were a gift from the childless Moshe to his niece and her husband, or whether he just wanted Eliyahu to redeem them.

Invoices sent in 1922 by Blum & Levy, Ironmongery, Hardware, Metals, Paints & Oils, for cement, wood, pipes, shutters, screws, and locks show that the bakery was undergoing renovations. (Blum and Levy

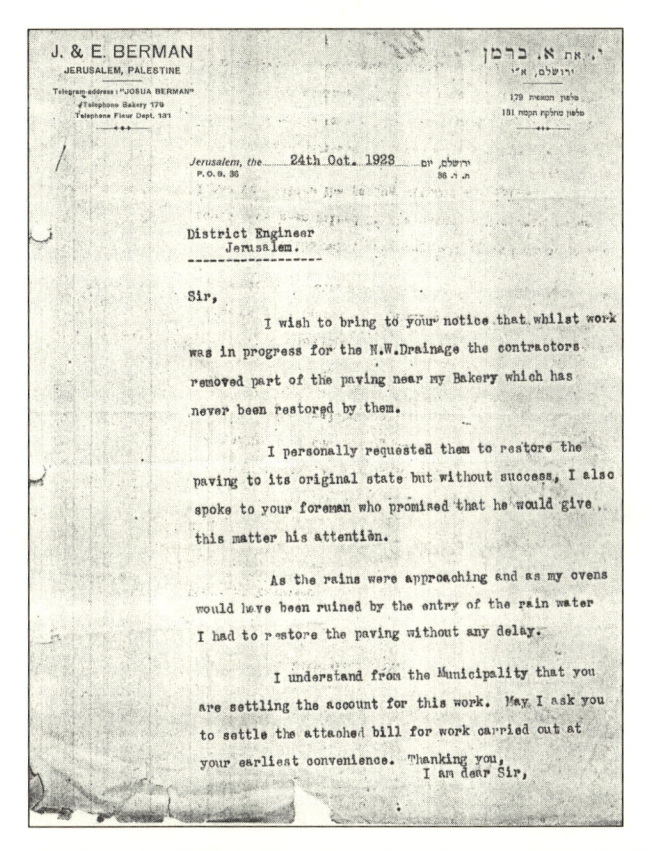

Letter to the Jerusalem District Engineer asking for a settlement for damages suffered when a drainage system was built, 1923
Courtesy of the Jerusalem City Archives

were Yehoshua and Eliyahu's brothers-in-law; their store was on Jaffa Road, across the street from the Bermans' shop.) But despite the renovations and the purchase of electric ovens, coal was still used at the bakery. One wagon, for example, loaded with 115 sacks of coal arrived from Hausdorff & Co. in Jaffa to be shipped to the bakery.

A carbon copy of a letter sent from the bakery, typed in English and addressed to Jerusalem's District Engineer, is the only document left in the Archives from 1923. In it the writer complained that when a central sewage system was installed in the city—one did not exist before the arrival of the British—the paving "near my Bakery" was damaged, and, despite a promise from the foreman, it was not repaired. "As the rains were approaching and as my ovens would have been ruined by the entry of the rain water, I had to restore the paving without any delay." Since the Jerusalem Municipality was reported to be settling accounts for similar incidents, the writer attached the bill for the repairs, hoping to be reimbursed. There was no signature on the copy, so I do not know which Berman wrote it.

In 1922 Yehoshua went on a buying trip to Austria. The bakery needed new carriages to distribute bread to its clients, since the old ones barely survived the war. Horse-drawn carriages were still the common mode of transportation after the war, even though the first car had appeared in Jerusalem in 1908 (driven by an American, of course). For very little money Yehoshua managed to procure carriages from a bakery in Vienna that had begun to employ cars. *Anker*, which means "anchor," was both the name and the logo of the bakery, and it was prominently displayed on all its carriages. And so, when the Austrian vehicles arrived in Jerusalem, the anchor became the symbol of the Berman Bakery. To this day the anchor still decorates the bakery's very modern fleet of trucks. Family tradition has it that the Viennese bakery used to supply bread to Emperor Franz Joseph, a man who was greatly beloved in his day by the Jews of Jerusalem: not only was he kind to their brethren under his rule but he had also donated the money for the roof of the Tiferet Israel Synagogue which was under construction when he visited the Holy City in 1869.

According to my uncle Avraham, the Bermans hired a pastry chef in the early 1920s, Miller Künig, reputed to have once worked for the British royal family. One section of the bakery was then turned into a confectionary, known as the *konditoriya* in Hebrew, a local version of the German word *konditorei*. My grandfather's oldest son, Meir, worked there for a number of years when he returned from the United States in

In the Aftermath of the War

Berman Bakery bread delivered to the old
Shaare Zedek Hospital, c. 1922
On right: Berman Bakery logo

the mid-1920s, after a marriage that resulted in two daughters, Miriam and Rochelle, and ended in a divorce.

Yehoshua's oldest granddaughter, Rachel Ben-Tovim Gretz, remembered the bakery as it was in the early 1920s. From the outside, she told me, it looked like a castle. Inside, fire and warmth and the smell of fresh bread reigned. It had two gates: a small one used by the family and the workers and a large one, painted green, which slowly opened to let out horse-drawn carriages laden with bread. On the floor above the bakery was the apartment Yehoshua and his family occupied, with many bedrooms, a spacious dining room where daily life revolved, and a terrace filled with flowers. Kreshe did not get along with her daughter-in-law and eventually moved to a small apartment on the ground floor. Kreshe was a difficult woman, said Rachel, hardened by her early struggles and always concerned with making money. She would question her sons daily

Kreshe Berman, c. 1905

to find out how much flour the bakery consumed and would immediately figure out how many loaves were baked that day and what the profit was.

Rachel was attached to Kreshe, her great-grandmother, who always smelled of yeast. She would share her meals with Rachel when she came to visit, comfort foods such as soup with beans or fresh rolls dipped in coffee. Kreshe used to take her into the bakery and show her, time and time again, how to make bread, and before Rachel left, pressed some coins into her hand. Rachel used to be scared of her grandfather Yehoshua who behaved like a "Turkish pasha" and seemed very remote. He was harsh with his wife at a time when it was very hard to raise a family, especially one with ten children, and while not a bad person, said Rachel, he liked talented, ambitious people, and did not tolerate weak ones, among whom he probably counted Rachel's father—husband of his eldest daughter Rashke—as well as a couple of his other sons-in-law. My grandfather

Eliyahu, whom Rachel adored because he was "a real gentleman," was most likely also considered too refined by his brother.

In the mid-1920s Yehoshua decided to retire. The business was then run by four of his sons, Todres, Baruch, Arieh, and Moshe, along with Eliyahu and his son Zalman. Yehoshua and his wife soon left the apartment over the bakery and purchased some property on the Street of Prophets—Rehov Hanevi'im—which consisted of a large yard with two houses. Yehoshua later added a third house to create a family compound (today numbers 19, 21, and 23). Several of his children and grandchildren eventually lived there, in separate units.

At this point I must add that relations between Yehoshua's and Eliyahu's sides of the family were not always ideal. Perhaps because Eliyahu joined the bakery late, all but one of the properties, past and future, were divided so that Yehoshua's side owned two thirds while Eliyahu's side got one third, and that was one cause of tension. Some deep-seated resentment also lingered because of Yehoshua's wife's objections to Eliyahu and Sarah's marriage. In addition there were the typical disagreement between partners in a family business although most of the quarrels, at least in my day, were among Yehoshua's sons.

Sarah and Eliyahu in the 1920s

Sarah was not thrilled when she realized, in 1920, that she was pregnant again. She was thirty-seven at the time and had already given birth to five children; by then Moshe was thirteen and Haya, her youngest, four. (Moshe, who assumed he would be sent to get the midwife as he had done a couple of times earlier, was embarrassed when he had to tell his school mates that his mother was expecting another baby.) According to my aunt Lily—the future baby's future wife—Sarah tried jumping off chairs and even took quinine in an attempt to induce a miscarriage but nothing helped. The baby arrived on February 19, 1921, looking like an angel with blue eyes and wisps of blond hair; he was named for David

My uncle David, aunt Haya, and uncle Avraham, 1924

Brandeis, my grandmother's late father. A severe snowstorm blanketed the city during the week after his birth, and few guests could attend his *brit milah*, the circumcision ceremony. "Do not be upset," said the ten-year-old Avraham to his mother, recalling the lean years of the war. "There will be more for us to eat."

Soon after David's birth Sarah began to suffer from acute dizziness apparently caused by an inner ear disorder. Some in the family attributed Sarah's woes to the onset of menopause; others whispered that she simply did not want to get pregnant again. Even today, in the second decade of

In the Aftermath of the War

My grandfather Eliyahu Berman, second from the left in the front row, holding the cup used to drink the curative water, Karlsbad, 1923
Courtesy of Eli Barr, Toronto

Inset on right: the actual cup from Karlsbad now in my possession through the generosity of Eli Barr

the twenty-first century, doctors cannot always diagnose the cause of dizziness or decide whether the problem is neurological or psychological. Sarah took to bed and moved into her mother's room, supposedly so as not to disturb Eliyahu. Then husband and wife began to travel to Vienna and Berlin to consult specialists there, and take rest cures in Karlsbad and Marienbad, but to no avail. Sarah stayed in bed off and on until my mother, Leah, got married in 1931. It took another ten years for her to move back into Eliyahu's bedroom.

The house continued to run fairly smoothly without the direct participation of the ailing Sarah. Esther supervised the cooking, and there was a housekeeper and plenty of other help. Eliyahu was in charge of purchasing supplies in bulk—boxes of soap, cans of olive oil, and other nonperishable goods. Sugar, flour, and legumes came through the Bermans' store on Jaffa Road and fresh milk and eggs were delivered to the house by people in the neighborhood: the wife of the electrician Oistreicher raised goats, and Eric *der Roiter*—the Red—kept cows, chickens, and geese. The older children took on additional responsibilities. Moshe used to put two of his youngest siblings on his bike—one in front, one in back—and take them to Dr. Avraham Ticho's clinic, when it was still located opposite the Italian Hospital, to have their eyes smeared as protection against trachoma, the dreaded blinding disease. Dr. Helena Kagan, the country's first pediatrician, was not far away, on the Street of the Prophets. There, in the courtyard, she sterilized her needles over a large Primus—an archaic kerosene burner—and, with the youngsters lined up in a row, inoculated whole families. No child was ever turned away from her clinic, rich or poor, Jew, Christian, or Muslim. The two-story house, today 64 Rehov Hanevi'im, is part of a compound set in a large courtyard with pines and cypresses and a water cistern. In the 1870s it was the residence of William Holman Hunt, the painter of the Pre-Raphaelite school famous for his biblical scenes, notably *The Scapegoat*.

In the 1920s, when Dr. Kagan lived there, so did the poet Rachel—who used her first name only—occupying a small shed in the yard. When she first arrived from Russia, Rachel tilled the fields of Kinneret, by the Sea of Galilee, a beautiful woman who wrote passionate songs to an unknown lover and died of tuberculosis at age forty-one, childless.

> *If I had a son, a small child*
> *Wise, with ebony curls*
> *To hold his hand and slowly walk*
> *Along the garden path.*

Did the Berman children ever come across Rachel? Would they have known who she was? Most likely they would have taken her for just another lost soul in the Holy City.

Moshe and Avraham were always good students, not so my mother. "She is so smart. If only she studied a little ..." sighed her teachers. Leah preferred reading to doing homework and indulged in the new books which arrived regularly at the house after Eliyahu subscribed to a book publishing house, Omanut, which issued Hebrew translations of world classics, books which enriched my mother's life as they did my own, a generation later. I remember Jules Verne's *Michael Strogoff,* Sir Walter Scott's *Ivanhoe,* H. G. Wells's *War of the Worlds.* There were also Thomas Mann's *Buddenbrooks,* Pierre Loti's *An Iceland Fisherman,* and books by Tolstoy, Twain, and Zola, and many more although not all Omanut volumes. At some point a piano was purchased and Leah and later Haya took lessons while their mother was listening in the next room, albeit in bed, making sure they practiced. The children, especially Moshe, loved charades and play-acting and often improvised scenes at the drop of a hat, draped in sheets or towels. Haya was an excellent mimic and even when I was growing up she could still be persuaded to parody some of her childhood acquaintances. A certain Hemda was her favorite: *Ma, lilbosh hatzait kahol vegarbayim yarok?* "What? To wear skirt blue and socks green?" Haya would imitate the scandalized lady's reaction to fashion in the backward city, expressed in broken Hebrew, an insult to the memory of Ben-Yehuda who had lived on the same street. As they grew older, the children were frequently sent off to Safed during the summer, to the house of Hinke and Eliyahu Klinger, whose own children were close in age to my mother and her siblings. *Der Fetter* Klinger, as the children respectfully referred to their great uncle, was a no-nonsense guy and it was hoped that he would manage to discipline David who was rather wild. In retrospect it seems so clear that he was simply seeking attention, what with his mother in bed and his father totally preoccupied, torn between Sarah's illness and the business.

In 1926, a year after he graduated from the Hebrew Gymnasium, my uncle Moshe left for England, to study electrical engineering in Liverpool. (While waiting for a visa he studied with a Mister Roittenberg, translating poems by Saul Tchernichowsky into English.) Avraham was still at the Gymnasia, where he was considered a young genius, an *ilui,* in math. On summer afternoons half a dozen boys and girls could be seen sitting in our backyard where Avraham would coach them for their final exams with infinite patience. He was also unusually kind to David, who was ten years younger, and would let him tag along everywhere. Once, when Avraham went with friends to the Zion Cinema—a modern sensation when it was built in the early 1920s—David came with them but found the movie too scary. He went into the lobby and stood in the doorway behind the red velvet curtain. Avraham remained on the other side to watch the film, but he held on to David's hand until the show was over. Avraham loved cars and as the bakery gradually replaced its regal Viennese carriages with motorized vans, he became friendly with one of the drivers and used to ride around with him to distribute bread. When the driver and several of his friends jointly purchased an Essex convertible, young Avraham was allowed in on the deal and he became the proud owner of one seventh of the car. He courted many a young lady in the Essex and often took David along on dates, letting him sit in front and help steer.

An account book from 1927 that I found in the City Archives lists the private citizens to whom the bakery delivered bread. Many were relatives who received their daily bread free—sisters, aunts, cousins, in-laws: Blum, Levy, Ben-Tovim, Bruchstein, Rossin, Salant, Davis. The rest of the list reads like a Jerusalem Who's Who: Granovsky—head of the Jewish National Fund; Yellin—one of the more important leaders of the Yishuv and one time deputy mayor; Caspi—a family of financiers and lawyers; Soloveitchik—treasurer of the city's Jewish Committee; Levin-Epstein—member of the Zionist Commission; Dr. Salzburger, who once told me it would not hurt as he was about to lance an ear infection, and Dr. Magnes, future president of Hebrew University. There are a few Muslims' names on the list, among them two Khalidis, members of an old Jerusalem family of distinguished scholars and political figures, and other Arab families in Talbieh, Mussrara, and the German Colony. There was the Polish consul, and more.

My grandparents Sarah and Eliyahu in a passport issued in 1927

Grandpa's Passport

Silent steamer trunks piled up in my grandparents' attic bore testimony to many voyages, enormous trunks with brass fittings and silk-lined drawers, covered with stickers bearing names of hotels in far away places. Everyone in the family had heard of Grandmother's visits to doctors and spas in Europe, of Avraham's tonsillectomy in Vienna, and of Leah's love affair with Venice.

In 2001, seven decades after those magical journeys took place and when all the participants were dead, my cousin Daphne, Avraham's daughter, found an old passport among her father's papers. It was a British passport, No. 2469—with visas to Egypt, France, Italy, Czechoslovakia, Germany, and Austria—issued in Jerusalem on January 10, 1927, to our grandfather by "His Britannic Majesty's High Commissioner for Palestine." (Every official line in the passport was printed in English, French, Arabic, and Hebrew. Although the passport said "British," it was a special version issued to Palestinians, as both Arab and Jewish citizens of Palestine were called under the Mandate.) Elias [Eliyahu] Berman was described as a merchant, born in 1870 [1867] in Rossyn [now Raseiniai, Lithuania], a male with blue eyes and gray hair. On June 7, 1928, his wife's name was added to the passport: maiden name Sarah Elstein, born Tiberias, 1884 [1883], with gray eyes and black hair. Their son David, seven years old, was also included in the passport. In his photograph, Eliyahu appeared dapper, in a white shirt, striped tie and a tailored coat. He was hatless, with a short gray beard and, despite a receding hairline, looking quite handsome. The same cannot be said for Sarah, always self-conscious when photographed because she was slightly cross-eyed, the result of a childhood accident when she tipped a kettle full of hot water on herself. The photo shows her frowning, with her hair pulled back, her eyes squinting, wearing a frumpy sweater. She seems forlorn, overwhelmed perhaps by her affliction—physical or psychological.

Actual itineraries confirmed family lore. In mid-June 1927, my grandfather went by himself to Egypt for two weeks, on business I assume. In October he and Avraham—whose passport Daphne found as well—traveled to Vienna. They went by rail to Alexandria, then crossed the Mediterranean and Adriatic by boat to Trieste, a four-day voyage. Two days later they left by train via the resort town of Mirabor—in Slovenia, near the Austrian border—to Vienna, where Avraham had his tonsils and some nose cartilage removed by Dr. Neumann, a renowned physician, popular among Palestinian Jews. A year later, Eliyahu, Sarah, and Leah followed the same route. They spent about two weeks in Vienna, where Sarah was examined by several specialists, then traveled to Karlsbad, which was their favorite spa in Czechoslovakia, and then to Germany, to consult doctors in Berlin and to look at schools for Leah who had just graduated from the Laeml School for Girls in Jerusalem, where German and Hebrew were the languages of instruction. On their way back the family spent a few days in Venice—where my mother must have bought every available postcard—then left from Trieste by boat to Alexandria. They reentered Palestine on August 28, 1928.

In the Aftermath of the War

Eliyahu made arrangements for Leah to continue her studies in Germany. At eighteen, she had several suitors in tow, none of who was considered good enough by her parents. So, in addition to broadening her mind, they might have hoped to break off some budding romance by sending her away. But at the last minute, with trunks packed and ready to go, Leah sat down on the lintel of the back door humming melodies from her childhood, tears streaming down her face. She did not want to leave home, she said. Her father, who rarely refused her anything, relented and she never did get to study abroad, a decision she came to regret.

On June 20, 1929, Eliyahu and Sarah left for Europe again, for further consultations. Moshe was still in England, Avraham was about to graduate from high school, and Leah was in charge of the household because Esther was losing her eyesight and could no longer cope. The family had just purchased a large orange grove in Bnei Brak, in addition to the one they owned in Petach Tikva, a good investment since the orange trade was booming, with thousands of "Jaffa Oranges" exported to Europe each year. The Bermans needed someone to manage the two groves but in those days they would not even consider hiring an outsider to run such an important venture. So the cousins—Yehoshua's four sons who were my grandfather's partners—suggested that Avraham, about to be a high school graduate, take on the job. But Leah objected since the position required moving to Tel Aviv, to be closer to the groves, and those were dangerous times, she reminded the cousins. There were many disputes that year over the right of the Jews to pray at the Western Wall and rumors of Arab attacks persisted. What would Eliyahu say if Avraham left her to take care of Haya and David all by herself? Leah's protest was accepted and cousin Moshe, Yehoshua's youngest son, was sent to Tel Aviv while Avraham went to work at the bakery.

The Riots in 1929

The Palestinian Arabs had rejected the 1919 agreement between Faisal and Weizmann to develop the "Arab State and Palestine" and allow Jewish immigration "on a large scale." The Arabs had also tried unsuccessfully to change the terms of the British Mandate that called for an establishment of a Jewish national home in Palestine. In 1920, representatives of Muslim-Christian associations met in Haifa and eventually formed the Palestinian Arab Congress. At that point the British were attempting to create self-governing bodies for the country's Arab and Jewish populations but the Arabs decided not to cooperate. They later realized that it was a mistake to oppose the British suggestion—which the Jews had accepted and used to strengthen their communal institutions—and consequently the Arabs reached an agreement with the Mandatory authorities to appoint a legislative council. But, as happened and still happens so often in the country, the timing was wrong. And the clashes over the Western Wall in 1929 further undermined the agreement.

Some attempts were made by Jews and Arabs during the 1920s to reach an understanding but the British did not always support those attempts. There was also disunity within the Arab community: mayors and businessmen formed the National Party around Ragib Bey al-Nashishibi, mayor of Jerusalem, to counterbalance the more extreme Muslim-Christian organizations and the influence of Haj Amin al-Husseini, the Grand Mufti, who continued to spread hatred against the Mandate and the Zionists. The Jews were occupied with their own problems, mostly ignorant of the festering resentment within the Arab camp against Jewish immigration and the acquisition of land. In fact, most of the Yishuv's leaders persisted in their belief that once the Arabs realized the economic benefits the Jews were bringing to the country they would learn to adjust to the Balfour Declaration. At the same time the Arabs were hoping that some of the difficulties the Jews were experiencing in

Jewish men and women praying at the wall, c. 1908
From a stereograph, courtesy of Underwood & Underwood
Library of Congress Collection

the mid-1920s—when an economic recession caused some to leave the country and temporarily slowed down immigration—would convince them to abandon the Zionist dream.

Tensions heightened during the fall of 1928 over the issue of prayer at the Western Wall, Judaism's holiest site. Jews call the area Har Habayit, the Temple Mount; Muslims call it the Haram al-Sharif, the Noble Sanctuary. After the Romans destroyed the Second Temple in AD 70 and forbade Jews to enter the city, the Mount stood empty until the Arabs conquered Jerusalem in 638 and—by the end of the century—built both the Dome of the Rock and al-Aqsa Mosque atop the platform. Muslims believe that the Prophet Muhammad tied his horse, al-Buraq, to the Wall on his night journey from Mecca to heaven—via Jerusalem—so they too consider it a sacred place. For Jews, the Western Wall is the remnant of the precinct where the two temples stood, and they have been praying regularly there at least since the Middle Ages, gathering at the narrow alley in front of it.

Trouble began in 1928, on the eve of the Day of Atonement, when a beadle—a minor religious official—placed a *mehitza*, a portable screen, on the flagstones at the foot of the Wall to separate men and women worshippers. The Muslims—having heard the Mufti's allegations that the Zionists were planning to destroy the Dome and al-Aqsa—complained to the authorities that the screen was a violation of the status quo and marked the beginning of the Jewish takeover of the Muslim shrines. The British overreacted. On the morning of Yom Kippur, the most sacred Jewish holiday, they marched in with excessive force to remove the screen, an act that caused outrage in the Jewish community, both locally and abroad. In typical fashion, extremists on both sides continued to exploit the incident: accusations flew back and forth, demonstrations and counter demonstrations followed.

A year later, further inflammatory charges by the Mufti brought crowds of armed Arabs to Jerusalem on Friday, August 23, 1929. After listening to the Mufti's speech at the courtyard of the Haram al-Sharif, they poured into the adjacent Jewish Quarter, attacking its inhabitants. The violence spread throughout the country, and culminated in Hebron, where a small, Orthodox Jewish community had lived peacefully for centuries. Many of the attackers were villagers from the vicinity, while some Arabs within the city actually hid their Jewish neighbors. Nevertheless, some seventy Jews were slaughtered in their homes—a third of the community—and fifty more were wounded. It took the police until August 28 to restore some kind of order. By then 133 Jews had been killed throughout the country and 400 wounded. (My mother had seen some of the wounded from Hebron brought to hospitals in Jerusalem.) Eighty-seven Arabs died as well, mostly by British hands. The atrocities committed in Hebron reached a new level of brutality, with tragic consequences affecting the political struggle to this day.

༄

Sarah and Eliyahu, having spent the summer in Austria, Czechoslovakia, and Italy, returned to Jerusalem on September 19, 1929, after the riots. While they were gone, Leah managed the household fairly well with Avraham's help. Haya was no trouble—the expression "good as gold" might have been coined for her—but David was a handful. At some point he got mad at Leah, took a pair of scissors and cut all her dresses in half. When his parents got back, it was decided that he would be sent to a boarding academy operated by the Hebrew Reali High School in Haifa. Eliyahu and David took a bus to Haifa, since trains—confined to their tracks—were more vulnerable than buses after the riots. Eight-year-old David was very excited at the prospect of going away until he arrived at the school and discovered that the children spent the afternoons doing homework. He announced that he was not going to stay, but the principal and Eliyahu talked him into spending the night there. When the children were put to bed David could not sleep. He lay there listening to jackals crying in the fields which abutted the school, then he got up, found his clothes and sneaked out running as fast as he could to avoid the creatures lurking in the night. He knew that his father was planning to stay with the Segals, old family friends, and somehow he found his way to their house. The next morning he and his father went back to school where the principal tried unsuccessfully to persuade David to remain a bit longer. They collected David's belongings and returned to Jerusalem.

Having failed to convince either Leah or David to go away to school, Eliyahu was more successful with Haya. He sent her to England, while Moshe was still there, to a girls' school called Minerva, which she enjoyed. But David missed her company since, as the youngest two in the family, he and Haya had formed a special bond. He told me that he hated twilight because the kids in the neighborhood who played with him after school—he owned the best ball—would go home then and he had nothing to do in a household where everyone was so much older. In his frustration he once got angry at Moshe who was in Jerusalem at that time and let the air out of the tires of Moshe's car, his pride and joy: a light beige Austin, license plate 14. Eventually, David was sent to Safed—where Eliyahu Klinger resided—to the Scottish College, a high school, where he spent three years.

The Early Thirties

The Bakery from 1930 to 1933

As noted earlier, most of the material about the bakery in the Jerusalem City Archives dated from 1920 through 1922 and from 1930 through 1933, with a few additional items. One of those, a large account book from 1929, contained copies of invoices sent to organizations and institutions that were clients of the bakery. The heading on the spreadsheets said: "Bermans' Steam Machinery Bakery, Tel. 179, P.O.B. 36, Jerusalem." The sheets were divided into eight columns, for five types of bread plus *hallot*, cakes, and rusks. Among the hotels served by the bakery was the Allenby—formerly the Fast Hotel near Jaffa Gate—a "modern hotel" with electric lights and bathrooms with cold and hot running water, afternoon teas, and "a splendid panoramic view." There was also Hotel Amdursky, founded in 1891, "the central hotel ... famous for its accommodations, food and service." Then there was Baer—a European-style hotel fashionably furnished—and the Goldsmith and Lazarus pensions. (The descriptions are from contemporary advertisements.) Other clients were schools and charitable institutions, including six Jewish nursery schools and many secular and religious schools: Beit Sefer Lebanim (*beit sefer* means "the house of the book," or school, *lebanim* means "for boys"); the Teachers' College; Beit

Yeladim and Beit Hatinokot—a home for children and infants, respectively; Beit Sefer Lemelacha—a trade school; Landau, Laeml, and Spitzer—all girls' schools; Mizrahi Teachers' College; Talmud Torah Bukharim and Talmud Torah Sephardim—religious schools, one for boys from Bukhara and one for Sephardim in general; Alliance, a vocational school established by the French Alliance Israélite Universelle in the late nineteenth century; the School for the Blind, and the Weingarten Orphanage. The hospitals serviced by the bakery were the English Mission Hospital, founded by the London Society for Promoting Christianity Amongst the Jews; Shaare Zedek on Jaffa Road, run by Dr. Moshe Wallach, a German-born Jew who came to Jerusalem in 1891 (and, in 1934, delivered me into the world), and the Rothschild Hospital on the Street of the Prophets, first established in the Old City in 1854. Most debts amounted to a few pounds, except for the Bikkur Holim Hospital that owed LP 376. (LP stood for the Palestinian Lira, in use since 1927, and was then equivalent to one pound sterling. In Hebrew we used LE"Y, for Lira Eretz Yisraelit. Between 1927 and 1948 the pound sterling to U.S. dollar exchange rate fluctuated between $3.5 to $5 per pound. To calculate value in today's U.S. dollars, see Endnote 6.)

The majority of the bakery's clients were observant Jews, as were Yehoshua and Eliyahu. Kosher laws therefore were strictly enforced at the bakery and all products, especially imported ones, carefully examined. One of the four surviving documents from 1927 illustrates this point: It is a letter from the "Grand Rabbinat d'Alexandrie, Egypte," handwritten in Hebrew, but using a very elegant Aramaic script. The writer verified that he had inspected a certain yeast factory, watched the production from beginning to end, and even examined the books, and he could testify that the laws of *kashrut* had been adhered to, and that neither milk products nor any other forbidden items were used in making the yeast. But just as a precaution, the Rabbinat appointed a *mashgiah*, a religious supervisor, to oversee future production at the factory and stamp all yeast packages with his special seal.

The Early Thirties

I expected to find lackluster business documents in the Berman files, but instead discovered a microcosm of events in the country and in the world around it. The material reflects the expansion of the Mandate's bureaucracy and the growth of communal institutions within the Yishuv. Echoes of the Depression can be discerned in letters sent by suppliers from all over the world trying to find new markets for their merchandise, and, locally, in the growing number of requests for help from charitable organizations. In correspondence from the middle of 1933 came the first hints of the catastrophe looming over Europe. On a more personal level, the names of various historic figures with whom the Bermans interacted reminded me how small Jerusalem was around 1930, with the Jewish community numbering about fifty thousand out of a total population of ninety thousand.

I grouped the material into several categories, beginning with the increasing number of government regulations. In order to satisfy the Department of Health, for example, A. Clifford Holliday—the noted architect who designed the Scottish St. Andrew's Church in Jerusalem—was hired by the bakery to examine conditions there. On July 16, 1931, he reported that he found the general layout of the building reasonable, but proposed some improvements: enlarging the windows, painting all walls white, removing the stables from the vicinity of the flour storage area, repairing the roof over the courtyard, adding another lavatory and better facilities for washing up, and hiring a regular maintenance man to keep the place clean. Holliday noted that the repairs, which might cost up to a thousand pounds, would comply with current health regulations but that the Department of Health might eventually come up with further demands. At least one of Holliday's suggestions was soon followed: a Mr. Simha Glazer was hired to paint the walls, and he was promised a reward if he finished the job on time. He was to paint during the week of Passover, when the bakery was always closed. (Holliday thought that instead of trying to improve the property, the bakery should move to a new location—which it did, thirty-four years later.)

The limit set on importing flour in order to encourage local production was the regulation that most affected the bakery. The Bermans submitted to the Standing Committee of Commerce and Industry many requests for permits to buy flour abroad. On July 24, 1931, the Deputy District Commissioner, Jerusalem Division, Government of Palestine, asked the Bermans to meet with him at the Chamber of Commerce and furnish him with information regarding import permits and the allotment of flour. Many letters followed the meeting. Over a year later, for example, the Bermans explained to the Standing Committee that the bakery regularly used 150 tons of flour a month. Once the Government set limits on imports, the bakery reduced its consumption of foreign flour, but there was not enough local wheat on the market to make up the difference. The Bermans had requested permission to import 350 tons of flour for the first quarter of 1933, which, in addition to the 100 tons they bought locally, would have supplied the amount needed for three months. They received a permit for 225 tons but since they did not have reserves, they worried that due to shortages, the price of local flour might rise and bread would become more expensive. As owners of the largest bakery in Jerusalem, the Bermans were "a decisive factor in fixing the price of bread; should we have to raise that price, all other Jerusalem bakeries would do likewise to the disadvantage of the inhabitants." They hoped that the committee would permit another 125 tons of flour to be imported. There is no indication of how the matter was resolved. The files contain additional requests to import flour and a number of permits to do so.

A Workers' Compensation Law went into effect in 1927. On February 13, 1930, in reply to an earlier inquiry from the High Commissioner, the Bermans noted that during 1929 there were no incidents at the bakery in which workers were hurt. The bakery had insured its employees through the local agent of the London-based Guardian Eastern Insurance Company; the annual premium cost was about thirty pounds. On February 20, 1930, the old Ottoman commercial law dealing with

```
                GOVERNMENT OF PALESTINE.

        DEPARTMENT OF AGRICULTURE AND FORESTS.

                                           VETERINARY SERVICE,
  In your reply please quote                  DISTRICT OFFICE,
  No.  VJ-6-21-10                                  JERUSALEM.
  Telephone No.  812
  P. O. B. No.  956
                                        4th May,      1932


        Mr. Berman,   Bakery, Mea Shearim
        Jerusalem.

                    In accordance with the Rule 11 of
        the Rabies Rules you are hereby required to
        keep the donkey , which has bitten Yehoshua
        Milikowsky on 3.5.32 , securely tied up in the
        stable  and apart from any other animals untill
        further notice.


                              I have the honour to be ,
                                       Sir,
                              Your obedient servant,

                                    [signature]
                              VETERINARY OFFICER
                              Jerusalem-Area.
```

*Request from the Department of Agriculture and Forests
to keep a donkey away from other animals*
Courtesy of the Jerusalem City Archives

corporations was changed to one modeled on the British Partnership Law. Advocate M. Avniel in advance of the change sent a lengthy booklet on the topic, based on a lecture given by Dr. Moshe Smoira—a future president of Israel's Supreme Court—to the bakery.

On May 4, 1932, the bakery was warned by the Veterinary Service of the Department of Agriculture and Forests that, until further notice, the donkey which bit Mr. Mikilowsky had to be kept securely tied and apart from other animals, in accordance with the Rabies Rules.

A lot of progress was made in the country under the British Mandate. Telegrams became more common and were used by suppliers to announce the arrival of flour or other goods. On the official form for telegrams, the heading "Palestine Posts, Telegraphs & Telephones," appeared in English, Arabic, and Hebrew, the country's official languages. The relatively new Hebrew terms, *doar* and *mivrak* for "post" and "telegraph," are still used today, but *sah-rahok*, "distant-talking," soon gave way to "telephone." All letterheads on official stationary were printed in the three languages while the letters themselves—judging by the ones in the Archives sent out by the government and by the Jerusalem municipality—were mostly typewritten in English. Among the few exceptions was a notice from the Water Department informing the bakery that the charge for water for March 1933 had been "reassessed to one Palestinian lira instead of the sum charged before." This was typewritten in English, on the left side of the page, with a handwritten Hebrew translation on the right.

The British Administration encouraged economic development. It periodically advised the Manufacturers' Association of new regulations and changes in the law, and the Association passed the information on to its members. The administration also cooperated with the Chamber of Commerce. In 1933, for example, the Bermans received an invitation from His Excellency the High Commissioner to join him, along with other members of the Chamber, for tea at Government House on December 13, at 4:30 p.m. when the Commissioner hoped to make a special announcement. (The files do not reveal what was said at tea.) From time to time the bakery was notified of the arrival of steam ships at Jaffa: in 1933, twenty-four ships had docked there between March 17 and 28, and thirty-six others were expected between March 30 and April 10. Other notices show the activities of a growing number of professional and trade organizations in the country: The Chamber of Commerce, the

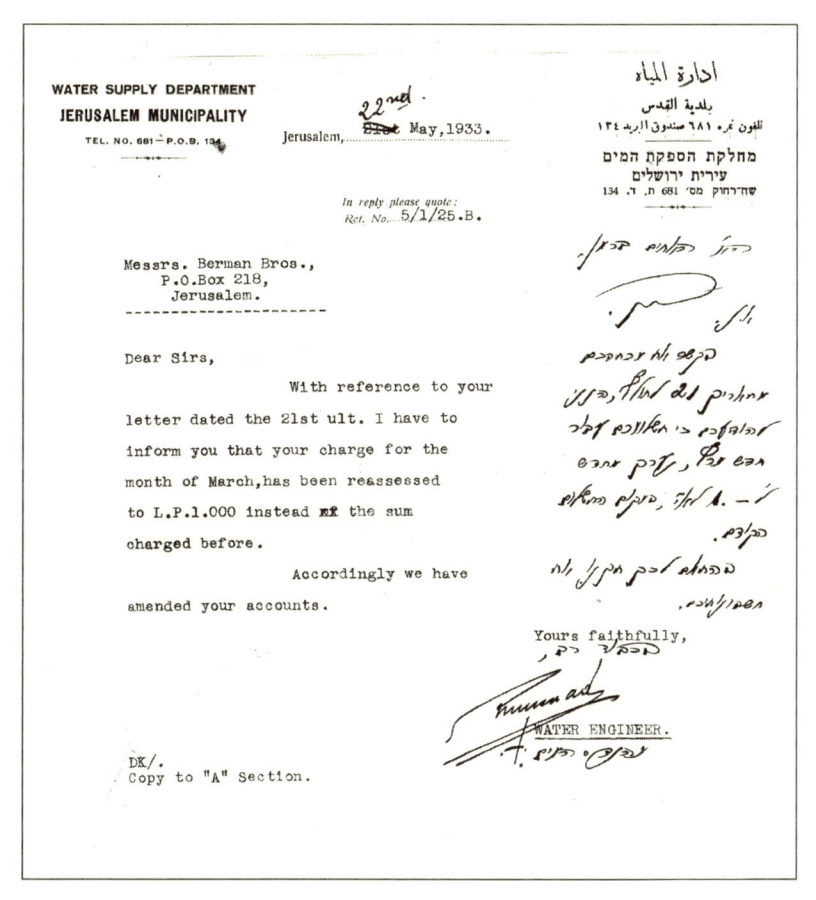

Letter from the water department informing the bakery that the charge for water for May 1933 had been reassessed
Courtesy of the Jerusalem City Archives

Manufacturers' Association, the Middle Class Organization. One of the few post-1933 documents in the files, dated November 19, 1935, is a contract made among the members of the Association of all Bakery Owners in Jerusalem, whose aim was to provide "Mutual Aid to Members in all Matters." Each owner agreed not to increase his bakery's daily production of baked goods.

The Bermans' main business was baking bread and trading in flour.

A schedule of the arrival of boats at Jaffa in March and April of 1933
Courtesy of the Jerusalem City Archives

They corresponded—in English, German, and French—with millers and firms in Australia, Canada, Czechoslovakia, Egypt, England, Germany, Holland, Hungary, Poland, Switzerland, and other places. They subscribed to several trade magazines and newsletters such as the "Market Letter," from the Hall Milling Company in St. Louis, Missouri, which reported in 1931: "Wheat futures declined sharply." "Slackening in export inquiries." "Buyers are perusing hand to mouth policy." The mood during the Great Depression is also reflected in the inquiries made in the early 1930s by suppliers of flour and other ingredients who had heard about the bakery through their consuls or chambers of commerce and were trying to push their goods. Peek-Frean, Biscuit Manufacturers in London "By Appointment to His Majesty King George V," learned from a note in the British Trade Journal and Export World that the Bermans were interested in "Dietetic bread," and recommended their own Vita-Weat. Matalon Commissionnaire, Alexandria, Egypt, complained that the bakery had not ordered flour for a long time. Most poignant were the numerous letters from Todres Epstein, the miller near Tiberias who was my great-grandmother Esther's cousin. On April 14, 1933, he wrote that he had already inquired several times about the samples of flour he sent the bakery but had received no answer. He still held thirty tons of flour in storage in Haifa that he was most anxious to unload. Would the Bermans name a price, any price? He was determined to sell, no matter the loss. The Bermans eventually answered, politely, that they were not interested in buying flour just then.

Samples of other goods arrived from far away places, butter from London, yeast from Alexandria. The Konditoreieinkaufsgenossenschaft [sic] in Munich offered *Torten Papier*, paper for pastries. The local agents for Cadbury-Fry recommended various kinds of chocolate for pastry. Northern Paper Mills in Green Bay, Wisconsin, inquired if the bakery was interested in establishing contact. A letter from Roneo in London announced the appointment of several new agents to its showroom in Palestine that displayed new office equipment: duplicators, copying machines, addressing machines, fire-resistant filing cabinets. In 1930 the bakery acquired two typewriters from the Palestine Orient Company: an English Mercedes and a Hebrew Empire and at a later date, new filing cabinets and folders.

The number of catalogs increased in 1932, arriving from all over Europe and even from Beloit, Wisconsin, advertising the latest equipment, from potato peelers and drying rooms to ceiling dough-chutes and machines that could measure and cut dough, knead it, and even shape rolls. A letter from Baker & Perkins Ltd. Engineers, Peterborough, England, advertised new equipment that could produce, per day, "6,000 kilo of round bread, 700 grammes weight and of long loaves weighing 1 kilo." The Bermans were apparently considering a "Rondo 2 Dough Divider" but on January 28, 1932, they wrote to Baker & Perkins: "In view of the present economic situation prevailing all over the world and especially in our county, we have retired our scheme of investing new capital in machinaries [sic] and shall have to wait for better times." On March 10, 1932, a letter from Daub & Verhoeven, in Tilburg, Holland declared that the company had heard through the Dutch consul that the Bermans were looking for dough kneading machines, and suggested they buy a Konditor-Knetmaschine "Excelsior." Despite the "present economic situation," the bakery was still upgrading. In July 1933 it asked a local agent for information about new kinds of ovens made in Hamburg and in England. A "major" firm in England offered a double oven, including iron parts, building materials, ceramics, and shipping costs to Haifa for a total of £550, and a "two story" oven for baking pastry for £328. (The pound was then worth about $3.50.) Invoices show that while purchasing electric ovens, the bakery was still burning coal in some of its older ones. A notice from Customs in the port of Jaffa, for example, announced the arrival of four cases of Bisques coal on the *Fernand Colignon*.

The bakery was gradually replacing its wagons with automobiles. At the beginning of 1931 a note came from Tannous Brothers, Chevrolet Distributors for Palestine, regarding a license plate for a car one assumes the bakery had purchased. In 1933 the Bermans answered a newspaper ad for an "automobile for sale, appropriate for bread delivery." In order to accommodate its growing motorized fleet, the entrance to the bakery's courtyard had to be enlarged and the Bermans leased a section of Mr. Salim Tahboob's abutting property for that purpose. At the same time the bakery was billed for repairs to one of its horse-drawn wagons.

Between 1930 and 1933 solicitations from charitable organizations mushroomed—testimony to the growing needs within the Yishuv. (There was only one letter asking for a contribution in the early 1920s files.) Requests for discounts or for free bread arrived from different institutions, such as the Jewish Women's Organization and Talmud Torah Beth Israel. The Mizrahi Teachers' College asked that its debt be forgiven since the school had to support many needy students. On March 14, 1933, Dr. Haim Yassky, the director of the Hadassah Medical Organization, asked if the bakery could lower the price of bread for Hadassah in view of "the difficult financial situation our institute is experiencing." Fifteen years later, on April 13, 1948, Dr. Yassky was among the seventy-eight victims killed in an Arab attack on a medical convoy carrying supplies to the besieged Hadassah Hospital on Mount Scopus.

Evidence of hard times can also be found in the reminders of overdue bills sent by the bakery to the Palace Hotel, to the Canteen of the British Police on Mount Scopus, or to Hotel Warshavsky where the last notice was accompanied by a letter signed by lawyers Max Seligman and Asher Levitzky to emphasize the urgency of the matter. Eliyahu Klinger in Safed was asked to help collect a small debt incurred by a customer in nearby Meron. A similar request went to Dr. Moshe Weizmann, noted chemist and brother of Israel's future president, regarding debts accumulated by the Students' Organization.

Most philanthropic organizations and individuals wanted cash, not bread. One request, from 1930, was sent to the Berman Brothers by the Vaad Leumi, Knesset Israel be'Eretz Israel—the General Council of the Jewish Community of Palestine. Between 1920 and the establishment of the State of Israel, the Vaad functioned as the executive body of the Elected Assembly of the Yishuv. The letter to the Bermans explained that the Vaad was engaged in preparing the Jewish community to vote for representatives to the Elected Assembly, according to the law approved by the High Commissioner. The Vaad was also planning to organize local communities, work with the Council of the Chief Rabbinate, and establish other communal institutions while continuing to deal with the Mandatory authorities and with Arab leaders. To do all that in addition to its routine work, Vaad Leumi required additional funds and a special drive was conducted among a limited number of the members of the Jewish community, such as the Bermans, who were assessed at five *lirot* or pounds. A Mr. Eben Ezra was going to call on the Bermans to collect the contribution. The letter was signed by Haim Salomon whose father, Yoel, had been one of the leaders of the old Yishuv. Haim's daughter Dalia, as yet unborn, was to become one of my closest friends in high school.

Keren Kayemet—the Jewish National Fund—requested twenty *lirot* for the Golden Book in memory of Lord Balfour. The Bermans sent half the amount and got a pithy letter back. The General Zionists Organization mailed a note about a promised contribution that had not arrived. In the spring of 1933 David Yellin, for a number of years the chairman of Vaad Leumi, wrote to my grandfather, his "dear and honored friend," to see whether he and his brother Yehoshua would contribute two pounds to help erect a memorial to Nissan Behar, as other friends of the deceased had done. Behar, one of the founders of modern Hebrew education in the country, died in New York in 1931 and his remains were brought to Jerusalem to be buried there. Joseph Yoel Rivlin asked Baruch Berman to help pay for a party given in honor of their old teacher, Ephraim Cohn-Reiss. Rivlin, a noted educator and scholar of Arabic who had taught at the Hebrew Gymnasium and later at the Hebrew University, was an important civic leader and founder of many organizations. Dr. Arieh Eigess thanked the bakery for items donated to a benefit ball given in support of the League for the War against Tuberculosis, held at the King David Hotel on December 9, 1933. Dr. Eigess was our family physician and, for many years, a tenant in an apartment building owned by the Bermans.

Another letter from Vaad Leumi, dated March 19, 1933, enclosed a report from its Social Welfare Department that had concluded that it was better to provide for the poor through social work rather than by giving money directly to street beggars. Henrietta Szold, chairman of the

*Letter to my grandfather from David Yellin requesting a contribution
for the establishment of a memorial to Nissan Behar*
Courtesy of the Jerusalem City Archives

Welfare Department, signed the letter, which of course asked for a contribution. The fabled, Baltimore-born Szold—who moved to Palestine after World War I—was a scholar, writer, and one of the founders of Hadassah. During World War II she served as the director of Youth Aliya and helped rescue thousands of Jewish children from Europe.

The Hebrew Writers Association of Eretz Israel informed the

"Brothers Berman" that they were among "those chosen few from the Yishuv to whom we appeal, who would understand and appreciate the need for the [Association's] work." The writer added that "as we lay the corner stones for building a *moledet* [a homeland] for our nation, we must not ignore the historic duty of laying strong foundation stones to fortify the spirit of Israel and its culture." The Association, which wished to launch numerous literary activities, was going to send Mr. Yehuda Burla to tell the Bermans all about their program—a good technique, as any one involved in fund raising knows. Burla, the "designated hitter," was born in Jerusalem in 1886 and was one of the first modern Hebrew writers of Sephardi origins. The letter was signed by one of the country's best-known poets, David Shimonovitz—later Shimoni—who was born in the same year as Burla, in Bobruisk, Belarus, and came to Eretz Israel in 1909.

A few months after Hitler became chancellor, the Bermans received the first letter foreshadowing events in Germany. It was sent by the Association of German Immigrants, on May 11, 1933, and recommended the services of an excellent baker, Mr. Hyman. That summer, on July 19, the Bermans were invited to a lecture at the B'nai B'rith Organization, titled: "The Condition of German Jews in Light of the Facts." Invitees were assured: "There will be no money solicitation." On August 14 came an appeal from the United Council of the Settlement of German Jews in Eretz Israel, signed by Henrietta Szold: "Although you had already agreed to contribute a hundred pounds, in view of the thousands leaving Germany, we hope you can contribute more." And on November 15, a letter from the Immigrants Housing Committee of the Township of Tel Aviv, signed by Meir Dizengoff, then mayor of Tel Aviv, and by his assistant and future mayor, Israel Rokach: "Hundreds of immigrants, refugees from the ruin and destruction in the Diaspora are seeking a roof over their head ..." On November 26, the General Council of the Jewish Community of Palestine invited Baruch Berman to a closed meeting. On the agenda were "Immigration" and *hamatzav*, "the situation." (The

The Early Thirties

Zeppelin over a street in west Jerusalem, 1936
Courtesy of the Library of Congress

term—which has come to imply a bad situation—has been in continuous use in the country for nearly a century.)

A notice from the Anglo-Palestine Company Ltd., dated September 9, 1930, informed Yehoshua and Eliyahu Berman that the firm had a balance of LP 8,395 in its bank account. (The pound was then worth about $4.80. See Endnote 6 to calculate current value.) By then the family owned the bakery, the mill, the flour-importing business, the store on Jaffa Road, two orange groves, and several plots of land in Jerusalem and Tel Aviv.

Then, in 1932, the Bermans began the construction of an apartment building on what was then Chancellor Street, named for the High Commissioner at that time. (In 1948 the street was renamed for Nathan Straus, the well-known American philanthropist and supporter of the Jewish Yishuv in Palestine.) The engineer, or architect, was A. A. Bruchstein—probably the brother of Moshe Bruchstein, one of Yehoshua Berman's five sons-in-law. On December 28, Bruchstein and the Bermans were notified by Gdud Haavoda—the Labor Brigade—of Ramat Rachel that the delays in construction were caused by the lack of cement. On the next day they were asked by the Federation of Labor to come to a meeting with Gdud Haavoda to discuss the delays. A solution must have been found because by February 23, 1933, the Bermans were asking the Electric Company to begin servicing the new building since all thirteen apartments, a total of forty-six rooms, were already rented. The Water Department was reminded that there were still some problems with the water supply to the tenants. The four-story white-stone building with its clean lines and symmetrical facade was designed under the influence of the International Style; in the back was a garden with palm trees and oleanders and a tennis court—the only private court in Jerusalem at the time. Over the years a number of Yehoshua's and Eliyahu's grown children and their families resided there—Todres, Baruch, Arieh, Meir, Avraham, Haya, David—and several physicians: Eigess, Phelsenthal, Weizmann. (The family sold the building in the year 2000.)

In 1932 the bakery had new stationery printed, in Hebrew and English: "J.&E. Berman, Bakers-Millers, Flour and Grain Merchants, Established 1879. Telephones: Bakery 179, Store 131, Mill 233, Telegrams: JEBER, Jerusalem, Codes: Bentley's. P.O.B. 218. In reply please quote: No. __." The bakery's trademark, the anchor, was on the letterhead nestled between the Hebrew on the right and the English on the left. (218 is still one of the bakery's official post office box numbers.)

The files in the archives end in 1933, except for a couple of letters. The last one, from April 1939, was a request for help from Beit Hinuch Yetomim, the Orphanage of the Sephardi Community, then in its thirty-eighth year. The world crisis and three years of rioting in the country had closed the gates of aid, the letter said, so could the firm please add the orphanage to the list of charitable organizations it supported and perhaps make a special gift in memory of Yehoshua ben Todres Halevi Berman, of blessed memory, who had just passed away. The letter—written in Hebrew as were all others requests sent by Jewish organizations—was signed by Jacob Meir, and stamped with a seal in Hebrew and French "Rishon Lezion [First in Zion] & Grand Rabbin de Palestine."

Love and Marriage

While quietly supporting various causes within the Jewish community, the Bermans were not directly involved in politics. Zahava Berman, who married Yehoshua's son Baruch, often complained that the family was not visible enough on public occasions. She was an activist who enjoyed participating in major events and only later in life, she said, did she come to appreciate the Bermans' reluctance to chase *kavod*, that is honor or recognition. While major changes were taking place in the country in the 1920s, the family concentrated on rebuilding the business after the losses suffered during World War I and continued to conduct its own life in private. Within Eliyahu's family the major concerns were Sarah's health and the education of the children. The ferocity of the riots in 1929 caught the Bermans and many others by surprise. The business had many Arab customers and suppliers who condemned the attacks—merchants always prefer peace—and they hoped that the Jewish and Arab communities could go back to living peacefully side by side. Even the bloodshed in Hebron did not shake the Bermans' hopes for normalcy.

Leah was nineteen years old in 1929, a spirited young woman with chestnut-colored hair, hazel eyes, and a figure "like a goddess," as my grandmother used to say. She had a good sense of humor and a sharp tongue, and was extremely efficient, running her parents' large household. She loved music and attended concerts organized by the Society for Music in Jerusalem—held in a large prefabricated wooden hut brought from England by the British Administration—as well as performances by an opera company that managed to survive in the country for a number of years. (A few years later, on December 26, 1936, Leah was present with three thousand other people at the birth of the Palestine Orchestra—now the Israel Philharmonic Orchestra—with Arturo Toscanini conducting the first concert. She kept the program till the end of her life.) Leah also went to see ballet and theater groups that sporadically appeared in the city, and she visited exhibits at the Bezalel Art School. There were many trips to Tel Aviv, always livelier than Jerusalem, and Leah regularly took part in the *adloyada*—the name comes from the rabbinical saying that during Purim, the Feast of Lots, one should frolic "until one did not know the difference" between the blessed Mordechai and the cursed Haman, the hero and the villain in the Book of Esther. Purim was celebrated with a parade of floats and bands. Children and even grownups dressed up in costumes and friends and neighbors exchanged *mishloah manot*, sweets and pastries delivered from one household to another. There were also fancy balls held on Purim and on other occasions which Leah adored; carefully folded evening gowns in the trunks in the attic—pastel-colored gowns in tulle, lame, or silk all with matching shoes—attested to her love of fashion and to her father's lavishness.

Leah went through a number of flirtatious relationships until she met Ronnie Ettinger with whom she fell in love. When she wanted to marry him, her parents objected vehemently. Sarah, I was told, worried that Ronnie was too young, without a profession, and that he would not be able to support Leah in the manner to which she had grown accustomed. For Sarah, raised by an aunt and uncle because her own mother was too poor to provide for her, stability was a major consideration. So the young couple broke up and Ronnie went abroad to study. Leah was soon introduced to Moshe Brown, who had graduated from the Hebrew Gymnasium in 1924, just a year ahead of Moshe Berman, Leah's older brother. Brown was a young physician who had recently received his diploma from the University of Geneva and, upon his return, opened a clinic at the intersection of Mamilla Street and Jaffa Road. Around the corner, at 55 Mamilla, was the clinic where his father, Dr. Eliezer Brown, practiced dentistry; the Bermans' store stood almost across the street, on Jaffa Road, and several family members were Eliezer's patients. Moshe's mother, Sarah, came from rabbinical lineage, from the Buchman

My mother, Leah Berman, 1930

family of Brisk, Lithuania; his brother, Eliyahu, was studying electrical engineering. The recent graduate seemed to be on his way to a promising medical career and his family was quite respectable. The Bermans crossed their fingers.

Leah and Moshe got married on June 2, 1931, less than a year after they began to date. She was twenty-one years old; he was twenty-five. Her parents were so delighted at the prospect of her settling down that they built a second story over their house for the newlyweds, at a cost of a thousand pounds. It was a large apartment, elegantly appointed. Nothing was too good for Leah. The furniture was made to order by a Mr. Elkeles, an early refugee from Germany, deeply influenced by the Bauhaus school. The silverware was English, the glasses Italian, the rugs Persian. Several sets of dishes bore Meisner and Rosenthal trademarks. The linen closet was stocked with enough sheets and towels to last for generations. Everything was there for a perfect married life.

After working at odd jobs in the bakery for a couple of years, Avraham followed in his brother Moshe's footsteps and went to study in England. He sailed from Egypt to Marseilles and on to Dover, then spent two years at the London School of Economics where he received his Academic Diploma in Public Administration on July 21, 1936. He had hoped to continue his studies, but instead was called back to Jerusalem, to take his father's place in the bakery: Eliyahu had been on the way to the United States to buy new ovens, traveling with his nephew Arieh and his wife Jeanette. They stopped for a few days in Paris where the young couple decided that Uncle Eliyahu should visit some of the famous nightspots in the City of Light. They took him to a cabaret and there, while the *jeune filles* were doing a *cancan*, Eliyahu began to have chest pains and was rushed to a hospital, apparently suffering a heart attack. The episode was blamed on his agitation at the sight of so much naked flesh, a sin for an Orthodox man to behold. Upset or excited, Eliyahu did not go to the States and returned home. He was sixty-nine years old and felt that he could no longer fulfill his duties in the business. He asked Avraham to replace him. As already mentioned, for reasons shrouded in late nineteenth-century arrangements, the partnership between the Berman brothers was such that two-thirds of everything was owned by Yehoshua's side, one third by Eliyahu's. (Their two sisters had been given dowries when they got married and were out of the picture.) The responsibilities of management were divided the same way. When Yehoshua retired, he had four sons working in the business, representing two-thirds of management, while Eliyahu and his son Zalman carried on the duties of the other third. When Eliyahu decided to retire, Moshe was already working as an engineer while David was still a child, so the burden fell on Avraham. A pity, because he was a gifted mathematician and a born teacher who should have had a more satisfying career. (Interestingly enough, despite the fact that it was a woman who founded the bakery, Yehoshua's and Eliyahu's daughters were not brought into the business by either one of the brothers. At one point, when my mother expressed

The Early Thirties

the desire to get a job, her father told her that it would be embarrassing for his daughter to work since she did not need to earn money.)

Moshe, who had finished his studies in 1930, accepted a position with General Electric in Coventry. A couple of years later the company received a large order, to install an automatic telephone system between Cairo and Alexandria, and Moshe was sent to Egypt, to a relay station in Tanta. He used to come home for visits, looking prosperous and elegant, or as his brother David put it, "fit and spiffy." Sarah, alarmed by rumors about Mabel, a non-Jewish woman Moshe was apparently seeing, urged him to apply for a job in Jerusalem, but Moshe just laughed and told her not to worry. A year later, perhaps when the Almighty got tired of my grandmother's supplications, new telephone exchanges and broadcasting systems were planned for Palestine and Moshe came to work for the British Administration in the Holy City.

Moshe moved back into his parents' house where Haya and David were still living, as was their grandmother Esther. My parents were installed upstairs, where one bedroom in the new apartment was given over to Avraham when he returned from London. My mother rarely cooked and my parents usually ate downstairs with the rest of the family. When I arrived on the scene, on April 15, 1934, the household consisted of four generations.

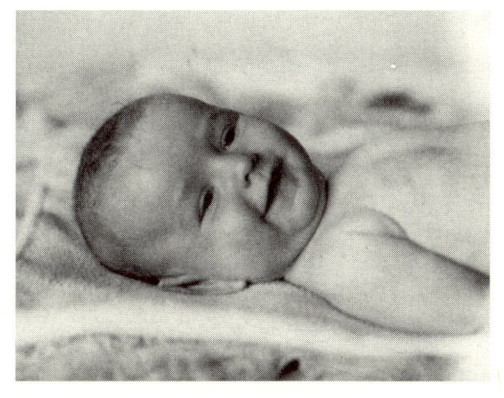

Nitza, April 15, 1934

*With my uncle Avraham, my mother, and aunts Haya
and Zahava on my fifth birthday*

part three

Within Memory

Hayei Adam Street, Jerusalem
The Berman house is located behind the trees.

Home and Hearth

My early childhood was spent on an enchanted island. All around there was turmoil: the world was in the throes of war, the conflict between Arab and Jew continued to smolder. But I was sheltered by the extended Berman clan, protected by my grandparents' house, the house my grandfather Eliyahu Berman built in the late 1880s, where my mother and her siblings were born. My whole identity as a child, my sense of belonging, grew out of that solid stone building with its large courtyards and tall trees. Along with the bakery next door, it implied permanence, security.

The House

Eliyahu designed the house, which still stands, and it gave him a chance to use his creative skills, frustrated by his failure as a cabinetmaker. Built of the ubiquitous local limestone, the facade contains few decorative details since the stone did not lend itself to fanciful carvings. Still, it has a pleasing effect. The masonry blocks, placed in alternating layers, create a certain repetitive pattern while protruding frames made of a finely chiseled stone emphasizes the doors and windows. The façade of the house is perfectly symmetrical, with a large door in the center, flanked by two pairs of matching windows secured by wrought iron grills that look deceptively delicate. The house was so well laid out that in 1904, when the construction of the nearby Zichron Moshe neighborhood was in the planning stages, David Yellin and other Yishuv notables came over to look at it and discuss architectural designs with Eliyahu.

Jerusalem's arid gardens grew no grass so the fenced and gated front yard featured a wide cobblestone walk with several large pines and cypresses on either side. A lone pepper tree, its branches drooping over the stone fence at the edge of the property, was the only climbable tree in front of the house because Eliyahu sawed off the lower limbs of all the other trees when my mother was a child. Some peeve had sent her scaling up the tallest pine and she refused to come down. So slender were the top branches that no one dared climb after her and the family spent several anxious hours coaxing her to change her mind. Grandfather repeated this story whenever my mother scolded me for tearing my clothes or getting sap all over them during my tree-climbing years.

The back of the house looked just like the front except for a long wing that contained the kitchen, a pantry, a bathroom, and storage areas. Originally, the kitchen was a separate entity, as was common at the time and the toilet, or outhouse, stood in splendid isolation in a far corner. After World War I, when the British installed a central sewer system in the city, all the separate utility rooms in the house were brought under one roof. A flourishing pomegranate tree that grew by the outhouse was sacrificed in the process of modernization, an event long rued by the family. A large stone-paved courtyard covered over half the property in the back of the house and under it was a cistern which used to supply the family with water, drawn by a hand pump; there was no running water in the city until the mid-1930s. Wooden crates where my great-grandmother Esther's garden grew surrounded the courtyard: the omnipresent geraniums, marigolds, roses, carnations, and several varieties of jasmine, which, basking in the sun all day overwhelmed us with their heady scent. One day Eliyahu decided that the yard looked cluttered with crates that were coming apart at the seams, oozing rivulets of mud whenever Esther

Home and Hearth

watered. But he really loved the flowers so he hired a mason to line the edges of the courtyard with red brick containers and transfer the plants to them. Then it was Esther's turn to complain: her flowers did not do so well in their fancy new receptacles, she claimed, but secretly she was very pleased. Between the courtyard and the back fence was a garden shaded by two enormous eucalyptus trees, some cypresses, and another pepper tree. In spring violets and irises bloomed beneath the trees and in summer we planted scallions, radishes, carrots, lettuce, and tomatoes in a small plot which we carefully watered by hand so as not to waste water. At the bottom of the garden stood another gate, a creaky gate, which was locked every night with a huge iron key. Since anyone could jump over the back fence, I never understood this ceremonial locking-up which began when the house was first built and continued till my grandmother sold it nearly seven decades later.

The walls in many of Jerusalem's old houses, including ours, were over three feet deep and the ceilings were very high which kept the temperature down in summer. When the weather turned cold and damp, oriental rugs were spread over the floors to lessen the chill. The floors of the bedrooms were made of tiles imported from Italy and each room had its own color scheme with the outer tiles forming a double margin to create a carpet-like effect

The spacious dining room served as an all-purpose room. Its floor consisted of highly polished slabs of Jerusalem stone that looked like marble—in colors ranging from ivory to pale yellow to a soft pink—and were ideal for playing hopscotch. The room was dominated by a long table, reflected in a large mirror that hung over an ornate buffet at one end of the room. A sideboard, topped by a glass cabinet, held the Shabbat dishes and the good silverware, and a built-in niche with wide doors held foodstuff and Grandfather's liquor supply—some schnapps and the sweet wine used for Kiddush, a syrupy liquid which for generations explained the low incidence of alcoholism among Jews. Life centered around the table since the room was in constant use, supervised by my grandmother

On the second floor with my parents, 1935

Sarah, with her endless patience, aided by my competent mother, and by our housekeeper Roh'keh. Esther, who was practically blind by the time I remember her, occasionally offered some unsolicited advice, known in Yiddish as *eitzes*.

There were a few interesting pieces of furniture in the house such as Eliyahu's worktable—a masterpiece carved in walnut, which sat on a central column supported by four lions, friendly lions with bunches of grapes in their mouths. When not in use, the table was covered with a velvet cloth with a floral design that reached the floor thus creating a perfect cave, igloo, chalet, prison, space ship, or submarine, depending on the book I was reading at the time. All the bedrooms featured wardrobes and bureaus but Eliyahu's room also held a rarely used safe, while Baba Esther's had a chamber pot hidden in a night table: the toilet, at the end of the long L-shaped addition to the house, took forever to reach at night, when the house was tightly secured and the doors in between rooms locked. A bowl and a pitcher stood in every bedroom to wash one's hands first thing in the morning, while saying the appropriate blessing.

The drawing room, which we referred to as the "salon," often doubled as a bedroom. It was furnished with couches and armchairs and an upright piano with the obligatory goldfish in a glass bowl on top. A large bookcase held countless treasures, volume upon volume, each providing me with a key to new worlds. On the walls were Van Gogh reproductions—*Sunflowers* and *Bridge at Arles*—and an Abel Pan watercolor of a dark-eyed beauty, of either biblical or Bedouin origin. Heavy ceiling-to-floor silk drapes from Aleppo adorned the windows. When the drapes were pulled shut, the deep windowsills formed perfect hiding places where, with a cushion, a snack, and a book one could spend many happy hours.

The second floor, added when my parents got married, was reached through an outdoor staircase. It contained three large bedrooms, a commodious living-dining room, a very modern—by the standards of the 1930s—kitchen, and a bathroom. Two balconies ran along in front and back of the apartment and a wooden staircase led up to the flat roof where an abandoned laundry room was used for storage.

My parents were living in the second-floor apartment when I was born, but I spent most of my time downstairs, where the action was. During World War II, when the thousands of refugees fleeing Europe caused an acute housing shortage in the country, a Romanian family temporarily moved into the apartment while my mother and I took over the drawing room downstairs. My father was gone by then. He spent the war years in Europe and North Africa, serving as a physician in the British army.

Dramatis Personae

In my father's absence, my uncles played a major role in my life. When Moshe, my mother's oldest brother, came back from England, I began to follow him around. Every morning, he would place me on top of the hamper in the bathroom where I would sit and watch him lather his face. *Sabon, mivreshet, ve'ein zakan,* he would explain anew each day: "Soap, brush, and there is no beard!" It seemed like magic. Always in love with science and engineering, Moshe tried to make me appreciate the wonders of technology. When I was about five, a new road was being paved near our house so he put me over his shoulders and together we went to watch the men at work. *Machbesh, hatzatz, veyesh kvish.* "A steamroller, gravel, and there's a road!" Moshe was somewhat disappointed by my lack of enthusiasm when he tried to illustrate how his beloved car worked, or to explain in simple language the wonder of radio waves, but he never gave up. Many years later, when I was living in the United States and came to Israel for a visit, he drove me all over the country to show me new broadcasting stations. He could not stop marveling at the landing of a man on the moon, which happened around the time of my visit. Avraham, a year younger than my mother, was already married by the time I remember him, but he too was very attentive. His wife Zahava told me that even while they were courting he would bring me along—a toddler—on their Saturday morning trips to the Dead Sea. It was fashionable to drive down in winter to the lowest point on earth where, in addition to the mild temperature, one could enjoy an elegant lunch at the Kalia Hotel. My youngest uncle, David, who was only thirteen years older than me, would come home during school holidays, either from Safed or Beirut, blowing in and out like a whirlwind. He taught me how to make faces, how to pretend to "fly" with the help of a mirror, and how to argue. He stood by me when I was disobedient and egged me on to mischief.

Haya, my mother's only sister, was like a streak of sunlight. A petite,

Uncle Avraham, my mother Leah, aunts Zahava, Rodia, and Haya, and uncle Moshe in the backyard of my grandparents' house, 1941

dark blonde with greenish eyes and freckles, she was always bubbling, laughing, telling stories. She usually had an admirer in tow, often British or Australian, whom she met at a Service Club. During World War II, mainly because of its proximity to the battlefields of North Africa, Palestine was a prime location for R&R and most of the women among our acquaintances volunteered to provide tea and a sympathetic ear to servicemen on leave. On Friday nights and on holidays there were usually several uniformed strangers at our table.

Baba Esther was always protecting me from all evil, real or imagined. Though she could hardly see, she insisted on washing my clothes, claiming that even our Yemenite laundresses, famous for their cleanliness, did not do a good enough job. I was the recipient of her stories, her guide to the women's section in the nearby synagogue, her helper as she tried to keep cultivating her flowers. When I was a little older, I began to read the newspapers to her and received my early political education through her pithy comments about events in Europe and the Middle East as World War II progressed.

Eliyahu was sixty-seven when I was born, his fifth grandchild. (The others were Miriam and Rochelle in the United States, the daughters of Meir, his eldest son from his first marriage, and Avraham and Yoram in Jerusalem, the children of Zalman, his son from his second marriage.) When I first remember him he was about seventy, a tall, somewhat portly man, with a trim white beard and mustache, always impeccably dressed in three-piece suits. Eliyahu was less demonstrative than Sarah but one learned to appreciate a pat on the arm, a twinkle in his blue eyes, or a smile *unter di vonzes*, "under the mustache," all of which signified approval. He never raised his voice, and that made us all listen carefully when he had something to say. One day he was crossing the courtyard while I was standing on the second-floor balcony holding a watering can. Eli, Eli, I called, using my grandmother's nickname for him, then poured the water over his head. The household held its collective breath, until even I—at age three—understood that I had done something wrong. Grandfather called me down, wiped his face and put me in his lap. "Don't ever do this again," he said sternly, then burst out laughing.

My grandmother Sarah was always there. By the time I was born she had recovered from whatever it was that ailed her for so many years and to me—her first grandchild—she was a haven, a shelter. She could calm down tempers, dispel anger with a word or two. If one of her children had a marital problem, she always took the other spouse's side, shielding the in-law. She accepted us all as we were, rarely criticizing. When neighbors complained that her children were not Orthodox, she would answer: "Yes, but they are honest." She was warm, big-hearted, and funny and her common sense never failed to amaze me. Her children and their spouses adored her, with the exception of Lily, David's wife, for reasons I never understood or perhaps did not want to know.

Home and Hearth

Sarah and Eliyahu Berman in our backyard, 1941

Sarah was very generous, perhaps because she knew what it was to be poor. Since I can first remember, there was a regular stream of fundraisers coming to her back door. Some came once a year, representing well-known establishments such as orphanages, or a home for the blind or for the elderly, and they would be invited in and served cake with tea or coffee. Others, collecting for less exalted causes, showed up every few months and were asked to sit on the chaise in the backyard and offered a beverage. And finally there were the weekly beggars who were just handed some cash. One of the regulars was called Isaac, reputed to be a former violinist who lost his mind, a disheveled and unpleasant person. I once joined a gang of kids who ran after him yelling "Isaac *der meshugener*," the madman. When Grandmother saw me, she, whom I had never seen angry before, chided me severely. A couple of things related to Sarah's piety worried me when I was a child. The first was that, since she was so good, she was sure to go to heaven as would many of her friends. Considering the alternatives, I too knew I wanted to go to heaven but I thought it would surely be a dull place what with all those virtuous ladies. I also worried about the End of Days, when all the dead would rise in the Valley of Jehoshaphat, after reaching Jerusalem rolling through underground tunnels. Since Grandmother had so many relatives, would all the resurrected ones come to live with us? I never dared asked her this question, feeling ashamed for being so selfish.

A detour. In 1958 I brought my one-year old daughter Leah to Jerusalem to show her to my grandmother. We came from Tokyo, after an exhausting flight that took forty-two hours in those pre-jet days. A couple of days after we arrived the following conversation took place, in Yiddish:

"My child," said Sarah, "if your husband were here I would not have to ask you any questions because I would be able to see how things are between you. Please forgive me if I embarrass you, but I am an old lady and I might not see you again."

"Fire away," said I.

"How is Henry with money?" was the first question.

"We are students and we don't have much money but what we have is in a joint bank account." After I explained how it worked she was very pleased.

"How is your sex life?" she continued, after apologizing again.

"I can't complain." What else do you say to your grandmother?

"Ah. That is even more important than money. And does Henry help around the house?"

"Grandmother, I cannot tell a lie. He barely knows where the kitchen is."

After a brief pause Sarah declared: "Oh, what do you expect? After all *er makht dokh kopf-arbeit*, he works with his head." (My husband is a professor. Whenever I tell this story he is willing to overlook my placid reply to the question about of our sex life because Grandmother forgave him for not helping! But back to the past.)

Home and Hearth

The Browns

During the years when my father was in the British army, Mother would occasionally leave me for a few hours with his parents. The Browns lived on Harav Kook Street in a two-story stone house with a large garden in the back. The garden was filled with snapdragons—lion's jaw in Hebrew—since my grandfather Eliezer was always trying to develop new strains. At the bottom of the garden stood a shed where my father's brother, Eliyahu, an electrical engineer, was carrying on his own experiments.

In the aftermath of the Arab Revolt (1936-1939), Eliezer moved his dental clinic from 55 Mamilla Street to his residence. (Many Jewish establishments in the Jaffa Gate area—including the Bermans' store—relocated to more secure neighborhoods in west Jerusalem.) I used to love to visit the clinic and sit, unafraid, in my grandfather's dental chair viewing all the instruments of torture with which I was familiar through visits to my own dentist. The models of skulls and dentures, neatly displayed in glass cases, provided additional spooky thrills.

Another great attraction at the Browns' house was the Biblical Zoo next door. From the windows of the second floor, one had an unobstructed view of the menagerie. It was a tiny place, a children's zoo, which boasted a pond with a few large turtles, some deer who mingled freely with hens and roosters, and a couple of caged monkeys. When the zoo expanded in 1941 and moved to Sanhedriya—where it featured a number of exotic animals and even camel rides—I deeply regretted the change. (Today the Biblical Zoo—enlarged and relocated again—is one of Jerusalem's most popular sites.)

My grandfather Eliezer Brown was a good-looking man, with olive-dark skin, a thick mustache, and large brown eyes. His father came from Graz, Austria. His mother, who was a Sephardi, was born in Constantinople, now Istanbul. The family moved to Palestine in the late nineteenth century and settled in Haifa. Like many other Jews in the country, they preferred not to be Turkish subjects and acquired Spanish citizenship that they could probably purchase because Eliezer's mother was Sephardi. The family still held it in 1934, as attested to by my birth certificate. By then the spelling of the name had changed from the Austrian "Braun" to the more British "Brown."

In contrast to her husband, my grandmother Sarah, née Buchman, was very fair, with blue eyes, and, by the time I knew her, silky white hair that she kept in a neat bun. She was born in Brisk (or Brest-Litovsk, now in Belarus), where her family owned textile factories. At a young age she came to Jerusalem with her father, Haim Yehuda Leib Buchman, who became a head of a yeshiva in Mea She'arim. (He was the author of *Mevaer Haim*, a religious tract published in 1914, in which he tried to "explain life.") Sarah dreamt of studying mathematics in Italy, but her father forbade it. Instead, she married Eliezer. It was not a happy union. He ruled the household with an iron fist and she, therefore, hid things from him. He wanted my father, for example, to take over his practice and did not realize that, with Sarah's help, his son was studying medicine in Europe, rather than dentistry.

Eliyahu, Eliezer's and Sarah's second son, had also married a Sephardi woman, Hannah Yehuda, niece of A. S. Yehuda, a well-known Arabist of whom she was very proud. Since the housing market in the country was extremely tight, the couple lived with Eliyahu's parents, on the second floor. They were unable to have children and Hannah turned bitter, which did not help the atmosphere in the house.

According to Hannah, whom I interviewed many decades later, Eliezer had a lot of charm and women simply "clung" to him—to use her word. At some point he wanted his parents to join the household but for once Sarah, who did not get along with them, put her foot down and objected. He then began to "take on mistresses," Hannah said, which Sarah bore in silence.

The Browns' house on Harav Kook Street   *My father's mother, Sarah Brown*

Sarah spoiled me by always preparing my favorite dishes. Because Eliezer was brought up by a Sephardi mother, he preferred Middle Eastern food at which Sarah became an expert, and meals at her house were more exotic than the ones served at home. I continued to visit Sarah on my own, when I was a young adult and she was a widow. She was a gentle soul who rarely complained and liked to pretend that everything within her family was perfect. She went on covering up "inconvenient truths" till her last day.

More Berman Weddings

Avraham was the second of Sarah and Eliyahu Bermans' children to get married. Though not tall, he was rather handsome, with dark brown hair, speckled green eyes, and a bemused expression on his face.

He was a bit of a dandy, and was reputed to have a girlfriend on every street in Jerusalem, in addition to Gladys (or was it Grace?) in London. Grandmother used to say that if Avraham stood anywhere in the middle of a city and whistled, half a dozen young women would appear. According to both Avraham and Zahava, he was driving along what is now known as Agron Street one Saturday morning, shortly after his return from the London School of Economics, when he noticed a car with a flat tire. Among those standing around the crippled vehicle was an attractive young woman, so naturally he stopped to offer assistance and helped push the car to a nearby garage.

"Where were you going?" he asked the young lady, Zahava Blau of Haifa, who was visiting friends in Jerusalem.

"We were on our way to the Western Wall. My mother told me to leave a note there asking God to send me a bridegroom," she teased.

"Then I'll go with you and ask for a bride."

Everybody piled into Avraham's new Baby Austin and off they went. When they returned later in the day to pick up the other car, its tire now patched, Avraham suggested that he drive Zahava back to her friends' house. They met again that night at a fancy ball—balls and "bazaars" were a popular way of raising funds for various charities. Each had come with a date, but while dancing together Avraham disclosed that he had a week's leave coming up and wondered where he should spend it. Zahava suggested that he come to Haifa where she would introduce him to some of her prettier girlfriends. She already had a beau, she declared. On the following Saturday at four in the afternoon Zahava was sitting at her parents' apartment having tea with several of her friends, waiting for Avraham. By the time he showed up, two hours late, they had all left. He then produced a pair of tickets to a popular movie and explained that he did not want to meet anyone else, he only wanted to see Zahava. Somehow she forgave him, and seemed to forget her old beau. Avraham continued to drive up to Haifa every weekend and soon brought Zahava back to Jerusalem to be inspected by the family. The Blaus, Zahava's parents,

Home and Hearth

At Café Lipsky in Talpiot, 1937

were originally from Safed so he was particularly pleased to introduce her to his grandmother Esther who used to predict whenever she was annoyed at him, that a *tzfaserke vet dich nisht nemen*, "a girl from Safed would not have you," since *tzfaserkes* were considered to be very canny.

Avraham and Zahava got married six months later. The ceremony was held on the roof of my grandparents' house on March 30, 1936, just before Passover. (Berman weddings usually took place on the eve of Passover because the bakery closed for a week and the bridegroom could take time off.) I was two at the time so I cannot possibly remember the wedding and there are no photographs to remind me of it. But there is an image imprinted in my mind, probably the result of oft-repeated tales: I am standing on the roof wearing my "training," as a popular children's outfit resembling a sweat suit was called. My back pocket is full of playing marbles. I am trying to watch the ceremony but all I can see are the bottom halves of men's dark suits. The young couple lived for a while in my grandparents house then moved a few blocks away to 14 Chancellor Street, the apartment house owned by the family, where at any given time various Bermans resided.

Once Avraham was safely married, the family's attention focused on Moshe, the eldest of Sarah's children who was still a bachelor at thirty-one with the threat of Mabel, the gentile girlfriend in England, looming on the horizon. But a solution was close. My mother had a friend, Ella, who grew up in Egypt and moved to Jerusalem after she married Asher King, a local attorney. Ella's father, Baruch Sachs, was a Jerusalem-born and Frankfurt-educated ophthalmologist who was exiled by the Turks to Egypt during World War I and eventually settled in Alexandria. He married Regina Grunhud, daughter of a Hungarian rabbi, and later—along with his sons Rudolph and Willie—served as King Farouk's eye doctor. In 1938, when the youngest Sachs daughter, Cecile, came to Jerusalem to visit Ella, my mother met her and decided to introduce her to Moshe. Cecile had several relatives in Jerusalem who also thought that a match between a Berman and a Sachs was highly desirable and they all hoped for good news.

According to Cecile, the first rendezvous was a near disaster. Moshe, who was rather short and stocky, had lost a lot of hair by the time he was thirty. (It was the bad drinking water in England, said Grandmother. No, it was a fish that ate his hair, Moshe explained to me.) His finer qualities—his intelligence, kindness, sense of humor—were not immediately apparent. Moshe often played at Café Lipsky's tennis courts in Talpiot, a suburb south of Jerusalem, and Cecile first saw him as he came off the court, short, bald, and sweaty. She was not impressed. She also had a boyfriend in Tel Aviv but rumors of her imminent engagement to Moshe—undoubtedly spread by her sister and my mother throughout the "right" social circles in Jerusalem—soon reached the young man. He

Home and Hearth

Moshe before he lost his hair, 1926

broke off the romance, Cecile stayed in Jerusalem and eventually married Moshe.

The wedding, which I actually remember, took place in the spring of 1939 in the large courtyard behind my grandparents' house. This time I was properly attired in a chocolate-brown velvet dress with a lace collar, especially made for the occasion. The young couple moved to a rented apartment in Talpiot, across the street from Cecile's sister Ella, and out of the immediate orbit of the Bermans.

The Arab Revolt, 1936-1939

The country's Arab population had benefited materially from the various Jewish *aliyot*—mass immigrations—since the economy grew and many found employment in Jewish enterprises. In addition, land, which was mostly owned by Arabs, rose in value. But tension between Arabs and

Jews persisted after the riots of 1929 and the Arabs continued to object to Jewish immigration that was on the rise, especially after 1933, when Hitler came to power. (Nearly 165,000 Jews entered the country legally between 1933 and 1936, plus thousands of others who came illegally. The number of Jews in the country rose to 400,000, a third of the total population.) When the Nuremberg Laws were announced in October 1935 and Jews were no longer considered citizens of the Reich, the Yishuv in Palestine demanded more visas for their European brethren, while the Arabs pressured the British not to allow more Jews in. Demonstrations, counter-demonstrations, and riots continued.

In April 1936 two Jews on a bus were slain by an Arab gang. The next night, in an act of revenge, Jews murdered two Arabs. During the funeral held in Tel Aviv for the two Jewish victims, riots broke out in nearby Jaffa and it took the British two days to suppress them while Arabs destroyed property and killed sixteen Jews. The Arab Higher Committee, founded to represent Palestinian Arabs to the British Administration and led by Haj Amin al-Husseini—the Mufti of Jerusalem and the main instigator of the 1929 riots—declared a general strike by Arab workers and a boycott of Jewish produce. The Arabs had three demands: stop Jewish immigration; stop Jewish land acquisition; and establish a representative government. The latter would have meant an Arab national government over all of Palestine.

Thus began the three years known as the Arab Revolt, years of violent assaults against the Yishuv and the British authorities, years in which their own people killed many Muslim moderates. Six months after it began, the strike was briefly suspended under pressure from leaders of neighboring Arab countries. Then, on November 11, 1936, a Royal Commission headed by Lord Peel arrived from London to seek a way to settle the strife. "Appeal for Peace Issued by Bishop and Chief Rabbi," read the headline of *The Palestine Post*, the country's English daily. But the Mufti considered it inappropriate to do the same since the Arab Higher Committee initially decided not to cooperate with Lord Peel. In

July 1937, the Royal Commission came out with a proposal calling for the partition of Palestine. It suggested establishing a Jewish state in the Galilee and along the coastal plain; an Arab state in the rest of Palestine and Transjordan; and a British enclave which would include Jerusalem and Bethlehem. The Arab leadership rejected the plan. Many Zionist leaders objected to it as well because of the miniscule size of the proposed Jewish state and their sense that part of the original Mandatory Palestine had already been granted to the Arabs when the Emirate of Transjordan—today's Jordan—was established a decade earlier. But others, transfixed by the notion of a sovereign Jewish state, wanted to further explore the plan.

Soon the second, more intensified, stage of the Arab Revolt began, with attacks on Jewish settlements, vehicles, and passersby, and on British forces and installations. Arabs who opposed the terror tactics were harassed, often assassinated. The government reacted by arresting many nationalistic Arab leaders, but the Mufti escaped to Syria where he continued to direct the rioting gangs. (In 1941 he was in Iraq, also a British Mandate, where he helped organize a short-lived revolt, supported by the Axis. He later visited Berlin, where he was welcomed by Hitler.) The British finally suppressed the revolt in the spring of 1939. By then, more than five thousand Arabs, four hundred Jews, and two hundred Englishmen had been killed.

It is interesting to note that while the British Administration did not officially recognize the Hagana—the underground founded by the Yishuv in the 1920s to provide protection from Arab attacks—it allowed the organization to arm during the Arab Revolt in order to better defend the Jewish population. Also, as the result of the Arab strike, which, among other things diminished their agricultural output, the Yishuv became more self-sufficient and that hastened the disengagement of the two economies.[32]

Yet even as the Arab Revolt was coming to an end, the British government in London was changing its policies. Fearing the possibility of another world war, England decided that it could not afford to alienate the Arab world with its vast lands, masses, and huge oil reserves. In May, 1939, the British colonial secretary, Malcolm MacDonald, issued a White Paper which stated that with over 450,000 Jews settled in Palestine, the Balfour Declaration had been met, and that His Majesty's Government "now declare unequivocally that it is not part of their policy that Palestine should become a Jewish State." Instead, an independent Palestine should be established in ten years, governed jointly by Arabs and Jews. Jewish immigration to Palestine would be restricted to a total of 75,000 over the next five years and after that, only with Arab consent. In addition, the sale of land by Arabs to Jews would be prohibited. Despite these concessions, the Mufti and other extreme Arab nationalists came out on the side of Nazi Germany in hopes of destroying the Jewish Yishuv.

I was five when the revolt ended and I only remember one incident from that period. My uncle Moshe was driving to Tel Aviv when he saw a gang of Arabs stop the car in front of his and stab the driver. Moshe somehow managed to turn his car around and escape. But the rest of the time, within my sheltered world, life seemed to be perfectly normal.

Weekdays and Holidays

The Daily Routine

Grandfather and I were early risers. Silently we would meet in the dining room where he would lower his pants, reach into a pot of boiling water for a sterilized syringe, and administer an insulin shot deep into his thigh. Next, he would recite his morning prayers while I waited, nestled in his armchair. Soon Grandmother would appear and start her day by reading from a Yiddish prayer book, a language, she assured her doubting granddaughter, the Lord understood perfectly well. The formal part of her prayers over, Sarah would proceed with a long list of private petitions on behalf of relatives, friends, or neighbors who needed help: a cure, a husband, a better job, a kinder mother-in-law, even better grades at school. Didn't God know of all those problems, I asked. The Lord was so busy, He needed reminders, she explained. Looking directly at me, she would often end her supplications with a sigh, hoping that God would let her live long enough to see me married. I was seven or eight at the time.

Normally we all had breakfast together, my grandparents, Mother, Haya, and whichever one of my uncles was at home at the time. There would be several kinds of fresh bread on the table, butter, jams, halvah, cheeses, and *leben*—similar to yogurt—and the ubiquitous salad of finely

*With my mother on the roof of our house
Mt. Scopus is in the background, 1939.*

chopped tomatoes, peppers, cucumbers, radishes, and parsley seasoned with olive oil and lemon juice. Roh'keh would serve each person with his or her beverage of choice: coffee, tea, or cocoa. (The latter, which I had to drink so my bones and teeth would be strong, said Mother, was made with hot milk, from which the skin was removed without benefit of a strainer. The remaining bits of skin floating around the cup were the bane of my existence.)

Everyone was rushing at breakfast, tempers were short, and there was little time for talking. But on days when school began late or during holidays, I lingered at the table as did Grandfather, who was the only one allowed to read the newspapers at breakfast, a privilege left over from the days when his presence at the bakery was more urgent and it was his only chance to glance at the news. When I was old enough to be interested in current events, I was very annoyed by this rule but since my regular place was on Grandfather's left, two seats down from the head of the table, I learned to read sideways, backwards, and upside down. (Once, when I bragged about this ability, Grandpa took me to a small Yemenite prayer house, not far from where we lived. The congregation was very poor and had few books; children and young men were studying around a low table, sharing one volume, and they could all read their portions from any direction.)

No sooner were the breakfast dishes cleared, than my uncle Avraham would stop by on his way to the bakery.

"Hello, Mother."

"Good morning, my child. Have you had breakfast?"

"Of course, Mother. Zahava would never let me leave otherwise." Aunt Zahava was famous for her good housekeeping, a model held up to lesser women. So why was Avraham here?

"You look a little pale this morning," Grandmother would continue while Avraham rubbed his temples, discreetly. "Do you have a headache?"

"Well, as a matter of fact, now that you mentioned it, I do feel one coming. It must be the heat." (In winter, it was the cold.)

This verbal waltz over, Grandmother would make Avraham a cup of Turkish coffee which he drank while standing, insisting that he was in a great hurry to get to work, ignoring her plea: "For the same price you could be seated." Half an hour later, he would depart. This daily ritual was Avraham's way of visiting his mother and assuring her that all was well. He was known in the family as *der shtiler hokhem*, "the silent sage," who showed affection in his own understated manner.

Next, almost without fail, two or three other Bermans would arrive from the bakery for a confidential chat away from the prying eyes and ears of the other partners. At any given time at least half a dozen family members were working in the bakery—fathers, sons, brothers, uncles, nephews, cousins. Relations were often tense, a natural phenomenon in a business run by three generations. Deep in his heart each Berman was convinced that he was the one carrying the main weight of the business on his shoulders while the others—innocent, incompetent, or wicked—did not fully appreciate his intelligence, devotion, or business acumen. So whenever there was a crisis or if alliances shifted, a not-so-secret conference would be held at our house, just a few steps from the bakery. Tea, coffee—Turkish or *au lait*—and cold drinks accompanied by homemade pastries were immediately produced for the conferees. "You cannot have people in the house without feeding them," was Grandmother's rule, strictly observed even when the guests were uninvited ones.

By one o'clock the consultations would end, usually without reaching any conclusions, and the table would be hastily set for dinner, the midday meal. The food was a fusion of rather heavy East European cuisine rescued by Middle Eastern touches. There was always soup, chicken soup with dumplings or a meat-and-potato soup and, in summer, a cold beet borscht or a fruit soup. The main course usually consisted of some form of chicken or meat, both tough and rather tasteless after being made kosher—salted, soaked, and drained—and cooked too long, accompanied by some form of starch, a lettuce salad, and a vegetable: okra or string beans stewed in a tomato sauce, deep-fried eggplant slices, cauliflower. Sometimes Roh'keh followed Baba Esther's Tiberias recipes and made cutlets or vegetables stuffed with ground lamb and rice, dishes far superior to the normal fare. For dessert we had fruit, usually oranges or watermelon, depending on the season. The meal was often a disorganized affair since each member of the household showed up at a different time, depending on work or school schedules, with Grandfather arriving from the bakery whenever he was overcome by hunger. So Roh'keh would be serving three-course meals to people as they appeared, any time between one and two thirty. It was worse than running a restaurant, she said, since we all had favorite dishes as well as ones we would not touch. To complicate matters, some unexpected visitors occasionally showed up.

"Oh, I would not dream of disturbing you," they would protest, having made sure to arrive a little after one o'clock. Famous for dropping in was Nehama, who was somehow related to Grandmother. She was a handsome if large woman, widowed at an early age with three young daughters to raise. Eventually she remarried, although we never saw her husband, who was reputed to be very old and very rich and own a "villa" in Ramat Gan in the days when everyone else lived in houses. Judging by Nehama's frequent visits, he could not have been very stimulating company, though even the most wicked tongues in the family agreed that she took very good care of him. Urged to join us at the table, Nehama would demure and announce that she had just eaten and could not possibly touch another morsel.

"You can't just sit there. How about a small bowl of soup?" Grandmother would suggest.

"I really shouldn't, but how can I resist your wonderful borscht?" The not-so-small bowl would soon disappear.

"Nehama, I know you are not hungry, but do try a little of this *kussa mahshi*. We stuff the squash just the way Aunt Leah in Beirut used to, may she rest in peace."

"Well, in that case, how can I say no? Aunt Leah, of blessed memory, was a renowned cook." To the best of my knowledge the two had never met.

Next she was coaxed to try a sliver of apricot torte. When she claimed that she was getting too fat—with which Mother and I agreed heartily if in silence because of Grandmother's chilling looks in our direction—she was told:

"Nonsense, Nehama, you look wonderful and you must stay healthy. After all you have three orphans to raise besides taking care of your new husband."

"Yes, eat, Nehama. Eat," Uncle Keith would mutter. Keith, who grew up in London's East End, the son of a poor Polish tailor, was an ardent communist sympathizer. When he married my aunt Haya, the daughter of a wealthy baker, he suffered deep guilt feelings since he was enjoying the fruits of capitalism. He felt better when others shared the wealth—and food— beside himself. The meal would end with a cup of Turkish coffee, after which Nehama, slightly embarrassed, would sigh and mumble, in Yiddish: *Der apetit kumt mietn esn.* "The appetite comes with the eating."

There was a brief pause in activities after the midday meal, when Grandfather dozed off in his favorite armchair, later claiming that he did not even shut his eyes. But he had the grace to chuckle whenever I picked up his *kippa*, his skullcap, which frequently slipped off his head while he napped. Tea was served after siesta, just before Eliyahu returned to the bakery. In the late afternoon there was a different class of callers; some were Grandmother's relatives of whom there were many, spread all over the country. They had to be well treated and offered the best, said Grandma, because some of them were less fortunate than we were. Thus the freshest fruit, the most delectable pastries, chocolate, and candies would soon vanish. Upon hearing some tale of woe, Grandmother would send the visitor off with bundles of food, clothes, or whatever else she felt would not be missed by the rest of the household. It was often at this point that Roh'keh, observing the disappearance of the food she had prepared for the next day, announced her resignation.

"Oh, please don't do that," Grandma would plead. "We are so lucky, and they are not. Besides, did you hear what happened to so and so's wife?" Some horror story would follow, whispered away from children's ears. It often involved marital difficulties or female troubles and it pacified Roh'keh who was really a kind soul. She would then go home, carrying a package of food for her own family, and return the next morning.

In the late afternoon Grandfather would go to say the evening prayers at the small synagogue that abutted the bakery and stood some twenty yards away from our house. Supper was served when he returned, an

Nitza, 1940

informal meal of salads, omelets, sardines, herring, fruit, and cheese, usually prepared by my mother. It was a relaxed meal, with most of us lingering around the table. Then the family did the washing up. The women in the family, that is. My task was to sweep the dining room floor to make sure that there was nothing left for cockroaches, ants, or flies.

Running the Household

Feeding the family plus the many visitors we had was a major undertaking, overseen by Sarah, with my mother doing the shopping, and Roh'keh the cooking. Thursday was market day and during summer vacation I would accompany Mother to Mea She'arim where an open-air market was held in the central square. Before reaching the semi-permanent stalls one passed by a group of Arab women in their traditional indigo-black dresses with embroidered frontispieces. They crouched behind large baskets which they had carried on their heads from villages miles away, baskets filled with pink radishes still covered with dew, bunches of scallions, parsley, dill, tiny cucumbers, shiny eggplants, yellow squashes, and baladi, native tomatoes—among the world's finest. In late summer they offered black and white mulberries, and plums ranging from tart green ones to luscious deep-purple Santa Rosas. Grapes, figs, and olives all came in different shapes and colors. Haggling with my mother in Arabic, the women drove a hard bargain.

"How much is a kilo of tomatoes?"

"As usual, ten piasters."

"What? That's more than I paid last week. Besides, these tomatoes look too ripe."

"Really," the seller would say to my mother. "Have I ever sold you a rotten tomato? I swear by the head of my little one that I picked those beauties this morning. Here, try one. They taste like honey, not like a vegetable."

"All right. All right. I will take two kilos for fifteen piasters."

"What, you want me to lose money? I'll give you three kilos for twenty-five piasters. I am doing this only for your mother, Madame Sarah, because she is a saint."

The fruit or vegetables would be placed in one dish of the farmer's scales, with balancing weights in the other. The weights were graduated stones that represented anything from five kilograms down. The stones were quite accurate, since every seller knew that each housewife could check the weight of her purchases on scales at home, and anyone who cheated would be ostracized by the regular clientele. The goods were then carefully laid into straw baskets that the shopper brought along, and one had to plan the order of procuring carefully so that delicate apricots lay on top of potatoes, rather than the other way around. When the baskets got too heavy, a *treger*, or "carrier" would suddenly materialize; once hired he would follow Mother, gradually disappearing behind his load.

Shopping took a long time. Once past the Arab women and the Jewish-operated stalls where goods varied with the seasons, one reached the regular shops where merchants stood in the doorways loudly praising their wares in Hebrew or Yiddish. Bargaining would continue, but only half heartedly, since the Jews lacked both the enthusiasm and the finesse of the *falaheen*, the Arab peasants. At the butcher's, Mother would place an order to be delivered later. The carcasses, hanging on large hooks, were less than appetizing and I tried to avoid entering the store. The quality of the beef raised in the country's arid fields was not very good to begin with, and after it was koshered—that is salted and soaked—it was tasteless and tough. Next we would stop for chickens at Mr. Sasson's, where a different ritual began. First there was a long conversation, each side inquiring about the health and well-being of various members of the two large families. Appropriate noises, expressing sorrow or delight at some mishap or a blissful event, accompanied the dialogue that was conducted against the background of clucking cooped chickens. Since we shopped at Sasson's every week, and our families lived not far from each other, the whole discussion was a waste of time but it showed respect, said Mother, and when you treated people properly, they served you well. Here there was no bargaining since we were old and valued customers and it paid to keep us satisfied. When both sides were certain that no family affair had been overlooked, the selection of chickens began. Old Mr. Sasson, a handsome, dignified man, would stick his arm into one of the cages which lined the shop from top to bottom; the chickens would panic and cluck, scratch, or jump, doing whatever possible to avoid his grip, but it was a lost battle. He would come up with a plump bird and hold her up for Mother to inspect, while talking continuously, both to my mother and to the hen, about the beauty, the tender thighs, and the limpid eyes—of the chicken, that is—and what a tasty dish she would make. Since the Friday night soup required more than one body, the selection process was repeated several times. For the sake of form either Mother or Mr. Sasson would occasionally reject a chicken and return her to the cage to await lesser customers. We never saw the chickens alive again since Mr. Sasson took them over to a kosher butcher next door, then to a woman who plucked off the birds' feathers; by the time we picked them up, they bore no resemblance to the white or golden creatures we had first encountered.

From there we would continue to the fishmonger's store, owned by Noah Epstein, one of Grandmother's second cousins. Without interference from Mother, who would not dare imply that a relative of Grandmother's could make a less-than-perfect selection, Noah would cast his net into a large tank and come up with several live carp. He would then bash the fish over the head, clean its insides, wrap it in a newspaper, and place it in one of the baskets the *treger* was carrying. Sometimes, when a two-day holiday preceded or followed the Sabbath, a lot of food had to be prepared in advance and shopping had to be done a day early. Noah would then give us several live fish and we would rush home to deposit them into a bathtub filled with water where the carp stayed overnight. Protests against this unorthodox use of the tub were useless. You could always take a sponge bath, said Grandmother, but you could not celebrate a holiday without gefilte fish. The carp, to which one got slightly attached if only through sharing the same bathtub, would then be hit over the head by Roh'keh, prior to being cut, cleaned, and stuffed. Trying to get a cold drink one day, I opened the refrigerator where Roh'keh had just left some freshly sliced carp. With reflexes still going strong, one piece wiggled and fell at my feet. After that encounter I stopped eating fish until, at age twenty-two, I found myself living in Tokyo where I became addicted to sushi.

Grandfather was responsible for some purchases. Large cans of olive oil and sacks filled with cakes of rough Shemen soap arrived from Haifa. Staples from the Bermans' store were delivered in large bags—sugar, rice, flour, several kinds of beans. Eliyahu was famous for being able to identify a ripe watermelon, and in the summer he would go in one of the bakery's delivery vans and purchase a couple of dozen melons and watermelons from Arab farmers in an open market near Damascus Gate. The watermelons usually dwelt under his bed—since his room was the coolest in the house—waiting for him to select one. He would then shake it, tap it, smell it, and listen to it until he was satisfied and then he sliced it—the inside was always red and sweet. Watermelons were served with a dry, hard goat cheese from Safed. The seeds were jealously guarded by Esther who spent hours washing and drying them. She roasted them on Fridays—to be enjoyed at leisure during the Sabbath—and divided them among her grandchildren, that is my mother and her siblings. I also received a portion but my uncle David, her youngest grandson named for her late husband, always got a larger share than the rest of us, to our great annoyance. Although we usually purchased additional roasted seeds from a nearby Yemenite shopkeeper, nothing tasted as good as Baba Esther's *popeetes*, distributed while still warm.

A milkman stopped by the kitchen door every other day, carrying a heavy tin container with a large measuring cup. He was handed a couple of pots into which he poured the unpasteurized milk which had to be brought to a boil then placed to cool on a window sill in Grandfather's bedroom before it was refrigerated. For many years a young Arab shepherd used to appear once a week in the courtyard with his herd of goats, scraggily creatures in brown or black-and-white coats that tried to get into our vegetable patch. Their master milked them right there, directly into one of our pots. That milk would be left in a warm place until it turned, then poured into cotton bags which were hung to drip over a sink until the remaining curds turned into cheese.

At some point in the summer, several *falaheen* from a nearby Arab village would arrive carrying baskets filled with green olives. White flour sacks—washed and bleached innumerable times—would then be spread over the courtyard and women and children helped bruise the olives with a hammer or a rock prior to pickling them, to remove the bitterness. Since each olive had to be hit individually with just the right amount of force to bruise but not crush, it was a great honor to be allowed to participate in the preparation. The olives were transferred into large tin containers, covered with a carefully balanced mixture of water, salt, garlic, dill, and sliced lemons. At the end of the day a tinsmith would show up to weld covers onto the containers which were then left to ferment in the basement for a year or longer. A similar process—except for the cracking—was used to pickle cucumbers. The results were the tastiest olives and pickles anyone could wish for. Jams were also made at home, a tedious job of stirring plums or apricots over a hot stove. Syrups were made from berries or lemon juice with lots of sugar, later combined with ice water to create summer drinks. Making noodles was Roh'keh's responsibility and once a week she would start the day by mixing the dough, letting it rise, rolling it out on the large worktable in the pantry until the dough was so thin it was almost transparent. Then she would drape the thin sheets over the roller and carry them one by one to Grandfather's bedroom—a nerve-wracking operation—and spread them on a clean linen sheet on top of the bed where they rested until Roh'keh deemed it was time to hand-slice them. Sometimes she concocted a slightly "eggier" dough, almost a batter, and deep-fried little squares, soup *mandalach*, or bow-like creations, which were sprinkled with fine sugar and eaten as dessert, known for some reason as "Baron Munchausen's trousers." Two women

Weekdays and Holidays

who worked in the courtyard, first mixing grainy semolina with water then pressing the dough through a huge copper colander onto a clean sheet, prepared couscous.

For other supplies we just went up the street to a small grocery store owned by Mr. Braverman who lived with his family on the floor above. We bought butter there, cheese, matches, candles, *lakerda*—a smoked fish, coffee, tea, and candy. The store was crammed with foodstuff in open barrels, plus cans and bottles stacked on rickety shelves behind Mr. Braverman's desk. He knew everyone by sight, and before you left the store he would jot down your purchases in his weighty black ledger and, at the end of the month, bring a bill to the house.

Basically, it was Leah who ran the household, a duty that fell on her when Sarah took to bed in the 1920s. When she recovered, Sarah did not return to her old duties and left them to my mother who continued to live above my grandparents in the second floor apartment they built for her when she got married. From the time I can remember, we always ate at my grandparents' table with whoever else of my mother's siblings was there at the time.

This may be a good place to comment briefly on Leah's social life. In general, there was not much going on in Jerusalem by way of entertainment, but if a concert or play was performed in the city, Mother was sure to be there. On Saturday night she often went to the movies with some acquaintances or family members, and she played cards once a week at a friend's house. A lot of social activity took place in cafés. Occasionally Mother would meet another lady for an afternoon coffee at Café Europa and bring me along. The café had an interior garden where a small band played. It also served heavenly, paper-thin potato chips just out of the fryer. A lot more time was spent at Café Vienna, on Jaffa Road, across from Café Europa. There Mother and her women friends—all middle-class ladies, wives of doctors, lawyers, bankers, well-to-do ladies who did not work outside the house—met every weekday morning. On Thursdays they would go to a beauty salon, to get their hair and fingernails done. To their credit, they were all involved in charitable work, organizing bazaars and balls to raise money for good causes. My mother's favorite was the League for the War against Tuberculosis. Since Jews and non-Jews rarely mingled socially except at formal events sponsored by the Mandatory authorities, or at musical and theatrical performances, the charity balls provided meeting places for Jerusalemites of different backgrounds. There were also New Year balls, usually at the King David Hotel, which were frowned upon by the Orthodox. I always looked forward to the holiday—which was a regular workday for Jews—because Mother, who attended some of the New Year's Eve balls, would bring me back a cream puff wrapped in silver foil. In his autobiography, *A Tale of Love and Darkness*, Amos Oz describes the Jerusalem his parents could only look at from a distance, a Jerusalem where at the King David Hotel "culture-seeking Jews and educated Arabs mixed with cultivated Englishmen with perfect manners."

Social life for the Bermans at that time was centered around the family, with the children who had already left home coming back with their families for Friday night dinner or lunch on Saturday. No one in our family gave dinner parties as such, but teas on Saturday afternoons—soon to be described—were occasions at which one entertained a broader group of friends. There were other social circles where different activities went on—among the intelligentsia or the politicians—but those were not the circles in which my family moved.

Clothes

Bossy and competent, my mother normally saw to the family's clothing needs. There were two department stores in the city which carried ready-made clothes: Maayan Stub at the corner of Jaffa Road and Straus Street (then Chancellor Street), and Kol Bo, where Jaffa Road and Ben-Yehuda Street met, where, as their slogan said, "You could buy anything you wanted." While my mother bought me ready-made shirts and underwear, her own lingerie, from silk slips and underpants to bras and corsets, was made to order at a *büstenhalter*—brassiere—shop, run by a Hungarian couple, recent refugees. "Good" grownup clothes were made to order as well, at a number of establishments such as Klein, for women, and Heilig, for men. Most everyday clothes were made at home. We had a capable Russian seamstress, Miriam, who used to spend several days at our house every spring and fall, measuring, cutting, and sewing dresses for all the women in the household. (Like many other families in those days, we owned a Singer sewing machine.) Fashion journals from Paris and London began to appear in Jerusalem in the 1920s and my stylish mother was familiar with the latest trends, and so, with Miriam's meticulous trimming and stitching, we were always well dressed. During World War II and later, in the early years of Israel's independence, many things were rationed, including clothes. But we managed by remaking old dresses and using pieces of fabric bought over the years and kept in storage: you never know when you'll find such a nice pattern again, said Mother, to warrant her impulsive purchases. My mother was a prolific knitter, as were a couple of my aunts, and they produced an array of sweaters for the family. When wool was rationed yet children kept growing, old sweaters were unraveled, the yarn wound on the back of a chair, then washed, dried, rewound, and re-knit. Stripes became the style of the day, as two or three small sweaters were refashioned into a new one. A side benefit of knitting and dressmaking at home were leftovers—swatches of fabric, yarn, a selection of extra buttons—that provided hours of amusement on rainy days.

On special occasions, I was taken to Nelly, another refugee, Czech or Hungarian, who had a children's clothing "salon" on Ben-Yehuda Street. Once my cousin Daphne grew a little older, our mothers often ordered matching outfits for us. Nelly—a slim dark-haired lady in impeccable black ensembles who was always holding pins in her mouth—demanded many fittings, which I disliked intensely as she insisted that I stand straight and pull in my tummy. But the results were worth it. She once made Daphne and me matching navy-blue tweed coats with velvet collars that I can still see as if it were yesterday.

Daphne and I got new dresses and shoes for Rosh Hashana and Passover. The shoes were bought at Freimann & Bein where your feet were X-rayed by a special contraption in order to determine their size; you could actually look down into it and see your own bones. (No one realized the danger of this practice.) Mother had her shoes made at Gabardian, the best shoe store in the city, owned by an Armenian family and located on Jaffa Road, across from City Hall. After the war—that is World War II—she ordered a pair of gray suede shoes with crepe soles for which she paid five *lirot*—about $20—considered an outrageously high sum. Mother justified the expense explaining that she got clothes of high quality because they lasted for many years, which was perfectly true. But the shocked family remained unconvinced.

Cleanliness

Cleanliness was not merely a virtue but a necessity, protection against typhoid, typhus, and other diseases that periodically plagued the country. My uncle Moshe came down with typhus in the early 1940s and nearly died. (As is common practice among Orthodox Jews, he was then given another name, Haim—meaning "life"—at a ceremony in our synagogue. Esther gave God, rather than the doctors, credit for his recovery.) I was forbidden to use any toilet except the one at home and at my aunts' houses. In all my years at high school I remember going to the bathroom there once, when I was sick. Since flies thrived in the city where garbage was abundant, we washed dirty dishes immediately and swept the dining room after each meal; in the middle of every week a woman came in to scrub the floors throughout the house and they were wet-mopped again on Friday mornings. (The process was known as *sponja*.) The oriental carpets, used only during the cold season, were hung over a railing in the

Weekdays and Holidays

backyard once a week and beaten with an old tennis racket. My mother was so neurotic that she used to bend in half to check whether the floor under the refrigerator was cleaned. One time something snapped in her back and she could not straighten up and had to limp into bed where she spent an agonizing week, but when the maid came again, Mother practically crawled on all fours to repeat the inspection.

At school, posters depicted flies of monstrous proportions spreading germs with their hairy legs. "Never leave food uncovered," the posters warned. "Wash your hands after going to the bathroom and before every meal." Once a month the school nurse showed up with long knitting needles and searched our hair for lice. An afflicted victim would be sent home to have his or her skull rubbed with kerosene; smell and stigma clung to the poor tyke for days. To make sure nothing so disgraceful ever happened to me, Mother used to go through my thick mop of curly hair with a fine-toothed comb—a torturous exercise.

Bedbugs were considered to be another shameful sign of uncleanness so twice a year all beds in our house were dragged into the courtyard where the mattresses were sprayed with something known as Flit, an insect killer. Every corner of the metal bed frames where a bedbug might hide was scoured with kerosene. For several nights the fumigated beds reeked so badly that it was hard to go to sleep. I often wondered whether a few bedbugs would not be preferable. Once in a while other creatures made their way into the house such as cockroaches, both black harmless ones and the more repulsive brown variety, but they did not linger in the spotless kitchen. Creepy crawlers such as a centipedes or the rare scorpion required a grownup's help. If a dead snake was found in the garden we left it alone and placed a bowl with milk or flour mixed with sugar near it to comfort the bereaved spouse: everyone, including Huckleberry Finn, sooner or later discovered that if you killed a snake its mate would come to haunt you.

Another major effort in the war against dirt was dealing with laundry in pre-washing machine days. Two Yemenite women came to the house every Monday, a mother and daughter who lived in Kerem Hateymanim nearby, and spent the day scrubbing, rinsing, boiling, "whiting," starching, and hanging up laundry—pile upon pile of clothes, bed linen, towels, tablecloths and napkins. The women sat in the courtyard, sheltered by the balcony of the floor above, with two enormous copper tubs in front of them. When they finished scrubbing one tubful, they moved the laundry to the next tub and rinsed it in several changes of water. White fabrics were then boiled in a large cauldron that stood over a Primus—a kerosene burner—then fished out by a pole and dipped into another tub that contained bluish water "to make the clothes white," I was told. Table linen and shirts were briefly deposited into yet another tub with starch. After the laundry was wrung, it was carried over in large buckets to a vacant lot next door and hung on clotheslines supported by poles that were put up earlier in the day. Sometimes a gust of wind knocked over a pole and a line full of wet garments ended up in the dirt. If it rained, the washed laundry would wait in the copper tubs—and sometimes in the bathtub—for the next sunny day.

Even the efficient Yemenite pair could not handle all that laundry by themselves and other women in the household pitched in. Roh'keh often stood over the boiling cauldron removing steaming linen. (I was reminded of this sight when I first encountered the "Bubble, bubble" scene in Macbeth.) Mother and sometimes Haya helped hang up the laundry, a tricky job as one had to reach up for the line without dragging the wet laundry already on it into the dust. Semi-dry sheets had to be stretched and pulled to make ironing them later easier. At the end of the day, if all went well, the laundry was brought in, folded, and put aside to be ironed the next morning. Once that task was accomplished by Roh'keh, all the linen was deposited into a cupboard with military precision: bottom sheets, top sheets, pillowcases, towels. Each set of linen was marked by three stars embroidered in different colors to assure even rotation.

Mondays were so chaotic that there was no time for elaborate cooking so the midday meal consisted of noodles with grated cheese followed by a chocolate pudding. I loved Mondays.

Saturdays

My grandparents were Orthodox Jews. They kept a kosher home, they did not travel on the Sabbath, they said the daily prayers and all the appropriate blessings, and they gave money to charity. But they were not fanatic. Their children were not observant but when in their parents' home, they followed the rules. The Sabbath and the holidays were important to the whole family, and my mother's siblings, even after they left home, tried to come back and celebrate with their parents.

The Sabbath is the pinnacle of the week around which lesser days revolve. At our house preparations began on Wednesday and continued through Friday morning: The furniture was dusted, the floors were washed, the silverware polished. Food was purchased and prepared in advance, because cooking is work and is therefore forbidden on Saturday, the day of rest. Different kinds of cakes and pastries that were not available at the bakery were baked at home, including one of Esther's specialties: yeasty rolls filled with walnuts, cinnamon, and sugar and baked on Thursday, filling the house with a pre-Sabbath aroma. On Friday, a cold lunch was served after which the table was covered with a starched white tablecloth and napkins to match, and then set with the special china and glassware used only on Shabbat. Grandmother's silver candlesticks and the Kiddush cup stood at attention, as if anticipating the coming ceremony. Then a hush settled over the house as Roh'keh left early for her own home and most of the adults napped. (Roh'keh, who must have been in her late forties when I first remember her, was an *aguna*, a woman whose husband either abandoned her or disappeared for other reasons. Unless there were two witnesses to the man's death, his wife could not remarry. Roh'keh

My grandmother Sarah Berman's candlesticks, now in my home

lived not far from us with her son, who was a butcher, and his family.)

I was warned to play quietly and not to get dirty—the weekly bath was given on Thursday at bedtime. Before dusk we all got dressed up and Grandfather departed for the synagogue that abutted the bakery. Sometimes Baba Esther went to pray at the women's section that consisted of a small room with a tiny window into the main sanctuary. Since Grandfather and Esther, his mother-in-law, hardly spoke to one another, she would make a point of leaving separately, using the back door, but because she could barely see, one of us—usually me—had to walk her to the synagogue and back. After services we all gathered around the table and the usual Friday night ritual began. Grandmother said the blessings over the candles, Grandfather over the bread and wine. Predictably, the menu consisted of chicken soup—a very good soup—accompanied by Roh'keh's crispy *mandalach*, the tiny bits of fried dough. Next came gefilte fish, that is slices of carp stuffed with additional ground carp, not the type of balls made by Mrs. Manischewitz. Braised chicken usually followed, with a well-seasoned rice or couscous dish, and overcooked vegetables. For dessert we had fresh fruit or compote since one could not have anything made with butter or cream after eating meat or chicken. I often argued with Grandfather: "The law which prohibits mixing milk and meat comes from the biblical injunction against cooking a kid in its mother's milk. Right? It was a law meant to prevent cruelty to animals. Right? But chickens don't produce milk, so why does the law apply to them as well?" Grandfather would patiently explain that wiser heads than mine made the rules and it was not my place to question them. But he was amused, rather than annoyed, by my constant probing, and often suggested that I become a lawyer.

The meal over, *Birkat Hamazon,* a blessing after the meal, was hastily said, since my mother's generation was practically out the door before the end of the thanksgiving prayer. We did not sing *zmirot,* hymns chanted at the home especially on the Sabbath, as some of our neighbors did; I do not know if it was because of Grandfather's Mitnagdim —opposers of Hasidim—origins or because of my uncles' desire to get away. A temporary truce was declared between Grandfather and Baba Esther on the Sabbath and since she ate in her bedroom—claiming that, because she could not see, she tended to drop her food and did not want to mess up her daughter's table—he would bring her a glass of schnapps after dinner accompanied by a piece of *lekakh*, a sponge cake, which she liked to dip into the drink. It was her only known vice although it was rumored that in her youth she used to smoke a *nargile*—or *hooka*—a waterpipe.

On Saturday mornings my mother and I often went for a walk in the Old City, a mile or so away from our house. We would amble past Mea She'arim where men garbed in their Sabbath best were rushing to prayer, and continue down the Street of the Prophets to Damascus Gate, the most ornate gate to the Old City, built by Sultan Suleiman the Magnificent in the 1530s. The noises and smells of the *suq*, the market, assailed us as we made our way to the Three Covered Bazaars, built by the Crusaders, through lamb carcasses and sheep hindquarters dangling on hooks in Suq el-Lahhamin, the Street of the Butchers, to the Spice Market, Suq el-Attarin, where the goods—displayed in burlap sacks or glass jars depending on their value—were a feast for the eye and the nose. Sometimes a merchant, a customer of the bakery, greeted my mother and the two would launch into a long chat in Arabic, which I did not understand. We would then wander through the narrow alleys of the Jewish Quarter, eerily empty as most men were at prayer, their voices soaring toward heaven. Occasionally we lingered by the Hurva Synagogue, where my great-grandfather Todres Berman used to worship, or gazed at the golden Dome of the Rock, where the Temple used to stand. Before going back home we usually went down the winding narrow steps to the Western Wall.

When we returned in late morning we had visitors. My uncle Zalman—Grandfather's son from his second marriage—would drop by with his wife Rodia and their sons, Avraham and Yoram. (Yoram told me not long ago that he could never communicate with Grandfather: Eliyahu was hard of hearing and one had to speak loudly and clearly for him to understand.) Various Berman cousins came to pay their respect to their uncle Eliyahu who became the head of the family once his brother Yehoshua died; other friends or relatives stopped by as well. A few people remained for the midday meal which was usually *cholent*—a stew consisting of meat, potatoes, and beans flavored with onion, garlic, and chicken fat, sometimes accompanied by *kishke*, stuffed derma. Following a Sephardi custom, Grandmother added eggs to the *cholent* which turned brown as the stew simmered on a low fire from late Friday afternoon till midday Saturday when it was served, accompanied by a great vegetable salad and a tahini sauce brimming with parsley and lemon. (There are hundreds of versions of *cholent*, some lighter than others. My husband first tasted the dish on his first visit to Israel in 1961 at the house of one of my mother's cousins, and he claims that it is still lying in his stomach.)

In the early afternoon, grownups either read the Friday supplements—no newspapers appeared on Saturday—or napped. For me, it was a good time to get into trouble. I often went on long walks with Zahava—then nicknamed Goldie—my best friend and next-door neighbor, and together we explored forbidden territories lying at the edge of the city. Among our favorite haunts were the tree groves in Tel Arza, rather pathetic clumps of pines that we thought of as dark forests. The area was strewn with climbable boulders where cyclamens grew in winter. Sanhedriya also intrigued us, an area named for the multilevel burial cave with many niches where, according to tradition, members of the Great Sanhedrin were buried. The supreme judicial body functioned in Jerusalem during the Roman period, from about 63 BC to AD 70 when the city was destroyed. Zahava and I would marvel at the carved gable, decorated with pomegranates and acanthus leaves, then scare each other half to death by pretending to hear weird noises coming through the iron grille which covered the entrance to the cave. Nearby was an ancient wine press cut into a cliff where we would try to imagine life in biblical times. We never told anyone where we had been since those places were a few of miles away from home, considered too far for two pre-teenagers to explore on their own.

Sometimes my second cousin Izzy showed up on Saturday afternoons. He enjoyed playing with me, although he was four years older, perhaps as a reaction to his having an older sister. We were always in search of adventures and the bakery offered irresistble opportunities. First we would tiptoe past the sleeping Muhammad, the Arab watchman who guarded the bakery from Friday afternoon till work resumed late on Saturday night. Then we went into the storage area where hundreds and hundreds of bags full of flour were stacked in piles of different heights.

The piles soon became palaces, turrets, fortresses, or whatever else our hearts desired. We flew across from one pile of bags to another—cowboys and Indians, Saracens and Crusaders, British policemen and Jewish underground heroes—raising white clouds and somehow managing not to break our necks. Then we would sneak into the back of one of the bakery's delivery vans, lined with shiny metal floors, and glide from one end to the other until Muhammad woke up and chased us away. Once we discovered that the door to the first floor of the confectionary was left open, the floor where the ovens were located, as were the shelves that held the baked goods—alas empty on Shabbat. A dumbwaiter was there as well, a manually operated device which traveled between the first and second floors during the week, to lower trays with unbaked cakes, pastries, and cookies to the ovens from the second floor where all the ingredients were stored: flour, butter, sugar and spices, syrups, fruit, jams, and chocolate. Izzy talked me into folding myself in half and squeezing onto the dumbwaiter, then he slowly pulled the ropes until the contraption landed on the second floor where I got up and unlocked the main door for him from the inside. For the next hour we stuffed ourselves with everything sweet, sticky, and gooey. Then Izzy walked out, and I re-locked the door, got back into the dumbwaiter and was brought down by Izzy. Our escapade would have been classified as a mysterious raid by persons unknown except that I began to throw up as soon as I got back home. My mother, who always spoiled me, considered this bout punishment enough. To this day I have little use for sweets.

Saturday afternoon teas were highly fashionable in my mother's coterie, fancy affairs that allowed the hostess to show what a fine household she ran. Tables groaned under the weight of homemade coffee cakes, chocolate cakes, cheese cakes, fruit tarts and strudels, tiny pastry shells stuffed with tuna salad, and *burekas,* triangles filled with spinach or cheese. Decorative platters were piled high with dainty sandwiches in various shapes covered with cucumber slices, cheese, sardines, anchovies, egg

King David Hotel, c. 1946
Courtesy of the Royal Signals Officer of the Defence Security Office
of British Military Headquarters, Palestine

salad. Crystal bowls overflowing with pistachios and other nuts stood on every remaining surface. The tea itself, served in fine china cups, was almost incidental. Those elaborate teas came to a halt during World War II when sugar and butter were rationed.

Sometimes we went to tea at the King David Hotel, me in my best dress and party shoes, my mother and aunts properly outfitted in hats and gloves. Built in 1930 in the tradition of grand hotels, the decor inside the hotel was, and still is, quite regal with tall pillars bearing Assyrian and Babylonian motifs, highly polished floors, and vaguely Oriental furniture. Tall Sudanese waiters, each in white pantaloons, red vest and tarbush, glided silently across the floor carrying heavy silver trays laden with tea pots, toast wrapped in linen napkins, jams, marmalades, milk, lemon, and different kinds of sugar. After tea the children were allowed to play in the garden, which overlooked the Old City, but I preferred to disappear into one of the hotel's long corridors and slide along the floors. My shoes got scuffed, my dress smeared, and I would promise my mother never to do it again, until next time. Another favorite Saturday afternoon destination was the American Colony Hotel, originally built around 1870 as the private residence of one of the Nashashibis—a notable Arab family. Domes, arches, ceramic-tiled walls, and an exotic inner garden with a pond and fruit trees made the place a favorite choice, even without the afternoon tea. In the summer we often went to Ramallah, first sneaking into my uncle Avraham's car that was parked far from my grandparents' house so that none of the neighbors would see us driving on Shabbat. Once in Ramallah we stopped at a café owned by an Arab acquaintance of the family where tea was served outdoors, on tables set among tall pines. In 1967 my cousin Roni—born in 1948 during the siege of Jerusalem—was killed while unloading ammunition when the Six-Day War ended. I then went back to Israel to be with the family. A few days before returning to the States, I piled three of my aunts into a rented car and drove to Ramallah where we had not been for over twenty years. We somehow found our way to the café, where after some astonished looks and a brief conversation in Arabic, the owner and his wife threw their arms around my aunts and they all wept.

We did not turn the electricity on or off at home on Saturdays, following the command: "Thou shalt not light a fire in your houses on the Sabbath." Muhammad, the watchman, would stop by the house on Friday night and turn off the lights. (He often served as the *shabbes goy*—the non-Jew who can work on the Sabbath—for many of our neighbors.) But eventually some kind of a device was installed next to the electric meter, involving an alarm clock that turned the electricity off at eleven on Friday nights. My mother and her siblings did not observe Sabbath rules but none of them would have dreamt of breaking the law in front of my grandfather. Grandmother, however, had her own set of Halachic interpretations, and she also knew that, outside the house, her children did not observe all the commandments. So if for some reason she needed to see something after the lights were off, she would merely sigh: "It is so dark in here that I cannot find my medicine." One of us would then flip the switch.

The Sabbath, which begins on Friday at sunset, ends on Saturday evening when three stars can be discerned in the darkening skies. At that point the family would gather for the *Havdala* service, the separation between the holy Sabbath and the profane week. Grandfather would light the braided *Havdala* candle, shake the spice box, then we would all sing about Eliyahu Hanavi—the prophet Elijah—whose return will precede the coming of the Messiah.

Holidays

When I was growing up in west Jerusalem, nearly everyone around us observed the Jewish holidays. Schools, shops, restaurants, and offices closed, buses disappeared from the Jewish part of the city, and the streets emptied. Few people owned private cars so there was little traffic to disturb the quiet atmosphere. Schools followed the rhythm of the year and lessons reflected upcoming holidays. It was a way of life that could not have been duplicated in any other country and which by now has mostly disappeared even in Israel, except for certain areas where Orthodox Jews are the majority. In the following pages I try to describe how the holidays were celebrated in my grandparents' home.

The new year begins in the fall, with Rosh Hashana. For a whole month before the holiday Jews reflect upon the past year, prepare for the new one, and ask God to inscribe them in the Book of Life. The twenty-seventh Psalm is added to the daily prayers: "The Lord is my light and my salvation ... Hide not Thy face from me ... Cast me not off, neither forsake me, O God ..." After the morning prayers the *shofar* is sounded to awaken the people, and beginning on the last Shabbat before the new year, *Slihot*, penitential prayers, are recited at night. In my family, Baba

Esther and Grandfather used to spend the two days of Rosh Hashana in synagogue. The rest of us usually showed up in time to hear the *shofar* blown during the morning services. The food prepared for the holiday was slightly fancier than what was regularly served on Shabbat: round *hallot*, signifying eternity, were added to the menu as were apples dipped in honey for a sweet year. We also ate fruit new to the season so we could say the *Sh'hehiyanu* blessing, thanking the Lord for allowing us to live to this time, *lazman hazeh*. On the afternoon of the first day of Rosh Hashana, it was—and still is—customary to walk over to a body of water, empty one's pockets or throw a few pieces of bread into the sea or river, to get rid of one's sins and start anew.

Yom Kippur, the Day of Atonement, comes at the end of the Ten Days of Awe—that begin with Rosh Hashana—during which one continues to beg God for forgiveness. Shortly before the holiday Grandfather himself used to go to market, as if to emphasize the gravity of the occasion, and buy several live chickens and a rooster. When he returned, we took turns sitting in the backyard and reciting a prayer while Grandfather swung one of the birds three times over each head: "This is my substitution, this is my compensation, this is my atonement. This chicken will go to its death and I will enter into a good, long, and peaceful life." Some people used coins instead of poultry, tying the money in a handkerchief and twirling it around, then donating it to charity—a less nerve-wracking process. I, for one, always worried about what might happen when the bird was over my head and did not concentrate on pious thoughts.

On the eve of Yom Kippur, an air of solemnity descended upon the house, the neighborhood, and the city. Grandfather would put on tennis shoes—one does not wear leather on Yom Kippur—and both he and Baba Esther dressed in white, the symbol of purity. At the dinner that preceded the fast everyone was urged to eat a lot and to drink plenty of water. After the meal Grandfather went to his synagogue, Esther to the women's section next to it, while many of us walked to Yeshurun, a modern synagogue at the edge of Rehavia. After listening to the hazan chant

Kol Nidrei three times, the younger generation would sneak out and go home. Grandfather and Esther spent most of the next day in synagogue, Grandmother in bed, while Mother and Haya lounged around reading mystery stories. My uncles were nowhere to be seen. At the end of the day we would sit outside the front door awaiting the long piercing blast of the *shofar* to emanate from the synagogue next door. It marked the end of *Ne'ila*, the closing service. The Day of Atonement was over, the gates of heavens shut.

Then pandemonium descended upon the kitchen as fires were lit, water boiled, tea and coffee brewed, and trays of pastry passed around along with small glasses of schnapps. Avraham—who always claimed to have a headache—would show up with David who fussed the most about how hungry he was. Everyone but my grandparents knew those two did not fast, yet they were the first to be served and it made Mother, Haya, and Zahava furious. Real food was then reheated and, at the end of the meal, Grandfather would stand up, call me to go outside with him and hold a box of nails while he hammered in the first post for the Sukka, the booth used during Sukkot, the Feast of the Tabernacles, which begins two weeks after Rosh Hashana and lasts for seven days. The holiday celebrates the end of the harvest and commemorates the time when the Israelites dwelt in booths or huts during the Exodus. Sukkot is one of the three pilgrimage holidays, along with Passover and Shavuot, when the Israelites used to go up to the Temple in Jerusalem.

On the eve of Sukkot I often went with Grandfather to purchase the Four Species: the *etrog*—citron, the *lulav*—a palm branch, and myrtle and willow branches. The *etrog*—which looked like a large lemon and had to be without blemish—was kept in a lidded, glass-lined silver container. Every morning during the holiday Grandfather held up the *etrog* then waved around the *lulav* and the other branches while saying blessings "to rejoice before the Lord."

All year long I looked forward to decorating the Sukka, but I had to wait till the workmen, supervised by Grandfather, put up the wooden frame and Grandmother brought out from storage the beautiful fabrics which made up the Sukka's inner walls. Then, fancying myself as the creator of fantasies in paper, I produced cutouts, chains, and other rather pedestrian wall decorations. (Few ready-made ornaments were available for purchase at that time, so my works of art had little competition.) The roof of the Sukka consisted of wooden slats covered with greenery from which we hung pomegranates, grapes, and other seasonal fruit and vegetables to symbolize the harvest. We ate every meal in the Sukka, for a whole week. Gusts of wind or a rare rain shower only added to the excitement of eating outside. In households more Orthodox than ours, most men slept in the Sukka as well.

Simhat Torah comes at the end of Sukkot, marking the completion of the annual cycle of Torah reading. It is a joyous occasion, when members of the congregation dance in a procession holding Torah scrolls. It was one of the few times during the year when all children—even girls— were allowed into the men's section at Grandfather's synagogue and we marched around carrying flags with apples impaled at the tips of the poles. Burning candles were stuck into the apples and it was a marvel that nothing caught on fire.

Hanukka arrives two months after Sukkot, celebrating the victory of the Maccabees—or Hasmonaeans—over the Hellenistic Syrians in 165 BC. Established after the biblical period, Hanukka is not considered a major holiday in Israel and everyday life continues with schools, shops, and businesses operating as usual. Of course, we lit candles every night for a whole week to remind us of the small jug of pure oil found in the desecrated Temple that miraculously lasted for eight days. Our silver Hanukkiya was originally an oil lamp, with eight receptacles plus one for the *shamash*, the service light, decorated with a traditional motif of two lions upholding the Tablets of the Law. (I often regretted the switch from oil and wicks to the more practical candles.) We ate *sufganiyot* rather than potato latkes, a cloud-like version of the donut that our housekeeper

Hanukka at my nursery school where I am showing the teacher, Rebecca, a sufganiya, *the traditional holiday fare that resembles a donut*

Roh'keh deep-fried and served hot, sprinkled with powdered sugar. (There is no good explanation for the tradition of eating either food except for the use of oil.) We also played with dreidels, *svivonim*, and chanted Maoz Tzur and other songs with nationalistic undertones about the plights and victories of the few against many, both in the olden days and today, *bayamim hahem, bazman hazeh*. Children went around during the holiday collecting money, Hanukka *gelt*, from relatives far and near. The origins of this custom are also unclear but it predates the contemporary practice of giving children presents every night to outdo Christmas. I used to get money from everyone at home then go over to the bakery, a trip that resulted in additional gifts from my mother's cousins, some of whom were very generous, others less so.

At Christmas time, the tower of the YMCA was decorated with strings of lights. How nice for the Christian children, I thought, that they too had a holiday to celebrate during Hanukka! On Christmas Eve my uncle

Moshe, who worked for the British Administration's communication—or postal—services, used to go down to Bethlehem to supervise the broadcast of the ringing of the bells at the Church of the Nativity, and we all hoped for Moshe's sake that the sound would be heard around the world. Once, during World War II, my mother took me to Bethlehem on Christmas Eve in the company of some British servicemen. I was told not to say a word under any circumstances, which left me puzzled. I did not understand that a Hebrew-speaking child would not have been welcomed at the manger. The whole experience was frightening, the smell of incense, the unfamiliar chanting, the smoking candles in the dim nave, and worst of all, the crush of bodies, tall, suffocating adult bodies that blocked my view and sucked away the air. To this day, I try to avoid crowds.

I have a vague memory of a visit to another church at Christmas time, the Cathedral of St. Trinity in the Russian Compound in Jerusalem. My father took me there before he joined the British Army, so it must have been in December 1938, the last Christmas before World War II broke out in Europe. He had a number of Russian patients and knew several priests, one of whom greeted us, splendidly gowned if I remember correctly in green and gold. The priest allowed us to wander around the church and gaze at the Byzantine icons while he chanted and waved incense. Later we went to call on a Russian woman who lived nearby, a dental nurse who had worked for my father's father, Eliezer Brown. She had come to Jerusalem on pilgrimage in 1914 and got stranded there, first by World War I then by the Russian Revolution. We entered her small room in the former women's pilgrim hospice in the Russian Compound, and I was introduced to a good-looking woman in her late forties who, according to rumors I picked up decades later, was suspected of being Eliezer Brown's mistress. A Christmas tree stood in the room, sparsely decorated. She took a small bag off it, a bag made of golden threads and filled with chocolate—and gave it to me. I had never seen a Christmas tree before.

Weekdays and Holidays

Tu B'Shvat, the fifteenth of the month of Shvat is a minor holiday, the "New Year for Trees," observed in Israel by the planting of saplings. The country was practically deforested during the Ottoman period, when taxes were imposed on fruit trees and when timber was used as fuel. The holiday usually falls in February, and if the winter is mild, almond trees bloom across the land, pinkish-white puffs dotting the hills. Purim follows, the Feast of Lots. Purim means "lots" in Hebrew, and it refers to the lottery Haman used to select the date for killing the Jews but failed because of the courage of Queen Esther and her uncle Mordechai. The Scroll of Esther is read at synagogues on the eve of the festival, and whenever Haman or his ten sons are mentioned, the congregation is supposed to drown out the sound of their names by stamping feet, yelling, and spinning gragers, noise makers. Youngsters love it: imagine being told to be noisy during services! On the next day families deliver gifts of food—cakes, candy, fruit—to friends and neighbors, a duty I did not enjoy since Grandmother felt obliged to share her good fortune with as many people as possible, and I had to cover a lot of ground delivering the goods. I was also instructed, repeatedly: "First you knock on the door and wait till you are invited in. Then you enter and say Shalom." For security reasons, parties and parades were scaled down by the time I was growing up, but we still dressed up in costumes and put on plays at school and at home. One year I was a clown, another, a pussycat. I never wanted to be Queen Esther.

Then came Passover, my favorite holiday. It was a treat to take part in the well-orchestrated chaos that preceded it, to watch the house being turned inside out. Spring-cleaning began a week before the holiday, to make sure that no trace of *hametz*, of leaven, was lurking in some dark corner. The carpets were dragged outside, draped over a banister and beaten with the old tennis racket, then thoroughly brushed with damp tealeaves. Floors were scrubbed even more vigorously than usual. Windows were washed with ammonia then polished dry with newspapers; beds were stripped and all linen and pillows and blankets taken out to air; closets were emptied and every shelf wiped clean. Three days before the Seder, when the serious cooking was about to begin, Grandfather would carry a tall ladder to the courtyard and then climb into the attic above the kitchen and start lowering pots and pans, cooking utensils, and dishes, lots of dishes. There were two separate china services, for *mielkhik* and *fleyshik*, milk and meat. The dishes were all white, with small blue flowers on one set, while the other, the one used during the Seder, was decorated with fine blue and gold lines around the rim. Laws of *kashrut* do not apply to glassware so the glasses we used on Shabbat were washed and put aside for Seder. Two sets of silverware were brought out of the safe and polished. Families who did not own extra sets of everything placed their regular wares into baskets and lowered them into cisterns—found in the courtyard of every old house in Jerusalem—to soak and thus be cleansed for the holiday.

Cooking for Passover was complicated. There was always a crowd at Seder so a lot of food was required in addition to all the extra dishes that are part of the ceremony. A wonderful aroma enveloped the house while Roh'keh diced chicken fat and mixed it with chopped onions, then rendered it, pouring off the accumulating liquid. She meant to use the cracklings in her *kneidlach* but they smelled so good that they were usually eaten straight out of the pan by family members who rushed to the kitchen at the first whiff of the frying *gribines*. Preparations stretched over several days and the food had to be kept away from the *hametz* that was still around since daily meals continued to be served. The kitchen was scoured in stages—refrigerator, sinks, counters—while in one corner non-Passover food was kept until the last day.

On the night before Passover *Bdikat Hametz* was conducted: The ritual consists of discovering pieces of bread which were placed on strips of cloth and hidden beforehand, not too discreetly, so they could be found during the search. After supper the lights were turned off and we all followed Grandfather who was holding a lit candle and a feather with which

Weekdays and Holidays

to sweep up an occasional crumb. After collecting the bread, Grandfather tied it in a large piece of cloth and set it aside, with a wooden spoon. The next morning, after breakfast, the bread and any other *hametz* still in the house were burnt in the courtyard. The house stood purified, ready to embrace Passover.

It is customary not to eat *matzot* until the Seder begins, so lunch on the eve of the holiday consisted of boiled potatoes and a beet borscht, an easy meal to prepare. We ate at a table brought over from the pantry and placed in a corner of the dining room where the main table was already set for Seder, with extra chairs and place settings. The linen seemed whiter than usual, the silver brighter, the china prettier. Toward evening, a special Kiddush cup was filled for the Prophet Elijah and extra wine carafes were placed around the table to supply the obligatory Four Cups for each participant. Grandfather's armchair was piled with cushions so he could recline during the ceremony, as is prescribed, and the Seder plate was put in front of his place at the head of the table. The plate held foods meant to remind us of the Exodus, among them *harosset*, a mixture of fruit and nuts which is supposed to look like the mortar used by the Israelites to build the pyramids; bitter herbs to symbolize their hard life there; an egg, for spring or eternity; and a roasted lamb shank to commemorate the sacrifices at the Temple. Three *matzot* were set aside for the ceremony; half of the middle one to be used as the *afikoman* and hidden so children can find it and redeem it. (The *afikoman* denotes an old Greek celebration that took place after the end of the meal. Some say the custom keeps the children from going to sleep in anticipation of a reward. The Seder cannot be completed without the *afikoman*.)

The night of the Seder would finally arrive and I, in a new dress and shoes, got ready to ask the Four Questions. Children love repetition and there was something very comforting in hearing the story of the Exodus year after year. We always had guests for Seder, especially during the war when the campaign in North Africa intensified and many soldiers passed through the country. Most were not Jewish and coming to Seder was a new experience for them. By the time the Questions were asked and answered, the songs sung, the first part of the Haggada read, and the different parts of the ceremony explained to the guests, we were all hungry. When the food finally arrived, it resembled the usual fare eaten on Shabbat and other holidays except for the absence of *hallot* and the addition of *kneidlach* in the chicken soup, my favorite. After the meal, thanksgiving prayers were hastily recited and somehow, on an annual basis, we would persuade Grandfather that "this year" we would skip the second part of the Haggada. Then we drained the last of the Four Cups, sang our favorite Passover songs, and Seder was over.

There was one aspect of the holiday that continued to bother me throughout my childhood. While it was possible to cleanse the house of *hametz*, there was no way to do the same for the bakery. It was, of course, closed during the week of Passover but the machines, the ovens, and the flour and yeast supplies were still there. So every year the family symbolically "sold" the bakery to our Arab watchman for five pounds (or *lirots*). Muhammad was a farmer who lived near Abu Gosh and was said to be well to do, but he liked the extra income, so during the year he guarded the bakery every Saturday. He had worked for us for many years but despite assurances from Grandfather, I could not help wondering what would happen if he refused to sell the bakery back at the end of Passover. Muhammad often stopped by our house to talk to Grandmother. Several of his children had died in infancy and when he finally had a son who survived, he asked her to gather old clothes for the baby because he did not want to dress the child in anything new, fearing the evil eye. For many years, on the last night of Passover, as soon as three stars could be seen signifying that the holiday was over, Muhammad would show up at our house with a huge basket of fresh bread and pitas which had been brought up from his village. It was a welcome sight after a week of *matzot*. Muhammad always "sold" us back the bakery and remained a loyal employee until 1948 when it became too dangerous to come into the city.

During the week of Passover, someone would inevitably bring up the story of my arrival in this world. "Remember, Leah, how uncomfortable you were on the last day of Passover [in 1934] and how you went to the hospital the next day?" My poor mother spent a week in labor. When her brother Moshe called Shaare Zedek Hospital and heard that his sister finally gave birth to a daughter, he said: "Damn. Another girl. She too will have to go through labor."

Lag Baomer comes on the thirty-third day of the counting of the Omer—of the "sheaf"—which was brought to the Temple on the second day of Passover, symbolizing the first wheat harvest. It marks the day when, according to tradition, the plague that was killing Rabbi Akiva's students briefly stopped. Akiva, a humble man who became a great scholar, continued to teach the Torah in defiance of Roman edicts until, in 135, the Romans tortured him to death, tearing the flesh off his bones. His remains are said to lie in a mountain cave west of Tiberias. When Esther was growing up, hundreds of people used to leave the Jewish Quarter on that day, dressed in their fineries, and walk toward Rabbi Akiva's cave singing, clapping, and dancing. Once there they would light bonfires and continue to sing as the men whirled in a circle around the flames. Families feasted on delicacies they brought with them, while Arab vendors mingled with the crowds, selling candy and cold drinks. Everyone returned home at sunset.

A slight diversion: Baba Esther used to tell me about the biggest celebration in Tiberias which was—and still is—held at the tomb of Rabbi Meir Baal Haness, "the Miracle Maker," one of Rabbi Akiva's students who was reputed to perform miracles merely by calling: "God of Meir, answer me." Long before Jewish children learned to drop coins into the blue-and-white *pushkes* belonging to Keren Kayemet—the Jewish National Fund—households throughout the Diaspora featured the alms boxes of Rabbi Meir. This brilliant fund-raising technique was the brainchild of Haim Abulafia, the man who helped resettle Tiberias in 1740, and it benefited the city's Jews for many years.

Since the eighteenth century, a tomb on the shore of the lake just south of the city has been acclaimed as Meir's burial place. A complex of buildings now marks the site and thousands come there every year in the belief that a prayer said at the tomb could cure the sick, make barren women conceive, or heal troubled souls. In the nineteenth century, people used to gather by the city's main synagogue at midday on the fourteenth day of Iyar—in late spring—and carry the Torah scrolls to Rabbi Meir's tomb, about a mile-and-a-half away along the shore of the Sea of Galilee. Muslims and Christians often joined the parade; a few women and children were conveyed to the site by boat, the others over land, by donkeys. Laurence Oliphant—an English writer, former Member of Parliament, and a supporter of Zionism who settled in Haifa—came to Tiberias in 1884 to witness the festivities. He wrote about the participants, the Ashkenazim in the "long coat or gaberdine of Russia and Rumania," and the Sephardim, whom he preferred, in the "flowing robe of Asia." The women were "bedizened with ornaments, while their wigs were often a perfect garden of flowers." The wigs, made of black hair, never quite fit and he disliked the married women's "abominable practice" of shaving their heads. The celebrants, he wrote, waited till nightfall then lit two separate bonfires, one for the Sephardim and one for the Ashkenazim; the men danced around the blazing fires in circles while the women watched, nibbling sweets, gossiping, some puffing on *nargiles*, waterpipes.[33]

But back to the rest of the Jewish holidays. Shavuot, the Festival of Weeks, is celebrated when the counting of the Omer ends after forty-nine days. The holiday marks both God's giving the Torah to the Israelites at Sinai and the harvesting of the first fruits, *bikurim*, which the Israelites brought to the Temple. Our house was decorated with branches and flowers and, since my mother's birthday fell on Shavuot, it was always a special holiday in our family.

Tisha B'Av, the ninth day of Av, comes in mid summer. It is a day of fasting and mourning because both the First and the Second temples

Weekdays and Holidays

were destroyed on that day, the first by the Babylonians in 586 BC, the second by the Romans in AD 70. While Grandfather and Baba Esther fasted, the rest of us did not. Rosh Hashana follows Tisha B'Av some seven weeks later and a new cycle begins.

For lack of a better category, I am going to classify birthdays under "Holidays." Family and friends were invited to a lavish tea on the Saturday closest to my birthday, and a photographer was hired to commemorate the event. Black and white prints show my aunts and my mother's lady friends—no gentlemen were present except for an occasional uncle—and their various children, whether or not they were my age. All the ladies were elegantly dressed, most wearing hats. Presents were not elaborate, with a few exceptions. For one birthday Mother got me a small tent, a gay tent, with orange, green, and purple stripes in which I could actually

With family and friends at my seventh birthday party, 1941
My cousin Izzy, all in white, is first on the left; my best friend Zahava,
also in white, is in the middle of the front row. I am in the second row
with my mother, third and second from right.

stand. Some Australian soldiers were coming to supper and they pitched the tent for me and wrote "Villa Nizza" on it.

The gift I remember best came from Yaacov Klinger, son of Hinke, Baba Esther's youngest sister, who lived in Safed. As mentioned earlier, the families were very close and he was one of my mother's favorite cousins (actually a first-cousin-once-removed). Yaacov, who was a graduate of the London School of Economics, had brought me a unique gift from England, something unseen in Jerusalem at that time. It was a wooden dollhouse, complete with tiny furniture, and a carriage and horses in the stable. I used to spend hours rearranging the Victorian-style furniture, taking the family out for rides, brushing the wooden horses.

Yaacov worked for a while at the Berman Bakery. One September morning in 1937, on his way back to Jerusalem after visiting his parents in Safed, an Arab sniper shot at the bus he was riding and killed him. (His nephew, Shimshon Frankenthal, supplied me with the date. He recalls being yanked out of his first grade classroom when the tragedy happened.)

The Early Years

Elementary Education

In the fall of 1937 I began to attend a nursery school run by two sisters named Adelman: Hilda, who was huge, and Rebecca, who was tiny. I do not remember my classmates, but one photograph shows a group of us sitting around small tables and eating *sufganiyot*—donuts—during Hanukka. Other photos were taken at the school on April 15, 1939—my fifth birthday—with me surrounded by my mother, Haya, Avraham, and the pregnant Zahava. My father arrived late, just as we were leaving. He brought me two dolls, twins, he said, named Tzilli and Gilli.

Nineteen thirty-nine was a very eventful year. My grandfather's brother, Yehoshua Berman, died and I remember standing behind a group of men at prayer during *Shiva*—the week of mourning—all somberly dressed, my eyes level with their rear ends. In the spring a happier event took place at our house where, as mentioned, Moshe and Cecile got married. My memories from that occasion also include the backs of men in dark suits.

That summer Haya, Mother, and I went to Lebanon. I had never been out of the country so that was very exciting. On the long train ride from Jerusalem to Beirut we passed through the tunnel which had been cut

The American University of Beirut
Courtesy of the Library of Congress

into the white cliffs of Rosh Hanikra, at the edge of the Mediterranean, on the border between Palestine and Lebanon. In Beirut we stayed at the Saint Georges, a newly built fancy hotel by the sea. I was all dressed up one afternoon since we were going to visit distant relatives of Grandmother's—the family of the pharmacist Dr. Albert—when I ran outside to stand on the beach. A breaking wave got me all wet and my mother, who rarely reprimanded me, got rather angry and took me up to our room where she removed my shoes and sat me on the edge of the sink to rinse off my legs. Somehow I managed to fall off and badly bang my head, which is probably why the whole episode is still fresh in my mind.

During our stay we went to see the American University of Beirut where David, my youngest uncle, was studying and I faintly recall a beautifully landscaped campus that overlooked the Mediterranean and had its own beach. It was a place Grandfather loved. He became well acquainted with it on his frequent visits to Beirut to rescue David who, with his friend Sammy, regularly got into trouble. Once David was thrown out of school

My uncle David at graduation from the American University of Beirut, 1946
Photograph by V. Derounian

after he was caught in a nearby house of ill repute and it was Avraham and Zahava who drove to Beirut to deal with the situation, which was kept hidden from Grandfather. After much pleading, and perhaps because he was a champion tennis player, David was allowed back.

In late August, David, Haya, Mother, and I went from Beirut to Chtaura, a mountain resort not far from Baalbek. To me, coming from a parched Jerusalem, the place seemed like a setting out of a fairy tale, with tall cedars and a bubbling stream next to our hotel where swans were regally gliding. (David later told me that the region—famous for its wines—also produced a fine arak and people used to chill bottles of the anise-flavored beverage in streams kept cold even in summer by melting snows.) On August 29, just a few days after we got there, a telegram arrived from Grandfather: "Come home immediately." One did not question Grandfather so we hastily packed our bags—filling one with green walnuts from the old tree that shaded the balcony of our room—and were on the train the next morning. On the following day the Germans attacked Poland and World War II begun.

Although I have no recollection of his actual departure, my father left for Europe that fall and served as a physician with the British Army till the end of the war.

***

I do remember being taken by Mother to meet Mr. Pheeter—I am not sure if this is the correct spelling of his name—the principal of Gymnasia Sokolow, an elementary school near our house named for a well-known Zionist leader. I do not know what made my mother enroll me so late in the fall, after school had already started. I could hear children's voices as Mr. Pheeter, a diminutive man, questioned me, trying to decide if I was fit to enter first grade at age five-and-a half. I had to recite the alphabet and do some addition and subtraction and I must have passed the test since I was immediately taken to class, interrupting a lesson. The principal, with my mother hovering next to him, introduced me to the teacher, Rachel Fainsod, a large woman with a slight Russian accent and blond hair tied back in a bun. She took me in hand, told the other children that it was impolite to stare, and found me a seat. (Her daughter Shoshana—or Shoshi as she prefers to be called—is still one of my best friends.)

I liked school. After a few weeks I was allowed to walk there by myself, which gave me a great sense of independence even though Mother stood at the gate to our house and watched me till I reached the top of the hill—about a hundred yards away—where all I had to do was walk across a small field into the school. The day there began with all the students lined up in the courtyard, by class, and there we did calisthenics—although the term was not used then—for about ten minutes to

The Early Years

the tune of marching bands playing patriotic songs. The first grade was located in a large sunny room within the two-story building, originally a private house, and Mrs. Fainsod was a wonderful teacher. In second grade I was the teacher's pet: Mr. Levin was married to a close friend of my aunt Haya—a childless marriage—and he took me under his wing and encouraged me to write stories which he lovingly corrected. Things got tougher the next year, when after winning third place for a composition about the evils of chewing gum, I had to contend with the fact that there were at least two students in the class who were better than I was.

The school's proximity to our house was a mixed blessing. Since, at least in Mother's eyes, I was a poor eater, she showed up every day during recess with a half-pint of cream, or *shamenet*. She would stand outside the locked gate until she saw me playing in the yard or, if I tried to hide, she would get someone to find me. Then, through the grille work, she handed me the cream that I had to drink. Need I explain how embarrassed I was? The good thing about the school's location was that it stood next to the Berman family's apartment house where Avraham and Zahava were living with their daughter Daphne who was born a couple months before I entered first grade. Having no siblings, I was overjoyed by the new addition to the family and I often went to see her after school.

At some point Pnina Bruchstein Ralbag, one of Yehoshua Berman's granddaughters, began to give me piano lessons. She was about Mother's age, married but childless, and she was far too lenient with me. Both my parents were passionate about music, but that did not affect my lack of enthusiasm for practicing. The idea of ballet classes was also met with some reluctance, but at Mother's insistence, I continued to receive instruction in both art forms but became proficient in neither.

Books became an essential part of my life. Modern Hebrew literature was in its infancy in those days and most novels at home were translations of world classics—books that transformed me as they took me beyond the borders of my small universe. I explored the oceans with

In the Land of Israel

*With cousin Daphne on Grandfather Eliyahu's lap, 1941
Aunt Cecile and cousin Michal are in the back.*

Captain Nemo and sailed down the Mississippi with Huck Finn. I marched along with Pierre during the retreat from Moscow and cried with David Copperfield when his mother died. By the time I was eleven or twelve I had devoured practically every novel in my grandparents' house—some way above my head. Fortunately, about a block away stood the B'nai B'rith Library, a free lending library, a treasure trove where I stopped nearly every day on my way home from school. But there were problems, even in paradise: patrons were only allowed to check out one book at a time. Also, if a novel was printed in several volumes and a slow reader held the one following mine, I was left on tenterhooks for weeks, sometimes months. Imagine trying to get through *Anna Karenina* or the ten volume *Jean-Christophe* in the footsteps of a dawdler.

I loved reading beyond any other activity and during the summer I would go through a book a day. My uncle David could not believe how fast I read so he would often quiz me to see if I cheated, which I did not. He reminded me of this half a century later, shortly before he died.

I stayed at Gymnasia Sokolow through fifth grade, when my mother decided that the school was not demanding enough and transferred me to the Hebrew Gymnasium, Hagymnasia Haivrit, in Rehavia. The last episode I remember from the old school happened near the end of my final year there, when I was ten. On the way home I noticed a group of boys laughing at what looked to me like a small rubber tube caught in the school's fence. It was a condom, I was told, and when I continued to look puzzled, its purpose was crudely explained to me as were some other facts of life. Like many children in a more innocent age, I refused to believe that my parents had to do "that" in order for me to be born. When I told the other kids that I was going to ask my mother about it, they suggested that it is best to avoid discussing such topics with one's parents. But when I got home I took my mother aside, climbed onto her lap and demanded an explanation, which I was given along with the classic, if annoying, promise: "You'll understand it better when you grow up."

Childhood Ailments

One of the first things I recall is the operating room at Shaare Zedek Hospital where I was undergoing a tonsillectomy, performed by Dr. Moshe Wallach, the same man who brought me into the world four years earlier. I was clinging to my tiny black doll as I was being strapped to the operating table. "Is she made of chocolate?" asked the doctor, trying to put me at ease. "Can one eat her?" As he pretended to examine my doll he accidentally broke off her arm and that sent me into hysterics. Once I calmed down a nurse prepared the ether mask while the doctor challenged me to count to twenty. I was rather insulted by such an easy task and said I could do it backwards. Soon I was out and the next thing I saw, when I woke up in my hospital bed, was Mother carrying a huge bowl of ice cream, as she had promised to do before the surgery since ice cream was a real treat in the days before home freezers became common. I took one look at the bowl and started to throw up.

My tonsils were removed because every winter I came down with colds and bronchitis, but the operation did not solve the problem. I remained prone to ear infections and was often taken to see Dr. Salzburger, the man who, as mentioned before, promised: "This is not going to hurt," before he lanced an infected ear. My regular pediatrician was Dr. Helena Weizmann, sister-in-law of the man who would later become Israel's first president. We got along quite well until, when I was ten, I began to suffer from headaches. "Children don't get headaches," she declared. So at a very young age I came to the conclusion that doctors do not always know what they are talking about.

One night, when I was supposed to be asleep, I heard Grandmother saying that if *di kleyne*—that is me, the "little one"—continued to get sick all the time she would develop tuberculosis and will have to be sent to a sanitarium in Switzerland which would cost Grandfather much more than installing central heating in the house. Jerusalem winters are quite cold and our old house, with its thick stone walls, high ceilings, and tiled floors got very chilly. The only form of heat we had was a kerosene stove in the dining room that produced more smoke than heat. Grandmother usually got her way and soon everything was in an uproar. An ugly oil tank was installed in the front yard, a furnace in the basement. Floor tiles were removed in every room to make way for pipes and radiators. One morning, as Baba Esther was making her way to the bathroom, she stepped on a metal sheet that was covering a large gap in the dining room floor and she slid straight into the basement. By some miracle she was only slightly bruised and soon we all enjoyed the blessed heat emanating from the radiators. But I continued to get sick every winter.

A few months before my eighth birthday, I developed whooping cough, the respiratory infection against which there was no vaccine at the time. Spasms of dry, convulsive coughs shook my body, followed by "whooping" intakes of air that never seemed to fill the lungs. At times those seizures went on for hours, keeping me and the rest of the family up nights. One day Grandmother walked into my room and found me climbing to the top of a closet, where I thought I would get more air. She was convinced that I had lost my mind. After six weeks, when I was no longer contagious, Dr. Weizmann suggested that I get away from Jerusalem's winter clime and go some place warm to recuperate. Tiberias was the obvious solution.

Mother rented a room from Sarah Ashkenazi Cohen, Baba Esther's niece, the daughter of Yoel Ashkenazi. (Residents of Tiberias often augmented their income by renting rooms in the winter to people coming to enjoy the mild climate and the hot springs.) We knew the family well since we normally went to Tiberias for a few days every year to visit Yoel, who lived a couple of houses up the street from Sarah. Two houses in the other direction lived Sarah's son, Mordechai, and I often played with his sons. We spent a perfect month in Tiberias. In the mornings Mother and I would go to soak in the hot springs, famous since Roman times for their curative powers. Mother would pay the extra charge for

The Lido Hotel on the Sea of Galilee
Courtesy of the Library of Congress

a private room, rather than share the huge public bath, and she would often get a massage as well. After lunch at Sarah's table, we would rest for a while than go down to the Lido Hotel for tea, served at the terrace café by the beach, and there we sat watching fishermen on the Sea of Galilee or tennis players on the hotel's courts. Sometimes we would go to supper at one of the many small restaurants on the boardwalk by the water, and eat a freshly caught St. Peter's fish—Tilapia Galilea—surrounded by a salad and French fries. On the way back we often stopped at the Schorr Cafe, located on the first floor of Mordechai Cohen's house where Mother would have a cup of coffee. Later, in bed, I could still hear the orchestra at the café playing *"Bésame, bésame mucho"* late into the jasmine-scented night. By the end of the month I had gained back some of the weight I lost when I was sick, and I stopped coughing.

The Early Years

Long before I had whooping cough, and although photographs show evidence to the contrary, my mother—as already mentioned—was convinced that I was not eating enough. Every day she would put me on top of a bureau and there I stayed till I consumed a spoonful of cod liver oil, followed by a Gogol-Mogol, a dreadful concoction made with warm milk, an egg, and honey to which Mother would add a pat of butter, for good measure. I got even by frequently throwing up on an oriental rug. Matters improved once I learned how to read and was allowed to have a book in front of me at the table, and, while so distracted, Mother fed me. My food was kept warm by placing the plate over a pot of hot water. This appalling practice continued for years until, when I was ten, Mother and I spent a summer vacation in Nahariya along with Avraham, Zahava, and their daughter Daphne. My five-year-old cousin sat at the hotel's dining room, using a knife and fork perfectly, while Mother was cutting up my food. I was so embarrassed that I immediately began to copy Daphne.

I cannot leave the subject of ailments without mentioning *feltchers*, or medical practitioners, similar perhaps to the "barefoot doctors" in China. By the time I was growing up there were a number of fine hospitals and clinics in Jerusalem as well as doctors who specialized in nearly every field of medicine. When someone in our family got sick, a European-trained physician was usually consulted, but when even a big name, a "professor," did not cure the patient, a *feltcher* was called in. One lived in our neighborhood and Baba Esther trusted him implicitly. His two preferred methods of treating patients were the application of leeches—which I once actually saw him use on Baba Esther—and the other was *bankes*, or cupping. For those who do not know what it means, let me describe the process. The *feltcher* heated a number of small, thick glasses over a candle, and applied them to the back of the patient. The warm glass would then suck up some flesh so that the back looked like a strange terrain covered with reddish bumps that resembled anthills. I can personally testify that the method—which supposedly cleared up congested chests—was not painful since even I was treated by the *feltcher*. And judging by Baba Esther, who lived to be ninety, the *feltcher* did no harm. A final note must include the Yiddish saying which refers to any futile rescue attempt: *es helft vi a toytn bankes*, it helps like "*bankes* would help a dead person."

Friends

My closest childhood friend was Zahava Frank, a descendent of a distinguished family. Her paternal grandfather was Jerusalem's chief Ashkenazi rabbi, while her mother's father, Yehoshua Stampfer, was one of the Orthodox Jews who left Jerusalem in 1878 to found Petach Tikva, the first modern agricultural settlement in the country. Zahava, her parents, and her three older siblings lived next door to us in a house originally built for one of my grandfather's sisters. Our houses shared a common wall and we soon discovered that there was one spot inside a niche where—if we pounded hard—we could hear each other. So, in the days when private telephones were still rare, we developed a code: three taps meant "come over." One return tap meant "yes," two, "I can't." We played together almost every afternoon and during the long summer vacations, usually at our house which had more nooks and crannies and no older siblings. We built nests with pillows and created caves out of blankets and pretended to go fishing in crates in the courtyard. When we were hungry we walked into the kitchen and dipped thick slices of fresh black bread in olive oil, sprinkled them with coarse salt, piled tomatoes, scallions, and olives on a plate and climbed up a pepper tree to have a picnic.

After my cousin Daphne turned four, we occasionally allowed her to join us. By then we had adopted a room on the roof of the house as our playing field. A rickety set of steps led from the second floor balcony to the tarred and whitewashed flat roof from where rainwater drained into the cistern in the courtyard. Grownups rarely ventured up the steps so it was a perfect setup. Originally intended to serve as a laundry room, the space was eventually used for storage and it contained many treasures: elegant trunks filled with old evening gowns, a gramophone, old magazines, a classic leather couch from my father's clinic, and other discarded pieces of furniture. When the three of us played, Zahava took on the role of father because she was not always there and in her absence we pretended that she was at work. Daphne was the child since she was the youngest, and I was mother because I was the oldest and the bossiest: Zahava was a year younger than I and—since I started school a year early—two classes behind me at school, and Daphne was five years younger, so that gave me great power. Most of the time we played peacefully, recreating domestic scenes, but there were exceptions. Once, we tried to blacken a doll's face with a smoking candle and the celluloid doll caught fire. Luckily, the room had a working faucet and we managed to douse the flames. One hot afternoon, we lifted the lids off the three large water tanks that stood on the roof, stripped down, and jumped into the water to cool off. The fact that, unbeknownst to them, everyone in the house would be drinking the water in which we bathed never occurred to us. (The flow of water to the city was often interrupted so most houses had storage tanks on their roofs. The tanks were a big improvement over the old cisterns. They were installed in 1935 after the British finished building a pipeline to Jerusalem which pumped water to the city from Rosh Haayin, some thirty-eight miles away.) Another time I persuaded the two girls to climb onto the roof of Zahava's house, which, unlike ours, still had the original, steep red-tiled roof. One wrong step could have resulted in death.

Zahava and I shared the love of books. Our one disagreement was over Charles Dickens, whom we—naturally—read in Hebrew. Her favorite was *Oliver Twist* while I preferred *David Copperfield*. In addition to reading, we also spent time during our preteen years sitting in the pepper tree in the front yard, overlooking the street. We used to pretend that two boys from the class above mine at Gymnasia Sokolow were searching for us. Both boys were named Hanoch and neither one was aware of our existence, not to mention our harmless fantasies.

Two other boys filled an important part in my growing years. One was my previously mentioned second cousin Isaac Berman, nicknamed Izzy, with whom I used to explore the bakery. He too lived in the Bermans' apartment house, next to my school, and I sometimes stopped by to see him and play doctor, dominoes, or some other games. Occasionally Izzy came over to our house to see—literally—what was cooking and, since ours was a large household, something usually was. *Ma zeh Doda? Ma zeh? Ochlim et zeh?* he would ask my grandmother as she lifted the lid off a simmering pot. "What is it, Auntie? What is it? Does one eat it?"

The other young man in my life was Shimshon Frankenthal, my second-cousin-once-removed who lived in Safed, at the house of his maternal grandparents, Eliyahu and Hinke Klinger. Starting with my mother's generation, visits were often exchanged between the Jerusalem and Safed Ashkenazi descendants, and Shimshon, who is a couple of years older than I am, was always gracious and allowed me to roam around with him when we visited Safed. His paternal grandparents lived in Jerusalem where he was frequently sent during school vacations, and, since he did not know any other children in the city, he would come over to play with me. Our house was surrounded by Orthodox neighborhoods so we frequently ran into boys our age, on their way to or from *heder*. The sight of Shimshon, whose head was uncovered, climbing trees with a seven-or eight-year-old female clad in shorts and a sleeveless shirt really upset those kids. They yelled *prutza* at me, "prostitute," and pelted us with cones from the ubiquitous cypress trees. We retaliated, of course, and were sometimes joined by Zahava and even by her older brother Yaacov, despite the fact that they were scions of a famous Orthodox family.

Pets, Pests, and Vermin

Like most normal children I wanted a dog but I could not have one on account of Fido, my mother's dog who had to be shot at the end of World

The Early Years

War I because he was sick and his howling kept awake Ronald Storrs, the city's military governor. But there was no shortage of animal life around the house. The backyard abutted a vacant lot, a haven for mice and other small creatures. Ants, bees, spiders, and grasshoppers were frequent indoor visitors as were ladybugs that were gently picked up and released. Family rules allowed one to catch butterflies only for a school project, but it was all right to trap and kill moths since they feasted on sweaters, especially, or so it seemed, on handmade ones.

Fish, as most people realize, are not very satisfactory pets. There was the obligatory goldfish in a glass bowl on top of the piano. Every few weeks the occupant would be found floating on top of the water, having died of loneliness, or perhaps by my piano playing. It would soon be replaced, and the cycle would begin all over again. Birds played a small part in my zoological education. One memorable event occurred when a baby crow fell out of its nest and Roh'keh, our housekeeper, took pity on it and tried to put it back on a branch. An angry crow swooped out of the tree and pecked at her head.

Another encounter with birds came at the beginning of World War II, when food shortages were anticipated, and my mother's cousin Arieh decided to utilize some empty storage space behind the bakery to raise chickens. We were soon well supplied with eggs and an occasional stringy hen, but the birds were a lot of trouble. They cracked their eggs and ate them, a problem which was solved by building a contraption that prevented them from reaching the eggs. (I never understood how they were persuaded to lay their eggs where Arieh wanted them to.) They also used to attack each other and any hen with the smallest blemish would be pecked to death by her peers. To stop this, special blinders—which looked like tin sunglasses—were attached to the beak of each individual hen. They could look down and find their food, but could not see straight and were thus unable to assault their fellow birds of a feather. Neighbors complained about the smell which indicated the presence of a hen house, but since the Hoisemans next door kept ducks on the roof of their bakery, and a virtual farm—with cows, goats, chickens, and even a small duck pond—was located a couple of blocks away in the other direction, the family felt justified in its chicken-raising endeavor.

Then there was the episode of the pigeons that my mother got me when I kept asking for a pet. The birds were kept in the yard in an old air cooler, which they did not like. They were not ideal pets since one could not cuddle them, and the only time they noticed you was when you fed them. Every afternoon they were let out to fly around and, knowing where their supper was, they soon returned—until the day they disappeared. We suspected that they were lured over by the Langers, next-door neighbors who had a proper dovecote with several dozen birds, but this was never said out loud, Mr. Langer being a policeman.

When I finally realized that the trauma caused by Fido's unhappy end would not go away, I began to campaign for a cat and would regularly adopt a stray kitten—an easy task since the city was full of homeless felines. I would find a box for the kitten to sleep in, pad it, set a milk bowl next to it and bask in happiness. The family was less enchanted with my periodic acquisitions, often scraggly, flea-bitten critters. Mysteriously but consistently, the kitten would disappear while I was at school. Perhaps it went back to its mother, I was told. I had my doubts but could not prove foul play.

When I was about eight or nine I still had a part-time *metapelet*, a sort of nanny, a young woman who came to take me for an outing every afternoon. (This used to embarrass me terribly since I considered myself much too old for a *metapelet* and dreaded being seen with her by one of my schoolmates.) Once, on one of our walks, I noticed a cute kitten, black, with a white face, chest, and paws, who responded with great delight to my caresses. My companion tried hard to separate us, knowing full well that the last thing my mother wanted was another kitten, but I persisted and brought it home. I called it Mitzi, which proved to be a bad choice since it matured into a magnificent tom.

The Early Years

From the very beginning, Mitzi managed to outsmart everyone: As soon as I left for school, he would vanish only to show up again upon my return, waiting on the fence by the front gate. "This cat thinks he is a dog," mumbled the family, who could not wait for him to go away permanently. Eventually, the family got used to Mitzi's presence and he began to share my chair at mealtimes, to the great horror of Keith, my British uncle by marriage, who would complain about "Asiatics" and barbarians as he glared at Mitzi from across the table. My mother was not too happy about the seating arrangement either, but once Keith began to object she took up Mitzi's side. After all, who did this newcomer to the family think he was? I found the presence of Mitzi at the table very convenient: I disliked eating meat, not for any humanitarian reasons but because it was usually tough and stringy. Mitzi and I came to an understanding, and when no one was watching, I would sneak most of the meat off the plate and under the table; people always marveled at how handsome and well-fed Mitzi looked. Being a normal tom, Mitzi did his fair share of fighting with other male cats. Sometimes he would be gone for a whole night and return all cut up. On such occasions I would tuck him into a basket and march off to see Dr. Eliyahu Ralbag, a veterinarian who had married Pnina Bruchstein, my long-suffering piano teacher.

After one incident it was grudgingly admitted by all that perhaps Mitzi was an unusual cat. He was supposed to sleep in the bathroom, on a cushion near the radiator where he lay in wait until the rest of the family retired and then he moved into my bed. One night I was awakened by an agitated Mitzi, jumping on and off my pillow, behaving very strangely. Sleepily, I pushed him away but he kept running back and forth to the bedroom door. When I got up to see what was bothering him he led me into the bathroom where my mother was lying in the tub with water still streaming down from the showerhead. She had slipped, hit her head, and fainted and who knows what might have happened if it were not for Mitzi. The story of how he saved Mother's life spread around the neighborhood, and even Roh'keh began to brag about his intelligence. She was especially pleased to note that one could leave food out anywhere in the house and the cat would not touch it unless it was specifically offered to him. Who ever heard of such a cat? I shall return to Mitzi later on.

World War II

The War in Palestine

I was five-and-a-half years old when World War II began. At that point events in first grade seemed much more important than battles in faraway places, even though my father was somewhere on the front. I knew about Hitler and the Nazis because German Jews had been arriving in Palestine since the early 1930s and their plight was a frequent topic of conversation at the dinner table. Later, when I began to read the newspaper to Baba Esther, her criticism of the Germans, the Arabs, and the British—in that order—rapidly broadened my knowledge of current events and defined my political horizons. Grandfather subscribed to two daily papers, *Haboker*, "The Morning," which was published by the right wing of the General Zionists party, and *Hatzofeh*, "The Sentinel" or "Seer," issued by the Mizrahi, the national religious party.

When the war broke out, the Jews of Palestine declared their support of Britain. "We will fight the White Paper as if there is no war, and fight the war as if there is no White Paper," said David Ben-Gurion. (The 1939 White Paper basically repudiated the promise of a Jewish national home in Palestine and restricted immigration to seventy-five thousand over the next five years.) So while Britain and the Yishuv—the Jewish community—were united in their desire to see Germany defeated, a lot of tension existed between the two sides mainly because of Britain's immigration policy.

By the summer of 1940 it became clear even to me that a major war was going on. After France surrendered to the Germans, Syria and Lebanon came under forces loyal to the Vichy government and the front got closer to Palestine. Italy joined the conflict on the side of the Axis and its troops soon entered Egypt. Italian planes bombed Haifa in July, where they hit the oil refinery, and Tel Aviv in September, killing more than a hundred people. The government then ordered a blackout throughout the country and pedestrians were advised to wear white at night so drivers could see them. The volunteers of Mishmar Haam, the "People's Guard," patrolled the streets and made sure no lights shone through windows to guide enemy planes. In June of 1941 the two cities were bombed again. Twelve people were killed in Tel Aviv and many more wounded so, fearing further attacks, some residents left for Jerusalem since it was assumed that the Holy City would not be attacked.

At the same time the number of Allied forces stationed in Palestine increased and a Service Club opened in Jerusalem on Ben-Yehuda Street, staffed by Jewish volunteers. Mother, my aunts, and many of their friends spent a couple of afternoons there each week, serving tea, chatting with soldiers, often inviting some homesick soul to have dinner with the family. Australians and New Zealanders, with their big hats and funny accents, were very popular. When a major snowstorm blanketed Jerusalem in January of 1942, some Australians who had never seen snow before frolicked like children. A number of them hired a taxi, packed the trunk full of snow, and talked the driver into taking them to Tel Aviv so that their mates there could enjoy the snow as well.

By 1942 the Allies had lost control over most of Western Europe. The campaign in North Africa was also going badly. In June, under the command of Erwin Rommel, the Germans were advancing toward Alexandria and the Suez Canal, about to block that vital line of supply

World War II

Snow storm, with (seated) Daphne, Nitza, Avraham, Leah, and (standing) Haya, serviceman, and Zahava, 1942

⁂

and gain access to Middle Eastern oil. The British began to evacuate dependents from Egypt and many arrived in Palestine by train, bringing home the reality of war. Huge cones of concrete, known as "Rommel's teeth," were placed along roads south of Jerusalem, intended to block German tanks in case of an invasion. We closely followed the battles of El Alamein and, in the fall, rejoiced at Lieutenant-General Bernard Montgomery's victory over Rommel.

⁂

When the Yishuv decided to support Britain's war efforts, the Hagana—the Yishuv's "official" underground—followed that policy. But at the same time, disillusioned by the 1939 White Paper, the Hagana continued clandestine training. It also increased its efforts to bring ashore boatloads of illegal immigrants, called *maapilim* in Hebrew, "daring people." The Mandatory authorities, which had tacitly recognized the organization during the Arab Revolt, began to question the Hagana's loyalty and, soon after the beginning of World War II, arrested forty-three of its members, including Moshe Dayan. The prisoners were released in 1941 when the British authorities and the Hagana began to cooperate again as the Allies' situation worsened and an Axis invasion of Palestine seemed possible. The organization was consulted about likely targets in Vichy Syria and its members soon worked with British forces, gathering information and sabotaging roads and bridges. But after Rommel's defeat, when Palestine was no longer in immediate danger, the British army confiscated arms it had given the Hagana and when the latter retaliated, the organization was declared illegal again.

Other issues divided the two sides. One was the fact that while many Jews volunteered to serve in the British army at the very beginning of the war, they were not assigned to combat positions because of pressure from the Colonial Office which worried about Arab reaction to Jews gaining military experience. So it was not until 1942 that the Jewish volunteers from Palestine were allowed to join all-Jewish battalions and participate in actual fighting. (The Jewish Brigade was not formed until 1944.) But the main problems were Britain's limit on the number of refugees allowed to enter the country and the growing sense that the Allies, while opposed to the Nazis' plan to exterminate the Jews, were not doing anything about it. In 1943, for example, there was a suggestion that seventy thousand Romanian Jews could be ransomed for cash, but the British objected to it. The same thing happened with a Nazi proposal to exchange Jews for trucks. And there is the fact that the Allies never bombed any of the train tracks to Auschwitz or other death camps.

Rumors of events in Europe began in the summer of 1942, but neither the Yishuv nor Jewish organizations abroad made direct contact with the Jews of Europe. The governing bodies of the Yishuv organized mourning periods, strikes, and protests throughout the war, but it was only in April 1943, under public pressure in Britain and the United States that those two countries agreed to hold a conference in Bermuda and see if safe havens could be found for Jews who managed to escape to neutral

Jewish Brigade Recruitment, c. 1945
Courtesy of the Matson Collection, Library of Congress

countries. However, since neither the Foreign Office nor the State Department were anxious to see countries flooded with "alien refugees," the different proposals made at the conference achieved little. Eventually President Roosevelt established the War Refugee Board that helped rescue some 200,000 Jews. The British cooperated with the Yishuv on one occasion and trained Jewish volunteers, thirty-two of whom were parachuted into Nazi-occupied countries in the last two years of the war. Some did not survive but others reached partisan groups and ghettoes and helped organize local resistance; they also provided intelligence to the British. The person in this group who became most famous was Hannah Szenes who joined the partisans in Yugoslavia but was later captured in Hungary, tortured, and put to death.

The thing that I remember most clearly from the war, because it happened so close to home, was the fate of some of the European Jews who attempted to enter the country illegally, refugees who somehow escaped the Nazis and tried to reach Palestine on boats that were barely seaworthy. Unless caught, they would disembark onto remote beaches where they were met and smuggled into the country by members of the Hagana, or sometimes the Irgun—or Etzel—the more militant underground organization. But the British patrolled the seas and they captured most of the illegal boats and deported their pathetic human cargo to camps elsewhere in the Commonwealth where the refugees remained interned for the duration of the war. There were dramas on the high seas, and many tragedies. The *Patria*, anchored in Haifa's harbor in November 1940, held some 1,900 refugees whom the British intended to send to the island of Mauritius, off the African coast. The Hagana tried to sabotage the plan by blowing a small hole in the vessel, hoping to force the evacuation of the passengers. But the boat sank so rapidly that 267 refugees drowned as well as a dozen British policemen. The rest of the refugees were allowed to remain in Palestine, but a month later the authorities deported to Mauritius 1,645 immigrants who had arrived on the boat *Atlantic*. On December 4, 1940, *Salvador*, a ship with 326 illegal immigrants from Bulgaria left for Palestine. After a stay of about one week in Istanbul, the ship continued, but on December 14, it sank close to the Turkish town of Silviri with the loss of life of 213 passengers including 66 children.

The greatest disaster in the history of the illegal immigration was the sinking of the *Struma* on February 24, 1942. Crossing the Black Sea on its way from Romania to Palestine, the boat developed engine trouble and pulled into Istanbul's harbor. The Turkish government refused to let the passengers disembark, correctly assuming that the British would not allow them into Palestine. The boat remained in the harbor for seventy days, unbearably crowded, its passengers suffering hunger and disease. Finally, without allowing repairs to the engine, the Turks towed the boat out to the Black Sea where it was left adrift. When it was five miles away from shore, an explosion was heard and the *Struma* sunk along with nearly eight hundred people, among them some hundred children; there was one survivor. In 1978 the Soviet navy admitted that one of its submarines had torpedoed the boat, perhaps mistaking it for an enemy boat.

Within the Yishuv, relations worsened among the underground organizations—the Hagana, Irgun, and the most radical one, Lehi, or the Stern Gang—especially in 1944, after Menahem Begin became the leader of the Irgun. The organization then increased its attacks against British facilities, including police stations and government offices. The most damaging act was committed by two members of Lehi who murdered Lord Moyne in Egypt, the British Minister of State for Foreign Affairs, on November 6, 1944. This aroused great anger in Britain and shocked Winston Churchill. It is said that it changed his positive attitude towards the Jews in Palestine, even though the Zionist leaders strongly condemned the action. Pressure from the British Government on the Yishuv institutions eventually made the Hagana cooperate with the British police and hand over the names and whereabouts of Irgun and Lehi members, many of whom were arrested and a number exiled to Eritrea. This widened the split within the Yishuv, a split that never really healed.

My three Berman uncles, Moshe, Avraham, and David, were members of the Hagana at different points. David told me that during the Arab Revolt, in 1936, he met a Hagana officer who used to play tennis in the court behind the Bermans' apartment house—on what is now Straus Street—and he allowed David to join the Notrim, meaning "Guardsmen," who were an auxiliary of the Palestine Police, especially active in Jewish settlements. David, who was only fifteen, needed to get an identity card so he went to a nearby photo studio where the owner, Mr. Kovach, darkened his mustache and bundled him into a heavy army coat to make him look older in the photograph. The Notrim used to meet and train on Saturday mornings at the Alliance School on Jaffa Road where they would sign out guns under the command of Jacob Pat. But despite its support of the Hagana, the Berman family's unspoken sympathy was often with the Irgun and the measures it took both against the Arabs and the British.

As mentioned before, at some point during the war Mother and I moved downstairs while a number of Romanian refugees settled into the apartment upstairs. Other changes brought on by the war were food shortages, rationing, blackouts, and more men in uniform on the streets. But in many ways daily life continued as usual. In the midst of what seemed like a fairly normal routine to a young child, I had a very vague idea of what was happening in Europe. I knew of the Nazis and their hatred of Jews, of concentration camps, but the enormity of what actually happened in the camps did not become clear until after the war, neither to me nor to most other people. The scope of the tragedy and the cruelty and efficiency of the Germans—and of all the others who cooperated with them—were hard to believe, impossible to comprehend.

As children, we used the Hebrew word *Golah*, "Exile," rather than Diaspora, and deep inside our hearts we viewed *Golah* Jews with a slight disdain. With the arrogance of youth we failed to appreciate their enormous contributions or to recognize that for nearly two millennia they were the guardians of the faith that enabled Jews to survive as one people. When rumors about the Holocaust began and before we could grasp its evil or its magnitude, my eight-year-old peers and I thought that if all Jews had only chosen to return to Palestine—a simple matter in our eyes—the tragedy need not have happened. After the war, many of us wondered why Jews in the camps did not rebel and fight, completely failing to understand the constraints under which they lived, nor did we know much about the uprisings in the Warsaw Ghetto and in other places. Dr. Arieh Bauminger, a history teacher at the Hebrew Gymnasium and himself a Holocaust survivor, wrote about what was supposedly the attitude of teenagers toward the Shoah, the "calamity." They did not talk about it. On the contrary, in a way they were even ashamed of what happened to their brethren in the European Diaspora, and could not understand how millions went like "sheep to slaughter." (His piece appeared in *Sefer Hayovel*, the "Jubilee Book" published in 1962 to marked the fiftieth anniversary of the Gymnasia.) Dr. Bauminger taught a course about the Holocaust and found that his students' attitudes changed once they learned more about the evil and powerful forces that planned to exterminate the Jewish people.

Births and Weddings in the Berman Family

During the war Moshe and Cecile had two daughters, Michal and Liora, born in 1941 and 1943 respectively. It was very exciting to have more cousins, although I did not see them as often as I saw Daphne because they lived in Talpiot, on the southeastern edge of Jerusalem, a fair distance from our house. In 1945 Avraham and Zahava had a son, Adi, Sarah's first grandson. Both he and I had Sarah's coloring—brown eyes and curly brown hair—and being an only child, I was delighted when people thought he was my brother.

In 1939, when the war began, my aunt Haya was twenty-three years old and unmarried, which worried her mother. Haya—petite and lively—was good at tennis and dancing and did not lack for suitors. In a way it was a good time to be a young woman in Palestine, what with all the servicemen passing through on their way to or from battle. But the majority of the men Haya met were British—and most were not Jewish—which brought additional worries to her mother. Sarah was willing to close her eyes to a romance or two, but in the end, since it was marriage that counted, she was not happy about Haya's non-Jewish suitors. Eliyahu, Haya's father, was not that well informed about his daughter's adventures. At one point Haya hurt her back in a motorcycle accident and was ordered to remain flat in bed for several weeks. She was smuggled up to my parents' apartment, on the second floor, which Eliyahu rarely visited, and he was told that Haya was out of town, staying with friends. (I often suspected that Eliyahu knew exactly what was going on, despite the "Don't upset Grandpa" policy.) As the war—and Haya—grew older, Sarah saw to it that various more suitable candidates were introduced to her, children of respectable local parents, known to my grandparents or to their friends. Haya was less than enthusiastic but went through the motions to avoid battles with her parents. I still recall one gentleman from Petach Tikva who came to spend the weekend at our house so he could be inspected by both Haya and the family. He seemed to me like a nice enough fellow but before Haya had a chance to express her opinion, my mother, who never hesitated to express hers, announced that he did not bring a toothbrush with him so how could anyone even consider such a person? That was the end of that.

Then, near the end of the war, Haya met Keith Beecher, a Royal Air Force navigator who was recuperating in a hospital in Jerusalem after his plane crashed into a mountain in Jordan. Keith was born in London in 1914, to Jewish parents—he a tailor from Poland, she an English woman who deserted the family while Keith was still a young child. When Haya met him, he had dark-reddish hair, an impressive mustache of the same shade, and a great sense of humor. "I'll never be bored with him around," said Haya. Very properly, Keith came to our house to ask Eliyahu for his daughter's hand in marriage. He brought Haya a present, a beautiful leather handbag, which even my mother could not fault. The wedding took place in my grandparents' backyard and our neighbor Nahum Frank, father of my childhood friend Zahava, officiated. It was an elegant affair with lots of food and flowers and a tiered wedding cake with sugar figurines on top—a bride and a groom of course—a novelty in Jerusalem. Keith's mates, in their blue RAF uniforms, mingled with Bermans, Ashkenazis, and family friends. Keith and Haya lived in my grandparents' house for several months before renting an apartment in Baq'aa, on the way to Talpiot, not far from the old train station.

My uncle David's love life was much stormier than Haya's yet nobody seemed to mind—after all he was a man. But there was one exception, when he was having an affair with a married woman. This was never discussed in front of me, but Jerusalem was a small place and one day I happened to pass through a back alley behind Café Alaska, and there I saw David having coffee with a woman I did not recognize. Something made me suspicious of what seemed like a tryst and I decided not to mention it to the family. Then, at one of the charity bazaars in which my mother was involved, I saw the lady again, wearing a dress in three pastel colors: blue, yellow, and pink. So I asked: "Who is this woman in 'a spoil of dyed garments'?" (This is how the damsels of Sisera's worried mother described the loot he was going to bring home, while in fact he had already been slain by Yael. See Judges 5:30.) My mother and aunts burst out laughing and from then on David's friend was known in the family as *shlal tz'vaim*, the biblical phrase in Hebrew. Years later I found out that David became despondent when the lady broke up their affair. Sarah found him sitting on his bed with a pistol in his hand. In order to cheer him up she gave him the gold pendant watch she wore when she came from Beirut to Jerusalem and promised him a larger share of the percentages my grandfather owned in the bakery.

Lily Kolczycki

Sarah's ministrations worked. David soon brought home Lily Kolczycki, a beautiful young woman, to meet the family. They were married in Tel Aviv, on the roof of Lily's parents' house, on December 25, 1945.

Lily grew up in Riga, Latvia, where her maternal grandfather, Philip Gutman, owned a shirt factory. The family lived in a large apartment house—the grandparents, Lily's parents, her brother Shaul, uncles, aunts, and cousins. Lily's father, Miecheslav Kolczycki, was born in what is now Belarus, but his family moved to Poland, to Lodz, so that he would not have to serve in the Russian army. After he married Rosa Gutman,

Lily Kolczycki, c. 1945
Courtesy of her son Eli Barr

Lily's mother, they settled in Riga.

Kolczycki, who was always interested in world affairs, watched the rise of Fascism with great anxiety. In 1933 he traveled to Palestine where he bought a lot in Tel Aviv. According to Lily, he managed to get a residential certificate from the British authorities that he needed in order to own property there. A year later he went back to Tel Aviv, this time with his Gutman in-laws, and the family decided to build an apartment house on the lot he had purchased, at 97 Ben-Yehuda Street. Meanwhile, back in Riga, all the Jewish girls in the German school Lily had been attending were told to leave. Lily transferred to a Jewish school and, for the first time, learned not only about anti-Semitism, but also about Zionism, Herzl, and his dream of a Jewish state.

On June 23, 1940, some nine months after the onset of World War II, the Russians annexed Latvia. Lily, then sixteen, spent part of that summer working on a farm, which all Latvian school children were required to do. The family was nearby, at their summer villa on the seashore. When school resumed, under a Communist headmaster, Lily did well by drawing pictures of Stalin to decorate the schoolhouse. But then the factory was seized and Philip Gutman, its owner, was dismissed. "The State owns all properties," he was told, as he suddenly found himself a poor man. At that point the whole Gutman family wanted to leave for Palestine, but exit permits from Latvia and entry certificates to Palestine were not available. Lily's father, on the other hand, with his Polish passport and his Palestinian certificate, managed to get the right documents, but only after a long wait and a lot of bribe money. When the papers finally arrived, the Kolczyzkis had to leave within three days. It was total chaos as they packed the few belongings they were allowed to take with them. The whole family came to the station to say goodbye. As the train pulled away on a bleak, freezing day they did not know if they would ever see each other again. Lily said that January 17, 1941, was the most terrible day in her life.

Escaping Latvia was just the beginning of their hazardous journey. Everywhere they went they were searched and interrogated and barriers were put in their way. The train took them from Riga to Moscow, where Lily's father was held for hours by the Russian secret police. They eventually continued to Odessa, where they were told their cabin on the boat to Istanbul, for which they had paid long in advance, was not available. But at the last minute, just before their Russian visas expired and after the appropriate bribes were paid, they crossed the Black Sea and reached the enchanted Turkish city. There they were told that there were too many other refugees in the city with Turkish transit visas waiting to go to Palestine, and the British were not letting them in. Therefore, since the city was too crowded, the Kolczyckis were going to be sent back to Russia. But again, just as everything seemed lost, an influential local

Jew came to their aid and they were allowed to stay for a couple of weeks. Then they left by train for Aleppo and from there, by bus, to Beirut. They made the last leg of the trip by taxi to Haifa where they arrived on February 9, 1941, and from there to their apartment house in Tel Aviv. Lily never went back to school. The Kolczyckis had run out of money, and Lily got a job in a bookstore. She married my uncle David when she was twenty-one.

Seventy-five thousand Jews were living in Latvia when the Germans overran the country in July 1941. By the end of that autumn the Germans killed some thirty-five thousand of them. In December, with the help of the Latvian police, the Germans rounded twenty-five thousand Jews from Riga and executed them in nearby forests. The rest were murdered by July 1942. Only a thousand Jews survived the war in Latvia. None of Lily's Gutman relatives survived, nor did any of the Kolczyckis in Lodz.[34]

At the Hebrew Gymnasium

In September 1944, when I was ten-and-a-half-years old, Mother transferred me to the Hebrew Gymnasium—Hagymnasia Haivrit—in Rehavia, considered one of the two best schools in Jewish Jerusalem. I was not particularly upset when informed about the change since I thought I knew all about my future school. After all, at least a dozen Browns and Bermans had attended the Gymnasia: my father and his brother, two of my mother's brothers, several of her cousins, and some of my second cousins. Many of the children of Jerusalem's secular "elite" went there, and being a graduate of the school had a certain cachet. But, unexpectedly, I was faced with a number of problems.

I entered sixth grade along with two boys, and we were the only new students that year among some fifty kids, many of who had been together since first grade and were not particularly interested in the newcomers. The school was on different tracks in math and grammar from Gymnasia Sokolow so I found myself on a shaky academic foundation,

World War II

With my classmates at the entrance to the Hebrew Gymnasium, 1947

and since I disliked those topics anyway, I did not try to catch up and was content to glide along, just getting passing grades. And then there were political issues, as I will try to explain.

The Bermans were capitalists, and while they supported Zionism and hired only Jewish workers (except for the Arab watchman), they had little use for socialism. In their ownership role, they occasionally opposed some of their workers' demands, workers who belonged to the Histadrut, the labor union which encompassed about three-quarters of the country's Jewish labor force. Economically, the Bermans belonged to the upper-middle class as did the parents of most of my new classmates who lived in Rehavia, an affluent residential neighborhood inhabited by lawyers, doctors, bankers, professors, and other professionals. So when the school year began, I was surprised to learn that most of my fellow students belonged to Hatzofim, "The Scouts," a youth movement that had established several kibbutzim and, in my eyes, seemed rather sympathetic to socialism. My classmates' goal was to live in a kibbutz after graduating from high school and while I admired the idealism and moral values of the kibbutzim, I had no desire to live in one, and I did not think many of my fellow students would actually spend a lifetime there.

The following correspondence will illustrate my feelings. I am jumping ahead to October 2001, when I went to Jerusalem for my high school's fiftieth reunion. Shortly thereafter, back in the States, I received a letter from Ofra Brachyahu Katzir with whom I had chatted about our old days at the Gymnasia during the reunion:

> Enclosed are copies of four old photographs that clearly show that you were the cutest girl in the class. You were not with us in The Scouts, and did not live in the "hood." In addition, you did not study with us in the early grades. These are the reasons why you and I were not close. Most of us stuck together and did not bother to enlarge the circle. It was not easy for a stranger to enter a tightly knit, conservative group. We were the "cream" children, in today's terms, and it seems that we liked it.

World War II

I answered Ofra:

> You wrote about the past and the circle that did not bother to encompass anyone new. When I transferred to the Gymnasia, I did not really want to join you. I had strong political views and a somewhat cynical outlook so that even at age ten it seemed strange to me that the children of prosperous Rehavia belonged to a youth movement sympathetic to the Labor Party. I was glad to be a Beitariya. [Beitar was the youth movement of the Revisionist Party and while I never joined it, at that time I liked their ultra-nationalistic agenda.] At the reunion we spoke a little about "belonging." Since part of my family settled in Eretz Israel in 1809, it never occurred to me that I did not belong. Now, fifty years later, I think my attitude was somewhat foolish and that I would have learned a lot had I joined The Scouts.

Ofra's letter back to me, dated December 21, 2001 is the reason I am quoting part of our correspondence:

> I was surprised that at such a young age you had such set political opinions. I grew up in a household where politics were not discussed in front of the children. The Scouts for us was the place where interesting and varied activities took place. We dealt with topics such as mutual aid, contributions to the State, to society. There was also pre-military training, such as flag signals, knots, climbing ropes. We also played a lot, sang—mostly romantic and Russian songs—and we danced. The attraction to the movement was tremendous, mostly because that is where the *hevreh*, the "in group," was. The utmost goal was to help in the creation of the State and for that reason we worked in kibbutzim in the summer, clearing rocks in the Galilee, cutting corn in Hatzor. I remember it all as much more important than school. I feel we were lucky to live during such a meaningful and important period in the history of the State of Israel and were privileged to have even a small part in creating it.

At the fiftieth reunion I discovered that while most of the members of the class of 1951 spent some time in a kibbutz after graduation, eventually all but one left to pursue other careers. Yet looking back, and reading Ofra's letters made me realize that I would have gained a lot, had I chosen to join The Scouts.

I felt very grown up going to the Gymnasia because I could take a city bus there all by myself, and since the school was a couple of miles away from our house, my mother stopped bringing cream for me to drink during recess. School was in session six days a week, from eight in the morning until two or three in the afternoon, except for Fridays when it closed around noon. The building we were in, on Keren Kayemet Street at the edge of Rehavia, was built in 1929, the classrooms were spacious, and there were usually forty to fifty students in each grade, twenty to twenty-five in one room. In ninth grade we were divided into two groups, one where the emphasis was on science, the other, on the humanities—*megama realit* and *megama sifrutit*. The language of instruction was Hebrew. As already mentioned, the Gymnasia, established in 1909, was the first school in Jerusalem where Hebrew was the sole language of instruction. We had many good teachers; most were of Russian origin, others came from Poland, Western Europe, and Eretz Israel. Some had Ph.D.'s and a number of them went on to teach in the country's universities, to write books, and to win prestigious awards.

Although it was a secular school, a large part of the curriculum was devoted to Jewish studies, or perhaps one should say Hebrew studies. It was as if our teachers were on a sacred mission, to instill in us a passion for the language and a love for the land. One session a day was devoted to the Bible. Simple biblical tales were introduced in second grade and by the time we finished high school, we had studied almost every book in the Hebrew Bible. We examined the Bible as a source of history, religion, and literature. We memorized lyrical passages, like the song the Israelites sang after they crossed the Red Sea, when Miriam the Prophetess led the women, dancing and playing the tambourine (Exodus

15:21). We could recite David's lament after the Philistines killed Saul and Jonathan: "Thy beauty, O Israel, upon thy high places is slain! How are the mighty fallen!" (II Samuel 1:19). And we knew by heart many of the beautiful verses in the Prophets: "I remember the affection of your youth," says the Lord to Israel, "The love of your nuptials, Your following me in the wilderness, In a land that was not sown" (Jeremiah 2:2).

When I entered the Gymnasia in the sixth grade, our Bible teacher was Yaacov Yona, a short man with a red face, cropped gray hair, and round, steel-rimmed glasses. Everyone at school was terrified of Yona, a disciplinarian famous for meting out punishment at the slightest provocation. At the mere hint of disobedience he would order the hapless student to copy—four or five times—Psalm 119, the longest chapter in the Bible, consisting of 176 verses. (Six decades later, I still remember the terse opening verse, which in Yona's mind was most appropriate: *Ashrei tmimei derech, haholchim betorat Yehova.* "Happy are they who are upright in the way of the Lord." Had we been "upright," he would tell us, we would not have been punished.) In ninth grade we were rescued by Dov Kimhi, a prolific author who treated the Bible as a fountainhead of drama and mystery, bringing the ancient heroes and villains back to life. By the time we graduated we knew about every corner of the Land of Israel, from Dan to Be'er Sheva; from Jericho, where Joshua blew his horn, to Gaza, where the blinded Samson killed himself and numerous Philistines; from Hebron, where Abraham was buried, to Emek Haela, where David slew Goliath.

In the upper grades we were led through sections of the Mishna and Talmud by Dr. Avraham Arazi who, unlike most of the other teachers, made the boys cover their heads during his classes. He was rather pedantic and some of us found his classes a little slow so—instead of following the text—we often read novels or detective stories which could be easily hidden in the large volumes of the Talmud.

We spent several hours a week learning English. First we had Miss Fox, a gentle British lady. Then came Mrs. Tepper who was much stricter. "Brown," she would say to me. "Some day you will be chatting away charmingly at tea parties, but your grammar will remain hopeless." (How right she was in the second part of her analysis!) Shimon Krieger took us in hand during our last two years at the Gymnasia. We spent a year going through *Adventures in English Literature*. We started with Johnson and Boswell, followed by representatives of the Victorian age such as Macaulay, Huxley, and Stevenson. (A sentence by the latter in *El Dorado* stayed with me for years: " ... for to travel hopefully is a better thing than to arrive, and the true success is to labor.") Among twentieth-century writers we read Conrad, Saki, Maugham, and Woolf. In our final year we struggled with *Macbeth*, a play Krieger made us appreciate—almost enjoy—despite the tragic story and the unfamiliar words. (I always think of "Eye of newt and toe of frog" when I come across the word "ingredients.") Starting in eleventh grade, we had to study an additional foreign language, either French or Arabic. This was in 1949 and many of us, including me, chose Arabic. It was a big mistake in my case because Yaacov Landau, who taught Arabic, was also our Hebrew grammar teacher. I always had trouble with grammar in any language and skipped as many of his Hebrew classes as possible, so I could not show up at an Arabic lesson when I was supposedly absent from school.

Our most idiosyncratic teacher was Yehoshua Avizohar who was charged with introducing us to physics and chemistry. He was the classic absent-minded professor who did not know the names of any of his students—which may explain the fact that we all got passing grades. Few of his experiments worked in the lab but when they did he would shout *nitzahon lamada*! "A victory for science!" The students spent a lot of time trying to find the right formula to produce a smoke bomb or some smelly concoction that would necessitate vacating the lab. Yet Avizohar must have done something right because the Gymnasia continued to produce future scientists. Perhaps it was his enthusiasm. (One of my classmates, the late Dan Shalitin, was a pioneer in the development of Israel's nuclear power program.)

Other sciences—botany, biology and what ever else could be classified under *teva*, or "nature"—were taught by Amotz Cohen. He knew and loved every inch of the countryside and, with a "hands on" philosophy, made us share his ardor. He took us on trips to gather fossils, to examine a few surviving ancient oaks, to observe wild animals in their natural habitat. Cohen was in charge of *hadar hateva*, the "nature room," which was filled with samples from the animal, vegetable, and mineral worlds. Most inanimate specimens were displayed in glass cases and needed no care, others were pickled in formaldehyde. But from time to time a live critter was brought in by one of the teachers or by a student, like me. I occasionally captured some crawling beastie—a centipede, a scorpion, a snake—and brought it to school to show that I was interested in science. As a result, Mr. Cohen put me in charge of feeding the animals and cleaning their cages—there were sometimes rabbits, turtles, or frogs in the nature room as well. I was rewarded with good grades in whatever Mr. Cohen happened to teach that year and that helped balance my otherwise indifferent science grades.

I had little enthusiasm for math, algebra, or geometry. History was another matter. We spent one year with Dr. Zvi Yavetz falling in love with ancient Greece, another trying to follow the rise and fall of the Roman Empire. Dr. Ben-Zion Gat guided us through different chapters of Jewish history.

In addition to academic subjects, we also had drawing lessons, arts and crafts, and music. And there were several periods of physical education each week, another area at which I did not excel and where I suffered my worst experience at the Gymnasia. Our gym teacher, Ze'ev Feldman, wanted to put on a show for some occasion—I do not remember what it was—and so he tried to turn a series of exercises we had been practicing into a ballet-like production. To this day I do not understand why he put me in the front row since he knew how bad I was at that particular form of gymnastics. As a result, he had to keep correcting my steps and that only made me more reluctant to participate. At some point, after he chided me in front of the whole class, I muttered *eizeh hamor*, "What an ass." That was too much for Feldman who lost his temper and slapped me. Now, there was never any physical punishment at the Gymnasia, and no one—anywhere—had ever slapped me or hit me before. I ended up in the principal's office and my mother was asked to come to the school. She was horrified by the idea that someone touched her child, but the principal, Dr. Avraham Bartana, told her how lucky it was that Feldman reacted the way he did for otherwise I would have been expelled from school. An uneasy truce was declared and I was sent back to row one. But I was determined not to take part in the performance.

I began to complain about a pain in my knee. I was sent to the nurse's room where, after examining me a couple times, she passed me on to Dr. Eiges, the school doctor, who declared that he could not find anything wrong. I continued to complain so Mother took me to see an orthopedist, Dr. True. To make a very long story short, I ended up in a cast, from my ankle to my hip that I had on for six weeks. Needless to say, it got me out of gymnastics, but it was a bittersweet victory. (The experience also reenforced my opinion that medicine was not an exact science. On several other occasions, while in my teens, I managed to get out of tough spots by faking illness.)

Dr. Gedalia Alkoshi taught modern Hebrew literature. And here, a detour is required because so little is known in the general public about the revival of Hebrew. People are always amazed, for example, when they hear that my mother—who was born in Jerusalem in 1910—and her siblings spoke Hebrew to each other while they were growing up.

It was Eliezer Ben-Yehuda in the late nineteenth century who made Hebrew the vernacular of the Jews in Palestine after an interval of two thousand years. But Hebrew never ceased to exist as a written language. The Bible was followed by the Mishna and the Talmud, and by further commentaries, prayers, and other forms of prose and poetry. Yet postbiblical writing was mostly religious in nature until the Middle Ages when semi-secular literature began to appear in Italy, Provence, and in

Spain where, under the Moors, Hebrew poetry reached its "Golden Age." Then, in the late eighteenth century, modern, secular Hebrew literature made its first appearance. It started in Prussia with the *Haskala* (1770s-1880s), a movement influenced by the Enlightenment, which emphasized reason and good taste. The leaders of the movement were successful merchants and other professionals who considered Yiddish to be vulgar and were determined to return to Hebrew, the respected language of the Bible. In 1783 they established the first Hebrew monthly, *Ha-Me'assef,* "The Collector," which was published in Koenigsberg and lasted—off and on—for almost half a century. The first Hebrew novel, *Ahavat Ziyyon,* "Love of Zion," by Avraham Mapu, was published in Vilna in 1853, a story set in biblical times. Hebrew writers had rich sources to draw upon—the Bible, the Talmud, poems from Spain—but no one in Mapu's time was using Hebrew in everyday life so writing dialogue was especially difficult, hence the biblical setting.

Dr. Alkoshi had his hands full as he tried to make us appreciate the early fruits of modern Hebrew literature. I loved the poetry of the era, perhaps because its flowery language did not sound strained to me. But the novels seemed stilted, unable to compete with a lot of world classics that were being translated into Hebrew, and the essays, often written by the fathers of Zionism, left me cold. (It was the essays I disliked, not Zionism.) Dr. Alkoshi taught other subjects as well and it was under his guidance that we read Freud's *The Interpretation of Dreams,* which opened the door to a world unknown to me. He was also in charge of improving our writing and every week or so we had to write an essay on a topic he provided. One example that springs to mind is: "Out of the strong came something sweet," one of Samson's riddles (Judges 14:14). I was not good at writing essays so I often made up a short story that somehow incorporated Alkoshi's topic. Rather than admonish me for not following instructions, as other teachers did, he always encouraged me to continue writing.

After the end of World War II, as the struggle against the British intensified, many of the older high school students wanted to leave before graduation so they could join one of the undergrounds—mostly the Hagana, but both the Irgun and Lehi also had some followers at the Gymnasia. Those of us who were over thirteen began to stay after school for special training. We learned to do an "omega" which meant gliding off a roof on a tight rope with the help of a gadget shaped like the last letter of the Greek alphabet. We went on overnight hikes, slept on the ground, boiled water on an open fire after we collected enough wood. It all seemed very exciting.

On the whole, we received a sound education at the Gymnasia. When I eventually went to college in the States I got a year's worth of credits upon presenting my high school diploma.

Family Affairs

Back to My Parents

My father, who was born in 1906, graduated from the Hebrew Gymnasium in 1924. His parents then sent him to Paris, where he received his Baccalaureate from the Collège de France. (I believe that it was in Paris when he began to use "Maurice" as his first name, although in Hebrew he was still referred to as "Moshe.") He stayed in France and began to study medicine at the University of Montpellier but transferred to Geneva after one semester and completed his medical studies there. Upon graduation he returned to Jerusalem to open a clinic, but it was during the Depression and he had a hard time building up a practice. After he and my mother were married, on June 2, 1931, she often urged him to try and earn extra money by using his linguistic skills to translate medical texts. (In addition to Hebrew, English, and French, he also knew Arabic, German, and Greek.) But my father used to say that he did not spend all those years studying medicine in order to become a translator.

As soon as World War II broke out, in September of 1939, Moshe joined the Royal Army Medical Corps and served in France as a colonel with the British Expeditionary Force. Then, after being trapped by the Germans in Dunkirk, he was evacuated along with nearly 338,000 other Allied troops, between May 27 and June 4, 1940, in what Winston Churchill called a "miracle of deliverence." After a short stay in England, my father was sent to join the North African campaign in Egypt, and later, in 1944, he served in Greece. One can just begin to imagine the terrible carnage he witnessed as a physician. I only learned of the battles he was in many years later.

One of my favorite pieces of furniture in my parents' apartment was a large armoire that stood in their bedroom. I used to climb on top of it, then jump onto their bed, a few feet across the room. Though at age eleven I was far too old for such feats—long forbidden by Mother—I found myself by the armoire one day in the spring of 1945. As I stuck my hand under some linen to get a better grip on a shelf, I touched what felt like a piece of cardboard. It turned out to be a photograph of Hamish Dougan, a family friend.

"How can you keep a photograph of another man in your closet while your husband is risking his life in the war?" I asked my mother with all the righteous indignation I could summon. Putting her arms around me, she quietly uttered the sentence which brought my idyllic childhood to an end: "Your father and I got divorced years ago, before the war." It was no one's fault, she added. Things just did not work out. As her words sunk in, my first reaction was shame. I did not know one other child whose parents were divorced. I was too stunned to ask why no one had told me about it. Later I assumed it was because the common practice in those days was to shield children from bad news. But even after I found out about the divorce, the silence, the conspiracy within the family not to talk about it, surrounded me like a wall. It confirmed my darkest suspicions, that it was something disgraceful, better kept hidden. I did not talk to any of my friends about it, and withdrew into myself.

In my isolation I tried to recall life with Father before he left. The result was a collage made up of memories combined with bits of information. One early recollection was his late arrival at nursery school for my fifth birthday party, in April 1939. By then he was no longer living with us but I cannot remember how it was explained to me at the time. After he joined the British Armed Forces he used to send me hand-printed letters, punctuated with vowels so I could soon read them by myself, letters illustrated with cartoon-like characters. All correspondence had to pass through the military censor so my father could not reveal where he was or what he was doing.

Many things became clear to me, as I thought back. For example, the reason he did not stay at home on his rare, brief visits to the country during the war. On those occasions I was told that he had to return to a military base at night. He would meet Mother and me at the house of the Lefkowitzes, family friends in Rehovot, where my mother would remain while he and I spent the day together in nearby Tel Aviv. Father was never there for my birthdays—after all he was in the war—but he would mail me presents, usually government bonds. Once he sent me a watch, which I found very exciting, but then I accidentally overheard my mother making a disparaging remark about its quality. The only other negative comment that I can remember her making about my father came when I wanted to put on a new dress the minute I got it. "You are just like your father," she said. As far as she was concerned, one had to wait for the proper occasion to wear something new. (My grandmother later explained that it was she, Sarah, who forbade any criticism of my father. "You are his daughter, and anything bad said about him would reflect on you." She also told me that my father was a good doctor, an excellent diagnostician.)

Many years later, when I was interviewing the remaining members of my family, Zahava the Great, wife of my mother's cousin Baruch Berman, described the following scene to me: "I was visiting your mother one summer afternoon. She was lying on top of a bed, nursing you, with her skirt pulled up since it was a very hot day. Your father walked in and put his hand on her thigh. It should have made a lovely picture, a couple with their young baby, but your mother turned away from him as if she could not bear his touch. I knew then that the marriage could not last."

No one told me that my father had remarried in 1940 and so, like other children in similar situations, I continued to hope that my parents would get together again. Once the war was over, I fantasized, there was no reason why he could not move right back in with us. In my head I rearranged our apartment, making room for his clinic, and planned imaginary walks with my parents holding hands. In the meantime I blamed my mother for the divorce and hero-worshipped the father I barely knew.

After the war ended, my father spent a year in Cyprus, serving as the medical director of the camps where the British interned many Jewish refugees from Hitler's Europe who were attempting to enter Palestine. He returned to Jerusalem in 1946 and once again tried to build up a practice. Because he spoke so many languages, he soon established close relations with priests of different denominations, most of whom resided in the Old City. And this is how he became a minor actor in the narrative of the Dead Sea Scrolls, one of the most important archaeological discoveries ever made.

The story of the discovery is well known. In the spring of 1947, a young Bedouin shepherd found seven scrolls in a cave near Qumran, by the Dead Sea. Five were soon taken to Metropolitan Mar Athanasius Yeshue Samuel, the head of the Syrian Orthodox Monastery of St. Mark in the Old City. (It later turned out that two of the scrolls were the successive parts of the "Manual of Discipline" so Samuel actually had only four scrolls.) He recognized the Hebrew script and assumed the scrolls were old and after many difficulties—including doubts expressed by various scholars about the age and origin of the scrolls—he managed to buy the four scrolls. In October of that year, Samuel showed the scrolls to my father, who was visiting the monastery, and he, in turn, informed Hebrew University's President Judah L. Magnes of the as yet unidentified find.[35] Samuel continued to show the scrolls to different scholars, who thought they were more recent than they eventually turned out to be. During that time, the noted archaeologist Professor Eleazar L.

Family Affairs

Sukenik of the Hebrew University was out of the country. A few days after his return, on November 29, 1947, he acquired two other manuscripts and was given, free of charge, two pottery jars in which some of the scrolls were said to have been stored. On that fateful date, the United Nations voted on the partition of Palestine into two states, and soon attacks by Arabs made further communications between the Old City and west Jerusalem nearly impossible. But in December, through some complicated arrangements, Sukenik managed to see some of the scrolls held by the Monastery of St. Mark and he wanted to buy them. But a planned meeting with Samuel and Magnes never took place because of the hostilities. Samuel then brought his scrolls to the American School of Oriental Research in Jerusalem where scholars recognized their antiquity. (He allowed the school to photograph and later publish three of his four scrolls.) Eventually the Metropolitan smuggled the scrolls to the United States and in 1954 Yigael Yadin, Sukenik's son, purchased them for Israel. They are now housed and displayed at the Shrine of the Book in the Israel Museum.

The search for other scrolls continued, yielding a vast number of fragments and some more or less preserved scrolls dating from about 200 BC to AD 68, hidden—most mainstream scholars believe—by the Essenes of Qumran during the First Jewish Revolt against the Romans (AD 66-70). Among the finds are fragments of texts of all but one book of the Old Testament, plus commentaries, rules of faith, manuals, psalms, hymns, and other, non-canonical texts. My father remained interested in archaeology to the end of his long life.

It was only in the summer of 1947 that I finally realized that my parents' divorce was not the end of the world, and for that I am in debt to a fourteen-year-old boy I met that year in Nahariya, a resort town on the Mediterranean, near the Lebanese boarder. Founded in 1935 by refugees from Germany, the town seemed very exotic with wooden houses, green lawns, semi-tropical trees, and many pensions. Mother

Pension Tutti Loewy, Nahariya, mid-1940s

and I and Avraham and his family usually spent two weeks there—at Pension Tutti Loewy—but in 1947 Mother stayed in Jerusalem because my grandmother had to undergo some surgical procedure. So I was sent to Nahariya with Uncle Avraham, Aunt Zahava, and my cousins Daphne and Adi, who was two. The five of us were packed into Avraham's car, the luggage on the roof, with Adi's potty teetering on top of the largest suitcase. A convoy of British soldiers overtook us, cheering and clapping at the sight. That time we stayed in a hotel owned by Dr. Dr. Joseph Neuburger, a lawyer with two doctorates, who like many other German refugees could not practice his profession in Palestine and had to find another way to make a living. Every evening after dinner, while Avraham and Zahava put Adi to bed, Daphne and I used to stroll along the Gaaton—a little stream where there was hardly any water during the summer. Two young men, or rather teenagers, often passed us on their bicycles and sometimes stopped to say hello. Their names were Yossi Scheinman and Michael Strauss, they said, and they lived in Nahariya. (Michael's family was in the steel industry in Germany. In Nahariya his parents purchased some cows and started making cheese, then ice cream,

With my mother on a beach near Nahariya, 1940

and other dairy products. Michael eventually became one of Israel's leading industrialists.) One evening I managed to leave the hotel without Daphne and I ran into Yossi who was also by himself. We walked down to the beach telling each other our life stories and it was then that, for the first time, I spoke to someone outside the family about my parents' divorce. Yossi just continued talking as if he heard nothing unusual and even held my hand when he walked me back to the hotel. I began to think that perhaps a divorce was not such a disgrace.

Our family left Nahariya the next day, as scheduled. In the summer of 1948 Israel's War of Independence was not over and no one went on vacation. Other events followed, and we did not return to Nahariya so I never had a chance to thank Yossi.

Forbidden Love

By 1945 I had read enough novels to realize that my mother and Hamish Dougan were having an affair, although I am not sure I understood what that meant. At some point it dawned on me that during vacations, when Hamish used to stay at Pension Tutti Loewy in Nahariya at the same

My mother, Leah, in a café in Ramallah, 1941

time we did, it was not only because of his friendship with Avraham and Zahava.

Leah had been divorced for several years when she met Hamish in 1940 on the tennis courts of Café Lipsky in Talpiot. He was a tall, handsome man with blue eyes and straight black hair that he parted in the middle. Sometimes he brought me gifts—a pair of red suede gloves, a tartan scarf—and he took me swimming, that is I held on to his neck as he plunged into the waters of the Mediterranean off the coast at Nahariya where treacherous currents made it very hard to learn to swim. Hamish spoke a little Hebrew and I knew some English so we managed to communicate.

A Scotsman from Edinburgh, Hamish served for a number of years

Family Affairs

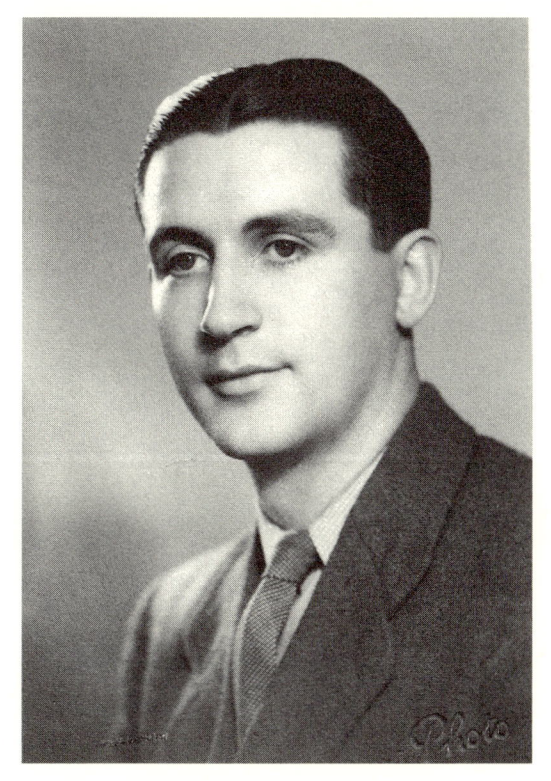

Hamish Dougan, early 1940s

with the Grenadier Guards—the most senior regiment of infantry in the British Army—before he was shipped to Palestine in the summer of 1938, together with over a thousand regular army men. Once in Jerusalem, he was assigned to the CID, the Criminal Investigation Department of the Palestine Police. Alexander T. Ternent, who met Hamish in 1940 after he himself was transferred from Jaffa to Jerusalem, told me that Hamish was "a real CID man who also served in Syria and Lebanon in 1941 and 1942 after the Allies vanquished the Vichy French and occupied the Levant." Hamish was a very kind man and a fine raconteur. Alex, who considered him his mentor, saw Hamish several times in Jerusalem in the company of "a tall, dark-haired, elegant lady."

It is hard to imagine today the obstacles that lay along the course of the romance between Leah, the daughter of a well-known Jewish family and Hamish, a CID officer. Tension between the British authorities and the Yishuv continued during the war since the British stuck to the policy of keeping Jewish refugees out of the country. So, for example, in the fall of 1943, at the height of World War II, a proclamation was issued by the Zealots' Alliance—an otherwise unknown Jewish organization—calling the public to join it in a holy war against the daughters of Israel who were dating foreign soldiers and bringing shame upon the honor of Israel. If the women did not change their ways, the Zealots planned to take forceful steps against them, beyond merely publishing their names and addresses. Eventually a couple of women were killed, some had their heads shaven, others were fired from their jobs.[36]

Once World War II was over the situation worsened. Lehi, the most extreme right-wing Jewish underground, and the Irgun continued to intimidate young women who had a relationship with the "enemy," and, on the other side, if a member of the Palestine Police married a Jewish girl, his future within the organization, I was told, "would have been dubious indeed." In addition, because of her closeness to her Orthodox parents, it was unthinkable for Leah to marry a non-Jew. It is not clear to me how she managed to hide the relationship from her parents for years since there were not many places in Jerusalem where couples could meet without being noticed. But I know that all of my mother's siblings and several of her cousins liked Hamish and helped cover up the affair. With time, especially after I found out that my father not only remarried but also had a son, I grew accustomed to Hamish's visits. One evening he asked me:

"Would you come to England if your mother went there with me?"

"Oh, I will never leave Jerusalem, and she would not go without me."

Hamish had warned some members of the Hagana, including my second cousin Amnon Berman, that the British authorities were becoming

Family Affairs

John "Hamish" Dougan in Malaya, early 1948
Courtesy of the Dougan family

suspicious of their activities. Probably because he was seen as too close to the Jews, Hamish was transferred out of Jerusalem in the early summer of 1947 and appointed Assistant Superintendent of the district of Hebron.

Hamish later played a heroic role in retrieving the bodies of the thirty-five young men—known as the Lamed-Hey in Hebrew—who left from the vicinity of Jerusalem on the night of January 15, 1948, to bring food and medical supplies to the besieged Gush Etzion—four kibbutzim near Hebron—but never made it past the Arab lines. At great personal risk Hamish saw to it that their bodies were brought to burial. Nearly everyone in Jerusalem knew one or more of the thirty-five or their families, and Hamish's role soon became known. Shortly thereafter he was sent to the Gold Coast of West Africa, to Ghana, then to Malaya. In May the British Mandate came to an end, Israel declared its independence and was invaded by troops from five Arab countries. Jewish Jerusalem was under siege, no mail went in or out of the city, and all contact between Leah and Hamish ceased.

The Road to Independence

The Displaced Jews of Europe

World War II in Europe ended on May 8, 1945, with the unconditional surrender of Nazi Germany. It was then that the full horror of the Holocaust began to unfold, with images of concentration camp survivors splashed over cinema screens and front pages of newspapers. Dr. Chaim Weizmann, writing to Prime Minister Winston Churchill, suggested that in view of the desperate situation of the survivors it was time to eliminate the White Paper and proclaim a Jewish state. Churchill replied that the problem could not be dealt with until the Allies were victorious on all fronts. On July 5, Churchill, the hero of the war, lost the election to the Labour Party which won by a landslide. In Jerusalem the Yishuv rejoiced. Based on earlier declarations, the Jewish leaders believed that the regime of Prime Minister Clement Attlee would be more sympathetic to the plight of the Jews. But the new government's Middle East policy was set by Ernest Bevin, the foreign secretary, who was alarmed by his country's empty coffers, depleted by the long war. Oil was crucial to England's economic survival and Bevin was determined not to jeopardize Britain's relations with the Arabs. When David Ben-Gurion went to London to demand that a hundred thousand Displaced

Persons—Holocaust survivors and refugees from the Soviet Union—be allowed into Palestine, the Colonial Office offered two thousand immigration certificates, plus another fifteen hundred a month. The Yishuv was in a state of shock.

In the United States, President Harry Truman, though well-aware of the State Department's anti-Zionist stance and its fear of antagonizing the Arab world, wrote to Attlee at the end of August, supporting the proposal to let a hundred thousand Jews enter Palestine. At the same time, in addition to American pressure, the British were facing increased underground activities in Palestine as installations were attacked and weapon depots raided. And at home loud voices were demanding to "bring the boys home." Ruling Palestine had become a costly affair, both in lives and in taxpayers' money. In November 1945, Bevin decided to form the Anglo-American Commission for Inquiry on Palestine.

Few Jews managed to escape Nazi-occupied lands during the war so illegal immigration to Palestine—Aliya Bet—nearly stopped. Now it resumed in force, organized and financed by the institutions of the Yishuv, with the help of the American Jewish community and Jewish soldiers in the Allied armies, and with the tacit approval of the American, French, and Italian authorities. Jews made their way to France and Italy and embarked on boats bound for Palestine, boats that were usually seized by the British blockade. In the summer of 1946 the British opened detention camps in Cypress to house the refugees they captured.

Reaction in the Yishuv

The Yishuv's desire to see the end of the Mandate intensified when it became clear that the Labour Government had no intention of lifting the restrictions on immigration. In October 1945, the three Jewish underground organizations, at times bitter rivals, formed a joint Hebrew Resistance Movement to coordinate their anti-British activities. Murders of Jews in Poland in 1946, including a pogrom in Kielce where some forty Jews were killed, made it clear that anti-Semitism was still alive and well in Europe, and that the survivors needed a new home.

The Anglo-American Commission, which heard testimony from Arab and Jewish leaders and visited Displaced Persons' camps in Europe, issued its report on May 1, 1946. It recommended that in view of the unbearable situation of the Jews, a hundred thousand of them should be admitted into Palestine. President Truman publicly endorsed the report while London rejected it. To reconcile their differences, Truman and Attlee set up the Morrison-Grady team that eventually suggested that the country be divided into autonomous Arab and Jewish enclaves with Britain remaining in charge of defense, foreign relations, and some other areas. Neither the Arabs nor the Jews accepted the plan. Later, after holding parallel negotiations with Arab and Jewish delegates in January and February of 1947, Bevin came up with another plan. It envisioned a five-year trusteeship for the country after which a cantonal self-government would be established. It also called for letting ninety-six thousand Jewish refugees into the country, over a two-year period. When both sides repudiated Bevin's plan, he announced that Britain would refer the problem of Palestine to the United Nations.

While the different committees were debating the issue, the Hagana, Irgun, and Lehi continued to raid military bases and police stations for guns and ammunition, and to sabotage railroads, radar installation, and airfields. On June 17, 1946, the Hagana blew up the bridges connecting Palestine to neighboring countries. The British retaliated with what became known in the Yishuv as "Black Saturday." Some seventeen thousand policemen and army personnel participated in the operation. A countrywide curfew was declared in the early hours of Saturday, June 29, and the British arrested twenty-seven hundred people, including many of the Yishuv's leaders, and put them in detention camps. Intense searches were carried on at the Jewish Agency and other institutions where documents were seized and arms caches were confiscated in kibbutzim and settlements. The operation lasted for two weeks after which the Hagana curbed its attacks against the British and concentrated its efforts on immigration, but Lehi and the Irgun became more extreme.

On July 22, 1946, the Irgun blew up a wing of the King David Hotel in Jerusalem where the offices of the Mandatory government, the Headquarters of the British Army, and part of the CID, the Criminal Investigation Department, were located. After managing to place large quantities of explosives in the building, a phone call was made to the CID with a warning to evacuate the place, but it was not taken seriously. Ninety-one people were killed by the blast, British citizens, Arabs, and Jews, and many more wounded. The British placed Jerusalem and Tel Aviv under a four-day curfew as they searched for the bombers.

Why was the telephone warning ignored? Some say because there had been many false alarms during that period, and also that the British could not believe that the heavily guarded hotel building was penetrated. A rumor persists that when informed of the call, Sir John Shaw, the Chief Secretary of the British Administration, said: "I don't take orders from Jews," and he did not allow people to leave the building. Yet he himself left before the explosion. A month later he was recalled to Britain. (Sir John vigorously denied the rumor.)

There are some moments you remember forever, like where you were when you heard that President Kennedy was assassinated. On July 22 a friend and I were playing in my bedroom, about to go down to lunch, when we heard the explosion. We went out on the balcony and saw a pillar of smoke and dust rising in the south and we knew something major had happened. I was only twelve at the time, but when the news came through later in the day I was horrified by the carnage, amazed that the Irgun managed to get into the closely watched building, and relieved that my aunt Haya, who worked at the switchboard at the Headquarters of the British Army, was not in the building that day.

The brief cooperation among the three underground organizations ceased after the bombing of the King David as Ben-Gurion and others condemned the action. Relations with the British continued to disintegrate since the Irgun and Lehi resumed their attacks and the British retaliated with curfews, searches, and arrests. On January 31, 1947, the British authorities announced the creation of security zones in the three major cities. Women, children, and nonessential personnel were evacuated from what were to become fortified enclaves. It turned out that it was mostly the Jewish population that was evacuated. By February 10, eight security zones were completed in Jerusalem, enclosing about a third of the Jewish areas. The main one, soon to be nicknamed "Bevingrad," was in the heart of downtown and enclosed the Russian Compound, the Generali building, the Central Post Office, and Notre Dame de France—a pilgrims' center. As if to show its disdain for the new security measures, the Irgun attacked an officers' club in Jerusalem on March 1, killing seventeen men, after which martial law was imposed in Tel Aviv and Jerusalem for two weeks. On April 16, four Irgun members were hanged in Acre's prison. Three weeks later, on May 4, the Irgun broke into the old citadel that served as Acre's prison, and freed forty-one Irgun and Lehi members. One hundred-eighty Arab prisoners escaped as well. On June 29, three more Irgun members were hanged. The Irgun responded the next day by kidnapping two British sergeants and hanging them in a grove near Netanya, an action that brought protests from around the world.

❦

When curfews were imposed, Zahava, my friend and next-door neighbor and I felt obliged to get together in an act of defiance. Since our backyards abutted each other—with the gates opening onto a tiny dead-end alley about ten feet apart—it did not take much courage to do so. Still, one would listen attentively behind a gate for the footsteps of the *kalaniot*, the "anemones," the nickname given to British soldiers for their red berets. If all was quiet, one dashed next door.

Since curfews disrupted normal city life, the British issued passes to

The Road to Independence

essential civilian employees and officials. Lewis Harris, a London Jew and British army officer who married my second cousin Aviva Berman, wrote in his memoir, *From Occident to Orient: The Memoirs of Lewis Harris, A Soldier's Tale*, that he helped Berman Bakery personnel obtain passes so they could deliver bread. Next he was asked by the bakery's truck drivers to escort their convoys as they negotiated the security barriers that were set up throughout the city. He would then sit in the leading truck, while my uncle Keith Beecher, Haya's husband, who was just released from the Royal Air Force, covered the rear. The bread distribution went smoothly until one day a group of British soldiers arrived at the bakery and arrested workers and owners alike and drove them to a detention camp in Rafah near the Egyptian border where they were interrogated for several days. Then most were released. At the same time other soldiers began to search the bakery for hidden weapons.[37] A few of them arrived at our house next door, and I remember a young soldier, looking rather sheepish as he kept his Sten gun pointed at my elderly grandfather who led the soldiers through the house, from the basement to the third-floor attic. No arms were found in either place although in his book Lewis writes that there was a well-hidden cache in the bakery—which I knew nothing about.

While all this was going on in Palestine, various Zionist leaders were presenting the Jewish case to the United Nations: the American rabbi Abba Hillel Silver, David Ben-Gurion, Chaim Weizmann. Ben-Gurion was furious with Menahem Begin and the Irgun, feeling that their actions were viewed most negatively by the international community, just when the Yishuv needed all the support it could get.

Meanwhile the Hagana continued its efforts to smuggle refugees into the country. Over the years Britain had gotten a lot of bad press over the issue, what with images of Holocaust survivors being forcibly taken off boats by British troops and put into camps. One such captured boat made world headlines, and probably helped create the State of Israel since the following events took place while the debate about the fate of Palestine was raging at the United Nations. On July 10, 1947, some forty-five hundred Displaced Persons from Germany were brought to a port near Marseilles and boarded a former Chesapeake Bay excursion boat, purchased in Baltimore and renamed *Exodus 1947*. The British Navy watched the boat all along, and even before it entered Palestine's territorial waters, destroyers forced the *Exodus* to Haifa. The passengers, knowing they would soon be deported, refused to disembark. Eventually the British opened fire, and three Jews were killed and a hundred wounded. Finally the refugees were transferred from the *Exodus* onto three navy transport ships and, since the detention camps in Cyprus were overloaded, or, some say, because he wanted to make a point, Bevin ordered that they be turned back to their place of origin. When the ships arrived at Port-du-Bouc near Marseilles, the refugees again refused to get off or to accept help from the French. After three weeks the French ordered the ships to leave the port, fearing that the appalling living conditions on board might cause epidemics that could then spread into the country. On September 10, the refugees were brought to Hamburg where again they declined to get off but were compelled to do so. The press was watching. The plight of the *Exodus* was broadcast all over the world and the sight of Holocaust survivors being forced by British soldiers into internment camps in Germany aroused a lot of sympathy for the Jewish cause.

On November 29, 1947, the United Nations voted to partition Palestine.

In the Berman Family

There were some additions to the family between 1945 and 1948. As mentioned, Avraham and Zahava had a son, Adi, born in 1945. Two years later Moshe and Cecile also had a son, Oded. On a sadder note, Baba Esther died peacefully at home in 1946, at age ninety. That evening, instead of going to bed as I was supposed to, I peeked through the keyhole of the salon next door into Esther's bedroom. And there I saw her

With Baba Esther, my great-grandmother, and cousin Daphne who is held by my mother, 1939

small, shriveled body lying naked on a wooden platform, surrounded by women who were cleansing her, washing her from head to toe before wrapping the body in *tachrichim*, in white burial shrouds. Then candles were lit around her body and several people came in and sat with her through the night, reading Psalms. Next morning, before the funeral, a man from *Hevra Kadisha*, the Burial Society, made tears in the garments of members of the immediate family. We then departed for the ancient cemetery on the Mount of Olives, where my uncles said Kadish and Baba Esther's body was deposited into the ground without a coffin, which is the custom in the Land of Israel because the soil there is holy. We came home to find the mirrors covered and food waiting for us, brought in by friends and neighbors. We sat *Shiva*, mourning for a week, while many of Esther's relatives, nieces and nephews from all around the country who could not get to the funeral on time, came to call and to tell Ashkenazi and Epstein family stories. Esther's death was not unexpected and she lived to a ripe old age, but until she died I did not realize what a major role she had played in my upbringing and how much I would miss her.

⁂

Two events I remember took place in the Berman Bakery in the years between the end of World War II and the War of Independence. One was a strike by the workers over the issue of working on Saturday night. Since all activity at the bakery ceased early on Friday afternoon because of the Sabbath, re-lighting the ovens and starting the dough had to be done as soon as three stars could be seen in the sky, signifying that the Sabbath was over, because fresh bread had to be ready for market by early Sunday morning. All the workers at the bakery belonged to the Histadrut, the Yishuv's powerful trade union. (In 1947 the Histadrut had a membership of 176,000, out of a total Jewish population of about 600,000.) Somehow the strike was settled although family members were not happy with the results and, being capitalists, they naturally blamed the union as they did during other strikes. Shortly thereafter the Bermans, who owned the oldest and at that point largest bakery in the country, went into partnership with their main rival, the Angel family, and with another bakery, Keter, owned by a family called Katz. They formed the Amalgamated Berman-Angel-Keter Bakery, which did not last very long. The partners separated and went back to their old businesses; the Berman and Angel bakeries are still operating in Jerusalem but Keter moved to Haifa and closed in the mid-1970s.

Jerusalem Besieged

On the night of November 29, 1947, everyone sat glued to the radio. After the United Nations approved the Partition Plan for Palestine, it seemed as if all of Jewish Jerusalem, me included, spent the night dancing in the streets. Even some British soldiers joined in. When morning came I went directly to school and continued to dance, with my teachers and classmates alike. A sense of euphoria engulfed even those of us who thought the area allotted to the Jews was too small and objected to Jerusalem's designation as an international city. But for the first time in two thousand years there was going to be a sovereign Jewish state. How could one not feel elated? That very day, November 30, seven people were killed when Jewish buses in several parts of the country were attacked. On December 1, the Arabs declared a three-day general strike. Two days later Merkaz Mis'hari, the new Commercial Center in west Jerusalem, was assaulted by a mob. Shoppers were injured and the stores set on fire. At the Gymnasia we watched pillars of smoke billowing as the principal gathered us and explained that we had to go home. (Hurrah, thought I. No Arabic exam tomorrow!) Later that day I found out that a Berman Bakery truck was burnt on Mamilla Street. The driver managed to escape and he hid until re-enforcements arrived and rescued him. The first stage of the Arab-Israeli war—known in Hebrew as *Milhemet*

Haatzmaut, The War of Independence, and as *al-Nakba* in Arabic, The Disaster—had begun. The second stage came with the invasion of armed forces from five neighboring countries after May 14, 1948, and lasted until January 7, 1949, with two periods of "truce" during which skirmishes continued nevertheless.

Soon after the United Nations' vote, two Arab armies of irregular volunteers entered the scene. The Arab League's Military Committee, operating from Damascus, helped arm and train volunteers who became known as the Arab Liberation Army. Led by Fawzi al-Kaukji, it consisted mainly of Syrians, Lebanese, Iraqis, Transjordanians, and Muslim Brothers from Egypt—an estimated six thousand men—who infiltrated the Galilee through Syria. Then the Army of the Holy War, led by Abd al-Qadir al-Husseini—nephew of the Mufti Haj Amin—arrived from Egypt with several hundred men, later joined by local volunteers. The Liberation Army operated in the north, while al-Husseini's men began the blockade of the road from Tel Aviv to Jerusalem.

All this happened before the British Mandate was to end on May 14, 1948. While the official position of the British government in London was to be impartial in the conflict, in reality there were contradictions and confusion. The British were in a difficult position. They resented their country's tarnished image because of its stand against the immigration of Jewish refugees, and were incensed by the actions of the Jewish underground organizations. And as always, the need for oil meant not provoking the Arab world. Many Jews felt that while the British rarely reacted to Arab acts of sabotage, they continued to confiscate weapons, conduct searches, and impose curfews on the Jewish population. (It should be added that Arabs sometimes accused the British of being pro-Zionist.) There were seventy-five thousand British soldiers in Palestine but at that point all they wanted was to get out of the country. As May 14 approached, they withdrew into their security zones and did not do much to stop the conflict.

While the situation of some three hundred Jewish settlements spread across the land was grave, Jerusalem presented an even worse problem. The city consisted of interspersed Arab and Jewish neighborhoods, the latter further isolated by the British security zones. In addition to the railroad that passed through Arab villages, there were four major roads that led to the city, from Hebron, Jericho, and Ramallah—roads controlled by Arabs—and from Latrun in the west, the main road over which food supplies arrived for the Jewish population. It was crucial to keep the Latrun road open but the topography made it difficult. As the road leaves the coastal plain and begins to climb up the Judean hills, it first goes through Bab al-Wad, the Gate to the Valley, a narrow passage between tree-covered slopes. There the Arabs set ambushes and attacked the convoys trying to reach the isolated city. The Hagana "armored" trucks with sheet metal and plywood in an attempt to make them bulletproof, but in the end the vehicles could not withstand the barrages from the hills, the road barriers, and the mines. By late March most of the cars used in the convoys were beyond repair and too many men had been killed, so no more food entered the Jewish part of the city. The Hagana then organized Operation Nahshon, named for the biblical hero in Exodus who was the first to jump into the Red Sea before God parted the waters. Some fifteen hundred fighters were recruited from all over the country, as were trucks and drivers, and they broke through to Jerusalem. They managed to hold the road for two weeks in April and bring enough food to the city to last for two months. The last convoy arrived on April 20, barely making it through Bab al-Wad. It brought *matzot*, eggs, and other supplies for Passover.

During those two weeks, in the brutal battle for the Kastel, the mountain dominating a crucial stretch of the road, al-Husseini, the commander of the Army of the Holy War, was killed which was a severe blow to the Arab side. On April 9, just as Hagana forces were trying to recapture the Kastel, about 120 Irgun and Lehi men attacked Deir Yassin, a village between Jerusalem and the Kastel. Each side in the battle tells a different

The last supply convoy reaches the outskirts of Jerusalem after the siege had been temporarily broken before the festival of Passover, April 1948.
Courtesy of *The Jerusalem Post*

story, but clearly crimes were committed by the underground organizations, even if not pre-planned: women, children, as well as men taken prisoner were killed. The numbers vary from 100 to 120, according to the Israelis, about 250, according to the Arabs and the British. The Arab media all over the Middle East continued to broadcast descriptions of the massacre which, rather than strengthening the resolve to oppose the Jews, had the opposite effect of lowering morale, spreading fear, and causing flight from Arab towns and villages.[38]

While the battle for the control of the Latrun road was raging, other conflicts were taking place within the city. Since the United Nations' resolution, hardly a day passed by without violence—shooting, sniping, stabbing—and the situation only got worse. In recounting the following events, I would like the reader to get an idea of how small the city was, and how—like me—each person living there knew someone who was killed or maimed during the struggle. On February 1, 1948, a stolen police car was parked in front of the offices of *The Palestine Post*, the country's English-language daily. Minutes later half a ton of dynamite went off, killing three people and injuring many more. The building was heavily damaged but the staff worked through the night and the paper came out the next morning in a reduced format, printed in a nearby small press. My uncle Keith, a sports writer for *The Post*, was luckily out of the office when the explosion happened. The building abutted the garden of my Brown grandparents but other than shock and broken windows, they too escaped unharmed. On February 22, some renegade British soldiers left three lorries packed with explosives on Ben-Yehuda Street, in the heart of Jewish Jerusalem. The early morning explosion killed fifty-eight people, among them my classmate Yehoshua Optovsky and his parents. On March 11, an Arab driver in a car believed to have been stolen from

Ben-Yehuda Street bombings
Courtesy of *The Jerusalem Post*

the United States consulate left the vehicle filled with explosives in front of the Jewish Agency building, a block away from the Gymnasia. The blast killed twelve people; one was the mother of a girl in my class.

The sister of another classmate was killed a month later along with eighty others, when a convoy carrying doctors and supplies to the Hadassah Hospital on Mount Scopus was attacked, and shortly thereafter the younger brother of yet another classmate died when the street where the family lived was showered with shells. Yisrael Horn, one of the Gymnasia's teachers, fell in battle, as did our schoolmate Ami Aricha, age seventeen. Ami was the commander of the paramilitary program run at the school at the request of the Hagana. As I wrote elsewhere: "Our beloved Ami managed to convince us that—for the good of the country—we had to learn to jump off the school's second-story roof unto a tarp held by our friends. And we did."

My reaction to each incident was a mixture of anger—"How could they do this to us"—and sadness, pity, for the ones who died and for those they left behind. (I could not imagine what it would be like to lose one's mother.) But not fear, perhaps because teenagers cannot envision their own death. I had no doubt that our side would win. In his magisterial autobiography, *A Tale of Love and Darkness*, the author Amos Oz describes a different mood, as a fear of annihilation gripped his family and their coterie in Kerem Avraham, a neighborhood a couple of miles away from our house. I did not sense the same apprehension in my family, probably because—with the exception of my aunt Lily's family—we had no relatives who died in the Holocaust. Of course we knew about anti-Semitism but we did not experience firsthand the humiliation suffered by Jews in Europe, the pogroms, massacres, or the Final Solution. We worried about the fate of Jerusalem and the rest of the Yishuv, and were aware of the threat of danger and death. But the possibility of annihilation was never mentioned.

An early blow to the whole Yishuv was the death of the Lamed-Hey, the thirty-five young men who, as mentioned before, were killed on

On an overnight hike, part of the Gymnasia's paramilitary program, 1947

January 15 on their way to Gush Etzion, and whose bodies Hamish Dougan brought to burial. Six of those killed, including Danny Mas, the group's commander, had been students at the Gymnasia. Altogether the school lost fifty-five students in the War of Independence, including Amnon Berman, my second cousin.

Whenever I think of Amnon, the words "golden youth" come to my mind. Born in Jerusalem in 1926, he was tall, handsome, with blue eyes and dark blond curls, a smart and kind person. He joined the Palmach, the fighting arm of the Hagana, during his last year at the Gymnasia. In September of 1947, following several skirmishes with British soldiers whom he barely managed to escape, and after warnings from Hamish that the CID was keeping an eye on him, Amnon left for the United States to study industrial engineering at Syracuse University. When he heard of the death of the Lamed-Hey—several of whom were his and his sister Aviva's friends—he left school and enrolled in a pilot-training program in Bakersfield, California. After 150 hours in the air, he returned to Israel on May 15, 1948, and began to fly missions to besieged settlements in the Negev, bringing provisions, mail, and arms. On July 7, 1948, he picked up a nurse from Revivim who needed an appendectomy. On the return flight the plane crashed as it neared the airport at Nir Am, near Gaza. It burst into flames and neither Amnon nor the nurse survived.

❦

By December of 1947, the outskirts of the city were deemed unsafe for Jews and my uncle Moshe, his wife Cecile, their daughters Michal and Liora, and the two-month-old Oded, moved from Talpiot to a small apartment in the building our family owned on what is now Straus Street. At the same time, my aunt Haya—who was eight months pregnant—and Keith moved from their place in Baq'aa to my grandparents' house where the ground floor with its thick stone walls was relatively safe, especially after flour sacks from the bakery were used to block the windows. At that point my mother and I—having only returned to the second floor apartment a year or so after World War II ended—moved back downstairs as well. On January 15, 1948, Haya gave birth to Roni, and the first floor became even more crowded, but it was a delight to have a baby in the family, a red-headed, feisty little boy, who was extremely spoiled what with so many adults hanging around, stuck indoors because it was too dangerous to go out. Every time Roni made a peep, someone would rush in and pick him up, and he was passed around from one family member to another, cooed over and admired.

The siege and the shelling continued. Next door to us, beneath a residential compound, was a winery owned by the Wiedman family. The office was on street level and behind it were several storage rooms. Underneath was a large cellar where wine aged in huge wooden vats. When the shelling intensified, many of our neighbors who lived in Batei Wittenberg, in rows of one-story townhouses, moved into the Wiedmans' cellar. They brought mattresses, blankets, and their rations of food and water, and settled in among the wine kegs, in overcrowded and unsanitary conditions.

The city was able to withstand the siege in part because of preparations made ahead of time. Shortages of food and kerosene were evident as early as December, when supply convoys were attacked and the British did not intervene. Several governing bodies within the Yishuv then got together and formed the Jerusalem Emergency Committee, headed by Dov Joseph who eventually became the city's military governor. His book, *The Faithful City: The Siege of Jerusalem, 1948*,[39] provides a detailed, firsthand account of events.

After the last convoy reached Jerusalem in mid-April, it was clear that no more food was going to get through. No one knew what would happen after May 14, when the British evacuation was to be completed, nor could anyone predict the outcome of the anticipated battle with the Arabs. "Would our supplies hold out, or would the city be forced to surrender through hunger?" wondered Joseph. A fair distribution system of the limited supplies was then established for the civilian population. Rationing books were issued with coupons required for water, foodstuffs, and kerosene.

Providing water to the city was problematic even in biblical times. In 701 BC, when King Hezekiah realized that Sennacherib "proposed to fight against Jerusalem," he "stopped the waters of Gihon and brought them straight down on the west side of the city of David." Hezekiah's foresight and the tunnel he ordered hewn saved Jerusalem and it withstood the Assyrian siege (2 Chronicles 32:2, 30). In December 1947, knowing that the Arabs could easily sabotage the pipeline which brought water from Rosh Haayin to Jerusalem, a special committee was formed to deal with the issue. The committee soon had all the cisterns in the city surveyed, repaired, filled, and sealed. Since the pipeline was installed by the British only in the mid-1930s, many houses in the city still had old cisterns where rainwater was collected. Our house, dating from the late 1880s, had such a cistern and Grandfather ordered it cleaned periodically, even though we rarely used its water (except for washing hair, which rain water was supposed to soften). Our cistern was sealed along with some eighteen hundred others all over the city. On May 9, 1948, the Arabs cut off the water supply and from then on, until August when a new pipeline was installed, water was rationed and distributed to each neighborhood twice a week by trucks—and later by horse or donkey-drawn carts—carrying large containers and manned by volunteers from Mishmar Haam. People stood in line with their buckets, pots, and pans to receive their quota which began as ten liters per person per day, about ten quarts, later reduced to six. The water was to suffice for drinking, cooking, bathing—that is sponge bathing—washing dishes, mopping floors, doing laundry, and flushing toilets. Frequently, while people stood in line, shelling started and everyone ran for shelter. Getting one's daily water ration was a dangerous endeavor. To help citizens cope with shortages, demonstrations were given at the Straus Health Center, right at the top of our street. There we learned how best to utilize the water we got and how to build outdoor stoves.

Fuel, like food, could no longer be delivered to the city. Private cars, taxis, and—after May 14—even buses stopped running. There was no fuel for home heating in the unusually cold winter of 1947-48. Kerosene for cooking was strictly rationed and citizens were encouraged to build campfires in their backyards, but soon there was no food left to cook. Loudspeakers were used to broadcast public announcements since the supply of electricity was cut down to a few irregular hours a week so radios were useless most of the time. The Emergency Committee also printed flyers with daily news since there were no newspapers, except for *The Palestine Post*, which was published in English. At night we read by the light of pre-Mandatory kerosene lamps rescued from the attic. Fuel was of course needed for baking bread. In the beginning of April, twenty-six bakeries were operating in the city; by the end of the month their number was cut down to five, including the Berman Bakery. By then only twenty-eight thousand loaves of bread were baked every day for a population of some hundred thousand, less than a third of a loaf per day when bread was the mainstay of the diet. The Emergency Committee calculated that the city would need forty-five hundred tons of food a month on a minimal basis, so before the Latrun road was closed, it tried to get as many provisions as possible, and store them in basements of schools, hospitals, and other large buildings. But for months there was no meat, poultry, or fish in the city, nor fresh fruits or vegetables, and no cigarettes. (Smokers said that the lack of tobacco presented the greatest hardship.) According to Joseph—who said that the backbone of the whole feeding program rested on the daily loaf—weekly quantities of food per person in June were about three-and-a-half ounces each of grouts, beans, coffee, and—for children only—powdered milk; two-and-a-half ounces of processed cheese and of margarine; and six ounces of bread a day. Those lucky enough to be sick received an egg or two. In the spring the population benefited from the ubiquitous *hubeiza* that was used in salads or turned into cutlets. (The word derives from the Arabic "bread" because of its breadlike fruit; in English it is bull mallow.)

By virtue of owning a bakery, our family fared better than most (as it did during World War I). Even my grandfather, exemplary law-abiding citizen though he was, closed his eyes to the fact that we brought home more bread than the ration coupons allowed. What he did not know was that Grandmother, accustomed to help any needy person who came to her house, could not turn away friends or neighbors who showed up begging for an extra piece of bread. As the siege continued and people ran out of whatever supplies they had in store, knocks on our backdoor increased. Grandmother began to wake me up at dawn, when Grandfather was still asleep, and we would sneak into the bakery and literally steal a couple of loaves of bread which she hid until Grandfather departed for the bakery and then, when someone came asking for bread, she would hand the person a slice or two. But man does not live by bread alone and I can still remember when we opened the last jar of jam, or the last tin of Australian cheese that Keith, while he was still with the Royal Air Force, purchased at the NAAFI—Britain's Navy, Army, and Air Force Institutes—which provided canteens and other facilities to servicemen and their families.

It is hard to describe the mood in the city where very little was going on except for the fighting and the shelling. Most people had no jobs, what with manufacturing and commerce at a standstill and most government offices barely functioning. It was too dangerous to venture outside. Schools were shut. All cafés and cinemas were closed, and at the few restaurants that were allowed to operate one had to use ration coupons. Stores were open for a few hours a day but stocks were very low. Yet there was no black market. People felt that the food rationing was fair and evenly distributed. We were isolated from the rest of the country, from the rest of the world, but we were united. Everyone in the city felt it was his or her war. The slogan was *ein brera*, "There is no choice." We had to hold on. There was no talk of surrender—with minor exceptions. Some ultra-Orthodox Jews, believing that only after the Messiah comes could there be a Jewish state, refused to serve in the army, and there was one incident in our area where the Military Police came in search of draft dodgers. They found the son of a neighbor of ours hiding in a bathroom.

It was a difficult time for the city's residents—suffering hunger, fearing the enemy, mourning casualties—yet whenever I think about the siege one of the first things that comes to my mind is Mitzi's disappearance. My poor cat really suffered when food became scarce and all I could offer him was bread soaked in water. At first he refused to eat it but eventually gave in to hunger. One Friday afternoon, after weeks of siege, Grandmother opened the last can of sardines for the Sabbath meal. She left it by a window to keep cool, the refrigerator being idle for lack of electricity. Mitzi, who had never stolen food before, demolished the content of the tin and ran away. After a few days, when he did not return, we were convinced that a shell killed him. I grieved in silence. Visiting a classmate who was wounded by shrapnel a few days earlier and seeing the agony of the other patients, crowded into a ward of a nineteenth-century hospital short of painkillers and other medical supplies, made the loss of a cat seem less important. Then one night Mitzi reappeared. He sat outside, on the sill of a kitchen window, until Grandmother noticed him.

She opened the window to let him in but he would not enter the house. He accepted some food when she brought it outside and then ran off, never to be seen again.

On Friday morning, May 14, 1948, General Sir Alan Cunningham, the last High Commissioner to Palestine, left Jerusalem along with the rest of the British civilians, police, and troops under his administration. The Mandatory authorities had made few arrangements for an orderly transition of power to Arab and Jewish future regimes. So badly organized was their withdrawal that tons of equipment had to be destroyed, as Edward Horne, who served with the Palestine Police, wrote: "As for the dumping, the sea some two miles out of Haifa received hundreds of tons of transport and equipment into its bosom." And dozens of armored cars were driven off a cliff near Mount Carmel and then set on fire.[40] No wonder the withdrawal became known as "Operation Chaos."

In Tel Aviv at four o'clock that very afternoon, on the eve of the Sabbath, David Ben-Gurion declared the establishment of the State of Israel. He read the Declaration of Independence at the Tel Aviv Museum, with the portrait of Theodor Herzl, the father of Zionism, behind him. The audience was small, invited to the ceremony only that morning for fear that at the last minute the British authorities might try to stop the ceremony, or that the Arabs would sabotage it. The text of the Declaration had been approved by Moetzet Haam, the People's Council, a temporary body representing all the parties in the Yishuv, established in April in preparation for independence. As Ben-Gurion banged his gavel on the table to open the ceremony, the audience spontaneously burst into *Hatikva*, the song that was to become Israel's national anthem. It took sixteen minutes to read the declaration of the birth of a new country, to be known as the State of Israel. Among other things the Declaration appealed to the country's Arab inhabitants "to preserve peace and participate in the upbuilding of the State on the basis of full and equal citizenship . . . " The new state extended its hand "to all neighboring states and their peoples in an offer of peace ... " When Ben-Gurion finished reading the audience sang *Hatikva* once again. An interesting aside is that when the text was under debate, the words "God of Israel" were not included. Instead, "Rock of Israel" was used, meaning either God or the Land of Israel, which, as Ben-Gurion suggested, each person could interpret in his own way. The event was broadcast on the new radio station, Kol Israel, "The Voice of Israel."

We did not hear the broadcast in Jerusalem since there was no electricity and radios were silent. In fact, when late that night rumors began to spread that a state was born, most Jerusalemites could not believe it. The morale in the city was low. We had suffered from cold, hunger, acts of sabotage, and the continual sound of gunfire and mortars. The Jewish Quarter in the Old City was cut off from west Jerusalem. And, after five months of siege, Kfar Etzion fell, one of the four kibbutzim that the Lamed-Hey—and many others—went to aid and instead met their death. The news was particularly grim because the commander of Kfar Etzion wanted to evacuate the area but was told by the Hagana in Jerusalem to remain in place since the kibbutzim constituted the only Jewish outpost on the road from Hebron in the south to the capital. On May 12, Arab irregular forces, joined by the Jordanian Arab Legion, attacked Kfar Etzion with artillery fire and armored cars. On the next day the defenders, who had no ammunition left, decided to surrender: they waved white flags and laid down their arms. At that point they were assaulted with submachine guns and grenades. Over a hundred men and women were massacred. According to the few who escaped, the Arabs were shouting "Deir Yassin"—the name of the village attacked by the Irgun and Lehi during the battle for the Kastel, where so many civilians were killed. Next day, May 14, the day the State of Israel was born, the three remaining kibbutzim surrendered—this time in the presence of the International Red Cross—and the survivors were taken to prison camps in Transjordan.

The Arab Legion was formed and financed by the British in the 1920s in order to keep tribes in Transjordan from fighting each other. In 1939, John Bagot Glubb became its commander and it was under his leadership that the Legion became a well-trained and well-equipped army. It entered the Arab-Israeli war even before the official end of the Mandate, and invaded in full force after May 14, under the command of "Glubb Pasha"—as he became known—and other British officers. In addition to the conflict in Gush Etzion, the Legion participated in the siege and the shelling of Jerusalem, and in the battles around Latrun for control of the road to the capital. Once the British left, additional armed forces, from Syria, Lebanon, Iraq, and Egypt moved across borders and joined the various fronts. The second stage of the Arab-Israeli war had begun.

During the month of May there were good and bad developments. The areas of Katamon, the German Colony, and the Greek Colony—on the southwestern edge of the new city—came under Jewish control even before the British departure. And on May 14, Hagana and Irgun forces captured "Bevingrad," the administrative center of the city, including Notre Dame de France, just across the street from the New Gate in the Old City wall. The Israelis also captured most of the other British security zones in west Jerusalem. But several attempts to reach the Jewish Quarter failed, although the Hagana managed to get some supplies and soldiers in there on May 18. That night the Arab Legion entered the Old City and the Quarter was attacked with mortars, hand grenades, and other explosives. By the next day the whole area between the Armenian Quarter and Habad Street was lost, almost half of the Quarter. Tiferet Israel, the great synagogue of the Hasidim, was taken by the Arabs and destroyed; two days later the same fate befell the Hurva, the synagogue where my great-grandfather Todres Berman used to pray. The majority of the Quarter's residents—under two thousand Jews, many old and frail, mostly Orthodox—had wanted to surrender, having lost faith in promises that help was coming since previous attempts to reach the Quarter and to parachute supplies there by air had failed. But the soldiers refused to give in and continued to fight over each house along the narrow alleys, while sending desperate messages to the Hagana Headquarters in the new city, requesting immediate reinforcements. Then, on the morning of May 28, two rabbis representing the inhabitants of the Quarter marched out of Zion Gate carrying a white flag—a sheet tied to two poles—to begin negotiating terms of surrender. In the end, 340 men between the ages of fifteen and fifty, including forty soldiers and some fifty lightly wounded men, were taken to Amman as prisoners of war, while the rest of the residents left through Zion Gate for west Jerusalem, walking between two lines of Arab Legionnaires who, to their credit, protected the Jews from local Arab mobs calling for revenge. The wounded were evacuated the next day.

The population of Jerusalem had become almost immune to the sound of mortar fire and machine guns. Concrete walls were erected along King George Street and in other strategic spots to shield pedestrians from snipers and we all learned to walk clinging to buildings, running into shelters when shooting resumed. But in April, just around Passover, the Arabs began using canons to bombard the Jewish neighborhoods. And after May 14, once the Arab Legion joined the fighting, explosions went off every couple of minutes, making it even more dangerous to step outside and difficult to sleep. It was estimated that some ten thousand shells fell on west Jerusalem in the first month after the arrival of the Legion. The constant shelling went on for weeks, until the first ceasefire, which began on June 11.

It was during the heavy shelling that my mother and my uncle Keith, her brother-in-law, had a bad fight. We had all been cooped up for weeks, with not enough to do, waiting for the next explosion. The frontline was a few blocks away from our house and everyone's nerves were frayed. There were rumors that our area was being heavily bombarded in the hope of damaging the bakery and disrupting the city's food supply. In fact, while phones were still working, Arabs sometimes called the bakery

Jordanian artillery bombarding west Jerusalem, 1948
Courtesy of Yad Yitzhak Ben-Zvi Photo Archives

at night to say that they will not leave one stone on top of the other in the Berman *furnus*, the bakery. My mother was always a bad sleeper and the constant noise was no help, so she kept a kerosene lamp burning on her night table so she could read. Our windows were all stuffed with bags of flour, and draped in heavy curtains because of the blackout. But Keith was convinced that some light was escaping, guiding the enemy's firepower toward our house. He stepped into our bedroom one night, and demanded that Mother put out the light. Not one to obey orders, she immediately refused and a shouting match ensued, the only time I remember people actually screaming at each other in the house. The rest of the family soon marched in and calmed down the combatants. Mother resumed her reading.

One of the most disheartening things about the shelling was that the Jewish side felt helpless because it lacked heavy artillery. Then David Leibovitch, an engineer, invented a homemade mortar, with shells filled with nails and metal scraps that created a tremendous noise upon explosion. Since the mortar was very light it was rushed from one frontline in Jerusalem to another, and the Arabs thought there were many of them. That, coupled with the noise the "Davidka" made and rumors that it was an atomic weapon, brought fear to the Arab side and raised the morale of the Jews.[41]

One day in early June my uncle David walked into our house and announced that there was only enough flour in the city to last for three days. The city was in danger of starvation. What we did not know was that the supply of ammunition was very low as well. And then, a miracle happened: a new road opened, the "Burma Road," named after the supply route built by the British during World War II. While the Israelis failed in their attempts to dislodge the Arab Legion from Latrun—the fort that controlled a vital section of the road between Tel Aviv and Jerusalem—on May 28 they managed to conquer several villages south of the fort, opening a narrow corridor between the coastal plain and the capital, bypassing Latrun. Using jeeps, the Israelis explored the footpaths connecting the villages and immediately decided to build a road there. But because of the dire shortages in the city, Jerusalem could not wait even for a few days. So while bulldozers were flattening the terrain, mules were used to transport supplies over part of the unpaved road. Then, over a three-mile section that even animals could not navigate, some two hundred men volunteered to each carry forty-five-pound sacks of flour over the last miles to Jerusalem. On June 5, workers started to surface the road and five days later it could accommodate civilian trucks. The siege was broken!

When the British Mandate came to an end, on May 14, 1948, the United Nations General Assembly appointed Count Folke Bernadotte, former head of the Swedish Red Cross, as a special mediator for Palestine. A week later the United Nations called for an immediate truce between the

My uncle David distributing bread during the period of martial law, 1946-1947
Courtesy of Keren Hayseod-UIA, Jerusalem

combatants. The Arab regimes turned down the demand, afraid to admit to their people that the victories they had promised had not materialized. But Bernadotte kept pushing and finally all sides agreed to a ceasefire that was to last from June 11 to July 8. On the night before the truce went into effect, it seemed to us in Jerusalem as if the Legionnaires were trying to exhaust their supply of shells in the heaviest bombardment of the city to date.

The quiet after the shelling stopped was eerie. At night I lay in bed unable to fall asleep, waiting for the next outburst. But the truce held and soon we were back in school. Electric lines were repaired and the blackout was lifted. A few cafés opened, and cinemas! Postal services were resumed, having stopped in late April, and suddenly we were in touch with the rest of the country, by mail, telephone, and telegraph. While the truce was in effect, I would meet two of my classmates in the afternoons, Ruth King and Alyssa Sperber, and together we would roam around the

"Triangle," formed by three of the city's main streets, Jaffa, Ben-Yehuda, and King George. Jerusalem was full of young soldiers and, for a trio of fourteen-year-old girls, it was a pleasant change to think about matters other than war. Amidst all those positive developments, we also had a chance to see the destruction brought on by the shelling.

On June 19, two convoys with one hundred forty trucks arrived in Jerusalem with food and ammunition. Two days later, each resident got one tomato, one cucumber, one green pepper, two onions, half a carrot, and some string beans. Eggs—one a day—were also added to the diet, and an occasional piece of fish. Bread portions were enlarged slightly and once in a while we got fresh fruit. There was still no running water in the city until a new pipeline was laid in August.

A tragic event took place on the shores of Tel Aviv during the truce, the sinking of the *Altalena*. The ship, on its way from France to Israel, was carrying over nine hudred immigrants and Irgun members, in addition to rifles, machine guns, and other ammunition purchased by the Irgun. Menahem Begin, leader of the underground organization, wanted the weapons to go to the Irgun battalions which were formed as separate units when, at the end of May, the Provisional Government issued an ordinance creating the Israel Defense Forces that were to include members of the Hagana, Irgun, and Lehi undergrounds. The Government objected to Begin's demand and wanted the *Altalena* and the arms placed under its command. Begin refused and, on June 20, the ship headed for Kfar Vitkin, north of Tel Aviv. Some of the passengers and ammunition were unloaded there, but soldiers were sent to stop them and in the ensuing fight a number of people were killed. The *Altalena* managed to escape and head for Tel Aviv while the Government issued an ultimatum demanding that the ship surrender along with the remaining weapons. Begin ignored the ultimatum and, at four in the afternoon, Ben-Gurion ordered the ship shelled. One shell hit the *Altalena* and it started to burn. Fearing an explosion, those remaining on the ship jumped into the water and swam to shore. The ship sunk, arms were lost, and, altogether, eighteen men died in what became known as "The *Altalena* Affair." At the time it seemed so terrible that when the country was still at war with its Arab neighbors, Jew was killing Jew. The justification was that a country could not have two separate armies, but the event only increased the resentment between the right and the left.

On July 8 the ceasefire was over since the Arabs turned down Bernadotte's efforts to prolong it. The Israelis had used the four weeks of truce to reorganize. Jerusalem was in a slightly better position, even though it was still surrounded by Arab forces, because there was a little more food in the city, more arms, and the Burma Road remained open. The renewed fighting lasted for ten days; the Israelis gained territory and the Arabs suffered heavy casualties. Under threats of sanctions from the United Nations, a second ceasefire went into effect on July 18. It was meant to last until some peace agreements could be reached.

In Jerusalem during the following months there was frequent gunfire—usually started by the Arabs with the Israelis reacting—and occasional shelling. Still, citizens began to go back to work and life was a bit easier. Somehow, my mother managed to get me a ride to Tel Aviv, in a truck which went over the Burma Road, and I spent a couple of weeks staying with Rosa Kolczycki, my aunt Lily's mother. Every morning I went to the beach, where I soon acquired an admirer who taught me how to ride on a *hasakeh*, a water sport similar to what some six decades later is becoming popular in the United States as stand-up waterboarding. The whole Tel Aviv experience was like being in a foreign country. There was no shooting, there was plenty of food and running water, people were sitting in outdoor cafés at night, and there was no evidence of destruction.

Israel's political situation was difficult during the second ceasefire. At the end of June Count Bernadotte, eager to bring about a peace settlement, declared that the United Nation's 1947 partition resolution had been "unfortunate" and came up with his own plan. Instead of two states, he suggested two independent members in a "union." Israel would keep

On the beach in Tel Aviv during the second cease fire, 1948

the coastal plain and part of the Galilee. The Arab territory—which was to include the West Bank, the Negev, and Jerusalem—would become part of Transjordan. Once the union was formed, there would be open Jewish immigration for two years, after which the United Nations would decide on the union's capacity to absorb more people. All Arab Palestinian refugees would be allowed to come back to their homes. The Arab leaders rejected the plan, including Transjordan's King Abddullah—even though he had the most to gain—because he could not go against the other statesmen. The Israelis rejected it as well: they could not accept giving up Jerusalem to the Arabs, after what the Jewish population there had gone through, nor the loss of the Negev, or the possible limit on Jewish immigration. And, as Benny Morris put it regarding the Arab refugees: "Without doubt the pan-Arab invasion of 15 May hardened the Israelis hearts toward the refugees. The onslaught of the armies, which threatened to destroy the Yishuv, left the Israelis with little room for errors or humanitarian misgivings."[42]

In September Bernadotte spent time on the island of Rhodes meeting with British and American representatives to work on another plan which proposed that Israel would get all the Galilee and the coastal plain, Jordan would still get the West Bank and the Negev, but Jerusalem would become an international city, administered by the United Nations. The notion of limiting Jewish immigration was abandoned. The Palestinian refugees would have the right of return. On September 17, as soon as the plan was submitted to the United Nations, Bernadotte left Rhodes for Jerusalem where, that very afternoon, members of Lehi, the Stern Gang, assassinated him. The murder shocked the world and embarrassed the Israeli government, putting it in an awkward position. At the United Nations, debate about the plan was postponed. Meanwhile, both the Israelis and the Arabs refused to accept it.

The state of no war and no peace, with continuous skirmishes, was very problematic for Israel. With foreign troops in the Galilee, the Negev, around Jerusalem, and elsewhere, the country could not risk reducing the number of men in the army, which at that point included most of the adult males of military-service age, and that played havoc with the economy. The Israelis worried that the West Bank and the Negev might become part of Jordan, and were tired of having to supply settlements in the Negev by air, since most of them were still surrounded by Egyptian troops. They were eager to attack the Egyptians but not wanting to be seen as the aggressors, they were looking for an excuse. It came when the Egyptians fired shots at a convoy on its way to bring supplies to settlements in the northern Negev, a procedure that was agreed upon in the July 18 ceasefire. The Israelis shot back and the Egyptians then sent planes to attack Israeli positions. The Israelis were well prepared and in the battle that followed they conquered Be'er Sheva and broke through to enclaves of settlements that were isolated since the beginning of the war. Another ceasefire was imposed by the United Nations on October 22, but both sides ignored it. At the end of October the Arab Liberation Army was pushed out of the Galilee, and in December, in another battle with the Egyptians, the Israelis freed most of the western Negev except for the Gaza strip. The last major operation of the war took place in March 1949, when the Israelis captured Eilat, at the very southern tip of the Negev, on the Gulf of Aqaba.

Finally, in the spring of 1949, armistice agreements were signed with Egypt, Lebanon, and Jordan, and then, in July, with Syria. Iraq, which does not share a border with Israel, withdrew its forces from the area in March. The agreements were supposed to be temporary, until peace agreements were signed. It was a very long wait. To date only two of the five countries at war with Israel have done so: Egypt on March 26, 1979, and Jordan, on October 26, 1994. The issue of a Palestinian state is still unresolved, complicated by Hamas being in control of Gaza and, as this book goes to press, by the as yet uncertain results of the Arab Spring.

The founding of the State of Israel was the most formative event in my life. In my early teens what was most important to me was not what I was wearing, not the gossip at school, flirting with boys, or any other worries of kids that age. What mattered was the conflict, the struggle for independence, dreaming about a state. Israel today is not the idealistic place it was in 1948, and the conflict with its neighbors is not over. In fact it is hard to believe that nearly sixty-five years later there is still no peace settlement between the Israelis and the Palestinians. The biblical injunction, "Pray for the peace of Jerusalem," is still relevant.

The End of a Chapter

Mother

On an early February morning in 1949 Mother noticed a lump in her left breast. Since she was going to play cards that night with her regular group, that included the surgeon Nahum Kook, she decided to ask his advice. Two days later she underwent a mastectomy.

I went to school as usual that day. When I came home I was told that Dr. Kook removed her breast, "just to be on the safe side," and that the operation went well. The hospital she was in—built in the 1890s by the London Society for the Promotion of Christianity Amongst the Jews— was terribly overcrowded, because of the loss of the Hadassah Hospital on Mount Scopus and the large number of civilians who were wounded during the siege. When I went to see her that afternoon, I hastily walked through a large ward, trying to ignore the sight of mangled bodies and the stench of rotting flesh. In one of the beds was a classmate of mine, injured by shrapnel, whom I had visited a few days earlier.

Mother was lying by herself in a small room looking very serene. She told me how successful the operation was. She came home a few days later, where Dr. Kook continued to treat her. On one of his visits he asked me to help him change her dressing. It was the first time that I saw the neatly sewn scar where her breast used to be and it was not as bad as I had expected. I soon realized that Dr. Kook did not need my help, but that he wanted me to face what had happened. Once the stitches were removed and the wound healed, another family friend entered the picture, a radiologist named Dr. Avraham Izmozhik. To save Mother the trouble of coming to his clinic for radiation, he brought a package with him—the size of an average book—which contained radium and which she applied to the site of her missing breast several times a week.

Mother seemed to be doing well. Soon she had some special bras made and tried to resume her old life. She slowly picked up her duties at home. She went out with friends. She looked well so she must be all right—I told myself—because I heard that people who had cancer lost weight rapidly. That summer, Miriam Brecher, my Grandfather's eldest grandchild, daughter of Meir, came from the States for a visit along with her two children, Ira and Lillian who were close to my age. They traveled all over the country and I joined them on most of their trips and enjoyed their company. They stayed at our house and their visit certainly improved my English conversation. Mother did not travel with us. Also that summer, my cousin Nurit was born to my aunt Haya and her husband Keith who were still living at our house, a red-headed and lively baby, just like her brother Roni.

Shortly after the Brechers left, Mother's situation worsened. The whole area of the breast turned into an open sore which would not heal, probably a radiation burn. More and more doctors were called for and often, when I came back from school, I was sent to the pharmacy with a new prescription. (We always used Moshe Bruchstein's pharmacy since he was married to one of Mother's cousins, even though there was another pharmacy much closer to our house. One always gave business to relatives.) The shortest way to the Bruchstein Pharmacy—which stood just off Zion Square—took me through Harav Kook Street where my Brown grandparents lived. A couple of times I ran into my father there, standing by the gate as if he knew I was coming. He would ask me in for

The End of a Chapter

a minute, glance at the prescription I was carrying, and shake his head.

After the siege, Haya and her family moved up to the second floor, while Mother and I stayed downstairs. Before her operation, Mother and I shared a bedroom on the first floor, in my grandparents' part of the house. When she came home I moved to the next room, to the "salon," so that I would not disturb her at night. Often, if I woke up and saw her light on, I would stick my head in to see if she needed anything only to find Grandfather sitting by her bed, holding her hand. The family kept reassuring me that she was just having some problems because of the radiation.

At some point, shortly after the High Holidays, a telegram arrived for Mother, a telegram from Hamish, from Kuala Lumpur. He told her he was due some leave, and would she meet him in Europe? Mother was ecstatic. "We will meet as soon as I am better!" she cabled back. What she did not know was that her siblings had somehow managed to contact Hamish in Malaya and had informed him of her illness. It brought Mother great pleasure to contemplate a trip to Europe and a meeting with Hamish. And even I, who had never wanted to see them married, was glad for her.

But she was not getting better. Soon nurses were brought in to stay with her around the clock. She was having difficulty breathing and an oxygen tank was delivered to the house. She seemed to be sleeping a lot. Then, one Saturday in late November, it struck me for the first time that she was dying. How could I have not recognized the symptoms before? How could I have ignored the hushed atmosphere around the house, the looks grownups gave each other, the doctors running in and out, the nurses, the smell? Denial, that's what it was. I did not want to know.

The next twenty-four hours passed in a thick fog. I sat by her side and held her hand and she smiled once or twice, in and out of consciousness. At one point she said "Baba Sarah will take care of you," so she knew it was the end. She died later that night, or rather early on Sunday morning, November 20, 1949. She was thirty-nine years old.

With my mother the summer before she died

The women who prepare bodies for burial—washing, wrapping in shrouds—must have come to the house, but I do not remember that. I do recall my uncle Moshe coming to my room and showing me the death notice he had written which was going to appear in the morning papers and asking me to walk with him to the offices of *The Palestine Post* to place the notice. In Jewish tradition a dead person has to be buried before

The End of a Chapter

the next sunset. Notices in newspapers and on billboards throughout the city informed friends and relatives of the sad event and gave details about the funeral.

Did I sleep that night? I am not sure. I just remember curling up on the sofa, which doubled as a bed, with my face to the wall, angry with my mother for leaving me, wishing I were dead. Next, as morning came and the family gathered for the funeral, I can still see Zahava the Great coming over and putting her arms around me. She said something to the effect of how sad it was and somehow I had the presence of mind to realize that her tragedy was greater. "Yes," I said, "but children bury their parents. You had to bury Amnon." While we stood there weeping, Haya Davis walked in—my mother's first cousin and Zahava's sister-in-law—wearing a necklace of large black beads and matching earrings. It was an astonishing sight in those days: who ever heard of funereal jewelry? Zahava and I looked at each other, smiled at Haya's eccentricities, and stopped crying.

Then I saw the street in front of our house, black with people from the crest of the hill down to the house. My teachers and my classmates were there and two boys from the class above mine, Avraham Weinberg and Haim Kaminitz, rivals for my affection. The funeral procession stopped for a minute in front of Grandfather's synagogue. Next, we were at the cemetery, a few miles away so we must have gone there by car. Who sat next to me? What was I wearing? Where were my grandparents? My mind is blank.

Only a couple of hundred people are buried at the Givat Ram Cemetery which was used temporarily in the late 1940s after the ancient cemetery on the Mount of Olives fell into Arab hands and before the ceasefire with Jordan which made more suitable burial sites safe from snipers who used to shoot at mourners during funerals. The city eventually grew around the cemetery. Today, looming above it are the Knesset and the Supreme Court with the Israel Museum a stone's throw away. Below it is Sacher Park.

From that day long ago I remember the voice of the *hazan* chanting prayers and the irritating sound of the alms boxes jingled by members of the burial society: *Tzdaka tazil mi'mavet*, they cried, "Charity saves from death." I was told that my father came over and stood by my side, but when he tried to hug me I pushed him away. That is one more episode I am blocking. But I can still see my mother's body, wrapped in white, without a coffin, slowly lowered into the freshly dug grave.

Nothing would be the same after that day. Oh, one continued to live, to eat, even laugh. And I was lucky to stay in the same house where I grew up, with my grandparents, and with Haya and her family who were now living in Mother's apartment where I soon joined them. My parents' old living room, the nicest room in the apartment, became my bedroom. We all ate downstairs, at Grandmother's table, the same as always. But for decades after Leah's death whenever I saw a mother and daughter doing something together—shopping, talking, walking down the street—I was on the verge of tears, envious, although that is not my nature. For years I cried into the soup as I got ready for Passover—my favorite holiday—because Mother was not there. She never knew her grandchildren and they missed so much by not knowing her. "You will have five children," she used to tell me when I became interested in boys. "And I will stay with them whenever you want me to so that you can travel around the world with your husband."

When we got back to the house after the funeral, it was full of neighbors who had brought food for the family. The week of mourning, the *Shiva*, passed very quickly as people stopped by the house from morning to night, family, friends, business acquaintances, the workers from the bakery, various dignitaries. We—the immediate family—sat on low stools, as tradition prescribes: Grandmother, Grandfather, Zalman, Moshe, Avraham, Haya, David, and I. At one point I tried to write to Hamish to tell him what happened—I did not know that he had already

The End of a Chapter

been informed by one of my uncles—but Grandfather told me that one does not write letters during *Shiva*. I remember reading a book about a Russian pilot who lost his legs during World War II yet learned to fly again. I cannot recall who gave it to me, perhaps with the idea that it would show me that one can overcome almost all difficulties, but it was not a good choice. The *Shiva* has a numbing effect as one is exhausted at the end of each day, and it has a curative effect, as you spend a week talking about the person you lost. During the *Shiva* I found out that Dr. Kook informed the family right after the operation that the cancer had metastasized and that there was little chance Leah would survive for long. They did not tell me about it, they said, because they did not want my mother to find out what the situation was and assumed that I would not have been able to conceal the truth from her. Were they right? It gave me, and perhaps Leah as well, several months of hope, but no chance to say goodbye.

I went back to school after the *Shiva* and daily life continued. Avraham Weinberg was very nice to me in the months that followed, waiting for me every morning at the top of our street so that we could walk or take the bus to school together. We were kind of dating. My cousin Izzy was also there. Soon after Mother's death Haya's children came down with the measles and so did I. They recovered in a couple of days while I felt at death's door with spots in my eyes, mouth, and throat. I could not eat. I could not bear any light in the room. I could not read. At night, Haya told me, when I had high fever, I used to ask for my mother. Izzy came to see me every day after school, and together we listened to Radio Amman across the border playing popular American songs.

When I needed new shoes I checked with Grandmother whether I should ask one of my aunts to go shopping with me. "No," she said. "Any one of them will be glad to do so but it would be better if you learned to do things by yourself." And she gave me money for the purchase. I hasten to add that my aunts and uncles hovered over me like mother hens. I felt like I had four pairs of parents and that entailed both pluses and minuses.

For example, my uncles dragged my old grandparents to court to declare that I was Leah's only heir and that they had no right to any of her property, which by law they were entitled to. This was done to protect me so that in later years no descendent of my grandparents would have any claim on my inheritance. Then my uncles had Grandfather change his will to be sure that one day I would receive the same share of his property as all his other children, that is, what would have been my mother's share. When Moshe and Cecile moved to Tel Aviv, where Moshe's job took him, I used to spend summer vacations with them so I could go to the beach and I felt completely at home there. For the rest of their lives my mother's siblings all treated me as if I were one of their own children. The down side of having so many people watching over me was too much advice. "Darling, what beautiful shoes you bought," said one aunt. "Nitza, how could you buy red shoes with such high heels. It makes you look like a street walker," said another.

In the meantime, my father and his wife left for Teheran where he ran a hospital for Displaced Persons under the auspices of the Jewish Joint Distribution Committee. They had a son, Ben, whom I have never met. The family later moved to Canada and then to San Francisco where my father taught pathology at the University of California's Medical School and where he died in 2001, at age ninety-five. I saw him only once after Mother died, in New York just before my wedding in 1956. But that is another story.

Hamish Dougan

And what happened to Hamish? In July of 1965 I arrived in Israel with my three young children. We were met at Lod airport by most of the Berman clan—aunts, uncles, cousins—and to my great surprise, Hamish. It was a chaotic scene, not conducive to a serious conversation and, since I was most anxious to talk to Hamish, we agreed to meet a few days later. But the meeting never took place. Instead, a letter arrived. Hamish wrote that he came to the airport to see me to make sure I was all right, because otherwise he would have wanted to help. But when he saw that all was well in my life, he could not bear the thought that Leah was not there. He never married, he added, because he could not find anyone like my mother. Hamish stayed in touch with Avraham and Zahava but I did not see him or hear from him again. Then, in 1971, my aunt and uncle found out that he had died at sea.

When I began writing this book, I wanted to get more information about Hamish. A friend in London told me about the Palestine Police Old Comrades' Association and gave me the address. I wrote and asked whether there were any files left where I might find some details about Hamish's life. But it seems that in the early spring of 1948, when the Criminal Investigation Department in Jerusalem was told to pack up shop, there was nothing for the CID to do but to destroy the files. "The whole memory system was consigned to the flames."[43] My query, however, was printed in the PPOCA newsletter and I received several replies from former policemen who had known Hamish in Jerusalem. One came from John H. Foster, General Secretary of the PPOCA who wrote, in September, 2001: "I knew Hamish Dougan whilst serving in Criminal Investigation Department's Headquarters in Jerusalem during the mid-1940s. We shared the same 'billet' in the Russian Compound and although I was one of a foursome (including Hamish) who played bridge regularly I must admit that I, like so many others, never really got to know Hamish particularly well. He always seemed rather secretive and reluctant to take part in any serious conversation about his work and where he was going." Others wrote that he was a great wit who "enjoyed a good dram o'Scotch," but when it came to discussing his job, his "mysterious lips [were] sealed."

The most detailed reply came from A. T. Ternent, "former British sergeant 2405 Palestine Police," whom I had mentioned before. Putting to good use his training as a policeman, Alex Ternent contacted the Church of the Sacred Heart on Lauristan Street in Edinburgh, where funeral services were held for Hamish in 1971, and where, thirty-one years later, the Dougans, who used to live practically next door, were still remembered. The secretary of the church located William Dougan, the only survivor among Hamish's eight siblings, and sent him Alex's letter. The following information is based on William's letters to Alex, and eventually a letter to me (an answer to my own to him), plus clippings from PPOCA newsletters that Alex forwarded to me. And then, out of the blue, when the book was in the final editing stages, I got an e-mail from Maurice Dougan who identified himself as a nephew of Hamish—"John" to the family; he got my address from his uncle William, with whom I was last in touch nine years earlier. Maurice was trying to gather information about Hamish, his "Uncle Johnny," so we exchanged notes and I learned some interesting facts about Hamish's early life.

Whenever Hamish was in Edinburgh, he used to play with Maurice. He taught Maurice how to get the better of his opponent when playing rugby, and how to defend himself if attacked by someone with a knife. Maurice told me that Hamish grew up in a flat where the living room had a sink and a hearth, two bedrooms with large cupboards that could be used for extra sleeping quarters (known as box rooms). There was a toilet but no bath and one washed in a tin tub. Hamish went to primary school at St. Ignatius, and then to St. Columbus. He left school at fourteen then apprenticed as a carpenter, and later worked in the Playhouse Theatre in Edinburgh. Eventually he joined the Liverpool police and may have served in the police in London before he joined the Grenadier Guards.

As already noted, early in 1948 Hamish was sent from Palestine to what is now Ghana where he organized the police force. ("When I went there," Hamish said, "Nkrumah was a prisoner. I made him president.") He then went to Malaya where he spent over twelve years and finished up as the commandant of the Police Training Academy. After that he joined the police force in the Bahamas where, in 1962, he supervised the security

The End of a Chapter

arrangements for the Kennedy-Macmillan talks two months after the Cuban missile crises. When he retired, he came back to the family home at 40 Lauristan Street, Edinburgh, where his brother William and his sister Winnie lived. William did not know him well since he was a child when Hamish—whom he always referred to as John—went overseas in 1938 and did not come back until World War II ended. William was in awe of his older brother who spoke several languages, read a lot, and liked to cook. When asked where he became such an accomplished chef he answered: "A Jewish lady taught me many of the fine skills of fine living."

Hamish used the Lauriston Street house as a base for further travel that was usually on government business. He was known as a "Roving Ambassador" or "Ambassador-at-Large." Some of his former colleagues thought he was a "King's (or rather Queen's) Messenger," a person who carries documents too secret to be trusted to the diplomatic mail. Others believed that he worked for British Intelligence or even for the Americans, for the CIA. Wherever he went there were parties for him given by friends or colleagues. Old photographs show him—the tallest man in any group, handsome and dapper—in Kuala Lampur, Melbourne, Nairobi, and more.

In 1965, the year I saw him at Lod Airport, Hamish was back in Israel at the invitation of David Ben-David, former secretary of Gush Etzion—the four kibbutzim near Hebron—and the families of the Lamed-Hey, the thirty-five young men killed on their way to the Gush in 1948. Ben-David always wanted to thank him for his role in bringing the warriors' bodies to burial. In 1970 Hamish was invited to Israel again, this time by the Soldier's Commemoration Department of the Ministry of Defense. He was asked to identify the spot where he had originally found the men and was interviewed extensively about the tragic event. Both his visits were widely covered by the press where he was lauded for his courage.

The average age of the Lamed-Hey was twenty; most were students who volunteered for the task. Their death so early in the Yishuv's struggle for independence was a terrible blow, and they became a symbol of heroism, soldiers in a hopeless situation who fought to the last man. Members of the Hagana and the Palmach—the Hagana's elite striking force—they left Hartuv on the night of Thursday, January 15, 1948, to bring medical and military supplies to Gush Etzion, some fifteen miles away. The besieged Gush had been attacked several times, as were convoys trying to reach it by road. Marching through the difficult terrain of the Judean mountains, the thirty-five could not get to the Gush that night and decided to spend the day hiding in a *wadi*, a dry river bed, near the village of Surif and try and reach their target the next night. But some local Arabs spotted two of their scouts and soon the hills were covered with villagers, Hebronites, and some Bedouin groups. The Lamed-Hey tried to fight their way out but were completely outnumbered and out of ammunition. By evening the shooting stopped. The Lamed-Hey were dead.

That morning, Friday, Hamish had heard rumors of a skirmish going on near Surif, and, as Assistant Superintendent of the district of Hebron, he rushed over there but was told by the head of the village that nothing happened. Yet later that evening he heard from an Arab policemen that a battle had in fact taken place that day. Hamish arrived back at Surif at dawn on Saturday morning and eventually the villagers admitted that fighting had occurred and Hamish got two young shepherds to take him to the site. After a long walk he saw the first naked body then others, strewn over several hundred yards between the top of a hill and the *wadi*. He counted thirty-five bodies. There were no survivors. Some must have been wounded early on because their bodies had bandages on them. One of the dead was clutching a stone, the last defense. The bodies were naked but not mutilated. Hamish concluded that on Friday evening the Arabs must have undressed the dead bodies and collected their arms to be distributed among the tribes who participated in the action.

By the time Hamish had the bodies gathered in one spot it was nearly five in the evening. The place where they were found was not approachable

The End of a Chapter

by jeep or even by horse, and the bodies had to be carried out by people. It would take about an hour to move each body to where a jeep could reach. Hamish then decided to surround the dead fighters with rocks and branches to protect them from hyenas during the night. He returned to Surif and tried for hours to persuade the villagers to help remove the bodies the next day. Hamish suggested that "the dead belonged to God" and should be buried. Then he threatened that the British Army will invade the village. Finally the villagers agreed to carry the bodies to the main road, but asked to be paid for each body. It was after midnight when Hamish got back to Hebron and called CID Headquarters to ask what to do with the bodies. He was told to bring them to Jerusalem. Military vehicles would be waiting for him on the road to Hebron on Sunday at noon.

On Sunday, accompanied by the mayor of Hebron, Hamish went toward Surif but was stopped on the way by some Arabs who claimed that Jews in an armed vehicle had attacked the village. When he got to Surif, Hamish found three shivering naked men with the head of the village pointing a handgun at them. Hamish realized that the men were two British army officers and their driver who were curious to see the battlefield near Surif. They found themselves surrounded by Arabs, who, in turn, were sure they were Jews on the attack. He convinced the Arabs that they were not Jews—all three were uncircumcised—and they were let go. But the villagers who had promised to collect the bodies of the Lamed-Hey had stopped in the middle of their task when they heard of a "Jewish attack." Hamish had to request help from British soldiers stationed in the district who reluctantly volunteered to do it after he promised them all the beer they could drink. By then the bodies had been exposed for three days and worse: when the Arabs collecting them heard of the alleged attack, they tossed the remains back into the *wadi* and stoned them. Several of the British soldiers got sick at the sight.

Later, Hamish persuaded Headquarters in Jerusalem to let him take the bodies to Kfar Etzion in the Gush, so as not to shock the city where

John "Hamish" Dougan, center, with Prime Minister Harold MacMillan, far left, and Foreign Minister—and later Prime Minister—Sir Alec Douglas-Home, far right, Nassau, Bermuda, December 1962
Courtesy of the Dougan family

most of the Lamed-Hey came from. When he approached the kibbutz with the trucks carrying the bodies, he was stopped at a security checkpoint, where the guards would not believe his story. Hamish walked with his hands up in the air, to allay their fears of a British "trick" but refused to let them look at the mangled bodies. He finally got through and, with the help of Ben-David, began to unload the bodies near the synagogue after first wrapping them in sheets. Not knowing of Hamish's part in discovering and protecting the bodies—at times risking his life—some people at Kfar Etzion were not friendly. When he said "Shalom" to one of them, the answer was: "For you there is no Shalom."

Later the people of Gush Etzion began to remember all the times when

The End of a Chapter

Hamish came to warn them of a possible Arab attack, how he increased the number of policemen in the area, how he got the pregnant women evacuated, how he—a lone British officer—could have been killed while ensuring that the Lamed-Hey would receive proper burial. "He symbolized the best of the original British decency," said one. And in 1965 and again in 1970, they finally thanked him. Hamish, when asked by a *Maariv* journalist why he took so much trouble in 1948 to help the Jews, he answered: "I was not pro-Jewish as I was not pro-Arab. I was humane."

⁂

In the late 1960s Hamish finally fell in love again. The woman's name was Pat Turner and they planned to get married. But like my mother, Pat was diagnosed with breast cancer and died in 1969. A year later, according to William, his brother wanted to get away from it all and boarded a freighter in Cardiff bound for the United States, Japan, and back to Rotterdam. But near the end of the journey, on February 14, 1971, Hamish died of a stroke on board ship, at age sixty. His body was then brought to Edinburgh and buried there. Two men in "wooly suits" came to the Dougans' house to look through his trunks and cases, but Hamish did not keep any secret documents. He left his remaining papers, letters, and photographs to his brother William who burnt them, which is what he thought Hamish would have wanted him to do.

Alex Ternent, who helped me find out so much about Hamish, became a good friend. We corresponded regularly until his death in early 2008.

Henry and Nitza Rosovsky, Izu Penninsula, Japan, 1957

Epilogue

THIS BOOK BEGAN with the idea that the story of one family could offer a glimpse into the daily life of segments of the Jewish population of Palestine between the beginning of the nineteenth century and the middle of the twentieth. Despite the fact that the second half of the book became my personal narrative—which was not my original intention—I hope the reader learned something about the country from the annals of the Epstein, Ashkenazi, and Berman families.

Here is some of what happened after 1949. The Berman Bakery is still operating in Jerusalem, in a different location, employing over one thousand workers. Several of Yehoshua Berman's descendants now own the bakery and my second cousin, Yitzhak Berman, runs it; our side—Eliyahu's family—got out of the business many years ago. My grandmother sold the house I grew up in after Grandfather died in 1952 and we—Grandmother, Haya, Keith, Roni, Nurit, and I—all moved to two connected apartments in the Bermans' building at 14 Straus Street. The house, which my aunt Lily ironically referred to as "The Chateau," is now an orphanage, its exterior changed beyond recognition, and the whole property neglected. My grandparents and my mother's siblings are all dead. Eliyahu and Sarah had ten grandchildren together. (Eliyahu also had two granddaughters from his son Meir—Miriam Brecher and Rochelle Gudeon in the United States, and two grandsons—Avraham and Yoram—the sons of Zalman, in Israel.) Of the other ten, four are still living in Israel and four—including me—in North America. As already noted, Roni, the redheaded boy born during the siege, was killed in an ammunition explosion after the Six Day War ended. Adi died of AIDS in London in 1989. I am still in touch with all of my remaining first cousins: eighty-four of us—with our spouses, children, grandchildren, and one great-grandchild—met in Israel in early 2010 for a memorable family reunion.

What happened to me? I graduated from the Hebrew Gymnasium in 1951. Grandfather then suggested that I should go to university and he would pay my tuition. I refused, saying that I did not want to depend on anyone. I got a job as a telephone operator at *The Jerusalem Post* and got married a few months later—when I was seventeen-and-a-half. The family was horrified, and told me that I was much too young, but Grandmother, perhaps regretting her interference in Leah's love life, let me go through with the wedding. Three months later I realized that I had made a bad mistake. When I confessed the situation to the family, no one said: "We told you so," and they helped me get through a difficult divorce. Ironically, part of the reason I got married was to be more grownup, to move away from the authority of so many family members. Yet during the few months of my married life, we lived in my grandparents' house.

In 1955 I came to the States for a short visit, met Henry Rosovsky, and decided to marry him on our first date. It took him a bit longer to reach the same conclusion. We lived for several years in Tokyo, then in Berkeley, where Henry taught at the University of California, and since 1966—after he accepted an offer from Harvard—in the Boston area. With all the moves we made, I never graduated college although I had spent some four years as an undergraduate in Jerusalem, New York, Tokyo, and Berkeley, but I did not stay long enough in any one place to accumulate the necessary credits there to be issued a degree. By the time

Epilogue

we moved to the East Coast, I decided I was not going back to school. With Linda Abegglen I opened a gallery, Art/Asia, where we carried contemporary prints and pottery, mainly from Japan. Later I worked for over a decade as curator for exhibits at the Harvard Semitic Museum. In 1978 Marty Peretz, then editor of *The New Republic*, asked me to write *Jerusalemwalks*, a guidebook. I spent the next four years working on it and when it was published I knew that I had done something good for the city and finally felt less guilty about leaving Israel. I have written many things since, mostly related to Israel, but never enjoyed anything as much as working on *Jerusalemwalks*.

Henry and I have three children and four grandchildren to whom we are very close. (One of our daughters is named Leah, one of our granddaughters Sarah.) The void left by my mother's death is still there. Hardly a day goes by when I do not think about her, or wish to tell her something about my family. But it gives me comfort to think that if she were still alive, she would have approved of the life I lead.

My family, 2000
Seated are Nitza with Ella in her lap, and Henry.
Standing are Judy, Rachel, Abigail, Michael, Sarah, Leah, Benjamin, and David.

Acknowledgments

In the Land of Israel has taken me a long time to finish. Over the years many people have read the manuscript or parts of and I appreciate their input. Special thanks go to Carney Gavin, Franklin Fisher, Marshall Goldman, Nachum Gross, Dorothy Harman, Yael Katzir, Morton Keller, David McIntosh, Martin Peretz, Michal Ronen Safdie and Moshe Safdie, Irwin Scheiner, Daniel Tassel, Peter Temin, and Leon Wieseltier.

Sarah Rosovsky McIntosh helped me with my Arabic; Henry Freeman sent me information about Berman ancestors; Dror Barak found material about Hamish Dougan's last visits to Israel; Avriel Bar-Levav led me to the early history of Hasidut in the country; David Gefen first identified members of my family in the Montefiore Censuses; my old friend Magen Broshi and his daughter Michal Broshi answered endless questions, provided me with correct definitions, and improved my Yiddish transliterations; Supratik Bose created my photograph which appears on the dustjacket. I am indebted to all of them for their invaluable help. For their meticulous editing—and their discovery of a multitude of typos, spelling mistakes, and other errors—I want to mention Sam Spektor, Elizabeth Thyne, and Marlene Gray. Marlene also found many of the photographs that enhance the appearance of the book. I am responsible, of course, for any remaining errors. At TidePool Press, I want to thank the brothers Jock and Frank Herron for their enthusiasm, good editorial judgment, and for venturing with me into new territories, away from New England. The book's design speaks louder than words of the talents of Ingrid Mach with whom it was a pleasure to work.

I am grateful to the following institutions for their help with my research and for permitting me to reproduce documents from their collections: The Central Archives for the History of the Jewish People; The Central Zionist Archives; The Jerusalem City Archives; The City Archives of Tiberias; Keren Hayesod-UJA; London School of Jewish Studies; the Montefiore Endowment in London; and at Harvard University, Widener Library and especially the Judaica Collection.

I had many insightful comments and suggestions from members of my family: my cousins in Israel and in North America; my children and grandchildren; and especially my husband Henry from whose support, patience, and proofreading ability I have benefitted for over half a century.

September, 2012
Cambridge, Massachusetts

Endnotes

Tiberias pp 1-53

1. Avraham Yaari, ed., *Igrot Eretz Israel* (Ramat Gan, 1971) 309.
2. Avraham Yaari, ed., *Masot Eretz Israel* (Ramat Gan, 1977) 139.
3. Yaari, *Igrot*, 316.
4. Oded Avisar, ed., *Sefer Teveria* (Jerusalem, 1973).
5. The results of the first census, *Mifkad Yehudei Eretz-Israel 1839*, were published by the Dinur Center, The Hebrew University (Jerusalem, 1987). The original data, *Censuses of the Jews of Palestine 1839 to 1875*, are housed at the London School for Jewish Studies and are available in michrofiche and now on the web. I made extensive use of the data in the Censuses.
6. Samuel H. Williamson, "Seven Ways to Compute the Value of a U.S. Dollar Amount—1774 to the Present," MeasuringWorth, April 2010. URL: www.measuregrowth.com/usacompare/
7. Yaari, *Igrot*, 360-61.
8. Aharon Surasky, *Yesud Ha'ma'alah: Divrei Hayamim Leyishuv Hahasidim Be'eretz Israel* (Bnei Brak, 1991).
9. Louis Loewe, ed., *Diaries of Sir Moses and Lady Montefiore comprising their life and work as recorded in their diaries from 1812 to 1883* (Chicago, 1890) vol. II, p. 68.

10. The description of the Montefiores' visit to Tiberias is based on *Diaries*, vol. I, 168-76 (The Project Gutenberg EBook # 26170, 2008).
11. William M. Thomson, *The Land and the Book* (London and New York, 1910) 386, 389. The book was first published in 1859 and became a best seller.
12. Yaari, *Igrot*, 134.
13. Yaakov Barnai, ed., *Igrot Hasidim M'Eretz Israel* (Jerusalem, 1980) 202-03.
14. Material about Teleneshti and Bessarabia comes from Yitchak Alfasi, *Hahasidut Berumania* (Segada/Tel Aviv, 1973); S. Ben-Zion, *Nefesh Rezuzah* (Tel Aviv, 1952): M. Landau, ed., *Al Admat Bessarabia* (Tel Aviv, 1964); and Rachel Peles, ed., *Ha'ayara Haktana Shebebessarabia* (Kfar Habad, 1981).
15. Israel Freidin, "The First Attempts to Establish a Hospital in Tiberias in the Nineteenth Century," *Cathedra* #22 (1982) 91-112; David Sarid, "The Difficulties of the Yishuv and the Archives of the Mission in Tiberias from 1884 and 1914," *Mituv Teveria* #2 (1983) 21-33.
16. W. P. Livingstone, *A Galilee Doctor* (London, 1925). See also Nissim Levy, *Prakim Betoldot Harefua Be'eretz Israel 1799-1948* (Tel Aviv, 1998).
17. Avisar, *Sefer Teveria*, 430-31.
18. Ibid., 201. The quote is from Ludwig August Frankl's *Yerushalayma* (Vienna, 1860) 396. The book, *Nach Jerusalem!* was first published in German (Leipzig, 1858).

JERUSALEM PP 54-153

19. I learned a lot about Lithuania from Elisa New's book, *Jacob's Cane: A Jewish Family's Journey from the Four Lands of Lithuania to the Ports of London and Baltimore* (New York, 2009).
20. W. M. Thackeray, *Notes from a Journey from Cornhill to Cairo, by Way of Lisbon, Athens, Constantinople, and Jerusalem: Performed in the Steamers of Peninsular and Oriental Company* (1846; reprint: London, 1903) 115.

Endnotes

21. Chaim Hamburger, *Sefer Sheloshah Olamot*, vol. II, 30 (Jerusalem, 1946).

22. Yehoshua Ben-Arieh, *Jerusalem in the 19th Century: The Old City* (Jerusalem and New York, 1984) 336-37. The book is a great source for data about the period.

23. Hamburger, *Sheloshah*, vol. II, 152-53.

24. Israel Bartal, "The 'Old' and the 'New' Yishuv—Image and Reality." *Cathedra #2* (1976) 3-19.

25. Robert St. John, *Toungue of the Prophets* (Garden City, NY, 1952) 48-49.

26. Zahava Berman, *Bedarki Sheli* (Jerusalem, 1982).

27. Ephraim Cohn-Reiss, *Mi-Zikhronot Ish Yerushalayim* (Jerusalem, 1967, 2nd edition) 82.

28. Bertha Spafford Vester, *Our Jerusalem* (Beirut, 1950) 273-74.

29. Tom Segev, *One Palestine Complete* (New York, 2000) 52-54; Jane Fletcher Geniesse, *American Priestess: The Extraordinary Story of Anna Spafford and the Life of the American Colony in Jerusalem* (New York, 2008) 268-73.

30. Yemima Rosenthal, ed., *Chronologia Letoldot Hayishuv Hayehudi B'Eretz-Israel: 1917-1933* (Jerusalem, 1979) 46.

31. J. B. Baron, ed., *Report and Geneal Abstract of the Census of 1922* (Government of Palestine, 1923).

WITHIN MEMORY PP 154-317

32. Howard M. Sachar, *A History of Israel: From the Rise of Zionism to Our Time* (3rd edition, New York, 2007) 200.

33. Laurence Oliphant, *Haifa or Life in Modern Palestine* (Edinburgh, 1883) 158-60.

34. Over the years Lily told me some of her family's history. After her death in 2006, her son, Eli Barr, sent me her unpublished memoir.

35. Millar Burrows, *The Dead Sea Scrolls*, New York, 1956) 6-8.

36. The novelist Ram Oren deals with the subject in *Yamim Adumim* (Tel Aviv, 2005). The book is now available in English, titled *Red Days*.
37. Lewis Harris, *From Occident to Orient: The Memoirs of Lewis Harris, A Soldier's Tale* (London and Tel Aviv, 2004) 125-29.
38. Benny Morris, *1948: The First Arab-Israeli War* (New Haven and London, 2008) 125-29. See also Chaim Herzog and Shlomo Gazit, *The Arab-Israeli Wars: War and Peace in the Middle East* (New York, 2005). For another perspective see Sari Nusseibeh with Anthony David, *Once Upon a Country: A Palestinian Life* (New York, 2007).
39. Dov Joseph, *The Siege of Jerusalem, 1948* (New York, 1960). The book provides a detailed firsthand account of the siege; most of the following quotes in this chapter come from it. See also Mordechai Naor, ed., *Yerushalayim Betashah* (Jerusalem, 1983), and Zipporah Porath, *Letters from Jerusalem* (Jerusalem, 1987).
40. Edward Horne, *A Job Well Done: A History of the Palestine Police Force*, 1920-1948 (Leigh-on-Sea, 1982) 577-78.
41. Larry Collins and Dominique Lapierre, *O! Jerusalem* (New York, 1972) 152.
42. Morris, *1948*, 299.
43. Horne, *Job Well Done*, 478.